Mark Leary, Ph.D.

Garonzik Family Professor of Psychology and Neuroscience
Duke University

Mark Leary is the Garonzik Family Professor of Psychology and Neuroscience at Duke University, where he is the director of the Interdisciplinary Behavioral Research Center. He earned his bachelor's degree in Psychology from West Virginia Wesleyan College and his master's and doctoral degrees in Social Psychology from the University of Florida. Professor Leary taught previously at Denison University, The University of Texas at Austin, and Wake Forest University, where he served as department chair.

Professor Leary has published 14 books and more than 250 scholarly articles and chapters on topics dealing with social motivation, emotion, and self-relevant thought. He has been particularly interested in the ways in which people's emotions, behaviors, and self-views are influenced by their concerns with other people's perceptions and evaluations of them and in the dysfunctional effects of excessive self-preoccupation. Professor Leary is the author of *The Curse of the Self: Self-Awareness, Egotism, and the Quality of Human Life*; *Social Anxiety*; and *Self-Presentation: Impression Management and Interpersonal Behavior* and is the coeditor of *The Oxford Handbook of Hypo-egoic Phenomena*. He was the founding editor of the journal *Self and Identity* as well as the editor of *Personality and Social Psychology Review*. Professor Leary blogs regularly on personality and social psychology for psychologytoday.com.

Professor Leary received the 2010 Lifetime Career Award from the International Society for Self and Identity and was the corecipient of the 2015 Scientific Impact Award from the Society of Experimental Social Psychology. He is a fellow of the American Psychological Association, the Association for Psychological Science, and the Society for Personality and Social Psychology. In 2015, Professor Leary served as the president of the Society for Personality and Social Psychology.

Professor Leary's other Great Course is *Understanding the Mysteries of Human Behavior*. ■

TABLE OF CONTENTS

INTRODUCTION

Professor Biography i
Course Scope 1

LECTURE GUIDES

LECTURE 13 Consistency and Stability of Personality 3
LECTURE 14 Evolution and Human Nature 26
LECTURE 15 Personality and the Brain 49
LECTURE 16 Genetic Influences on Personality 72
LECTURE 17 Learning to Be Who You Are 95
LECTURE 18 How Culture Influences Personality 117
LECTURE 19 Nonconscious Aspects of Personality 141
LECTURE 20 Personality and Self-Control 164
LECTURE 21 When Personalities Become Toxic 186
LECTURE 22 Avoidance, Paranoia, and Other Disorders 209
LECTURE 23 The Enigma of Being Yourself 233
LECTURE 24 The Well-Adjusted Personality 256

TABLE OF CONTENTS

SUPPLEMENTARY MATERIAL

Bibliography 280

Image Credits 291

WHY YOU ARE WHO YOU ARE:
Investigations into Human Personality

To live effective and satisfying lives, people need to understand both themselves and the people with whom they interact, whether they are family members, friends, romantic partners, people at work, or neighbors. Yet human beings don't come with a manual that explains how people work or why they turn out the way they do. This course offers an intriguing and engaging excursion into the nuances of the human personality based on decades of research in psychology and other behavioral sciences.

The course starts with a look at the nature of personality and the fundamental psychological characteristics that contribute to differences in how people think, feel, and behave. In addition to exploring the basic traits that underlie personality, you will examine differences in the motives that energize people's behavior as well as general tendencies to experience certain emotions rather than others.

Personality is also shaped by how people think and what they believe, so this course will focus on cognitive differences among people, including ways in which your beliefs about yourself, other people, and how the world works channel your life in particular directions. You will also learn about aspects of personality that involve personal values and moral character as well as traits that relate to how people interact and get along with others.

Having examined ways that people differ from one another in their traits, motives, emotions, styles of thinking, beliefs, values, and behavior, you will turn to learning about the processes that influence personality development. Starting with evolutionary mechanisms that underlie characteristics that you share with most other people, you will then investigate the role that the brain, neurotransmitters, hormones, and bodily rhythms play in personality. You will also explore the effects of genes on personality characteristics and the complicated ways in which people's genes and environments can interact in personality development.

You will dive into the processes by which personal experiences and learning affect how people turn out as well as how the culture in which people grow up affect their personality. You will also explore how nonconscious processes operating outside of awareness influence personality and learn about people's ability to manage their own personality by intentionally regulating their thoughts, emotions, and behaviors. Along the way, the course will address questions about the degree to which personality can change over time and whether it is important for people to behave authentically with how they really are.

Most of this course focuses on normal variations in personality, but a few lectures are devoted to personalities that are so dysfunctional that they are regarded as psychological disorders. The course concludes with traits at the other end of the spectrum—personality characteristics that underlie psychological adjustment and well-being. ■

CONSISTENCY AND STABILITY OF PERSONALITY

LECTURE 13

The concept of personality implies that people show a certain degree of consistency in how they respond across different situations and that their characteristic patterns of behavior are somewhat stable over time. But people don't act the same way all the time, and people's personalities do change over the course of their lives, at least within limits. This variability raises questions about the nature of personality. This lecture will examine these questions, first by discussing the consistency of people's behaviors and emotions across different situations and then by addressing the degree to which personality is stable over time.

CONSISTENCY

♦ All thoughts, emotions, and behaviors are influenced to some extent both by people's internal, psychological characteristics and by the features of the situations in which they find themselves. To understand these 2 sets of influences, let's consider the trait of agreeableness as an example.

♦ If we could send an invisible researcher to follow you around and record how agreeably you act in every situation that you're in for the next several weeks, we would find that your level of behavioral agreeableness varies a great deal across various situations. Sometimes you're exceptionally friendly, agreeable, and nice; sometimes you're moderately friendly and agreeable; and sometimes you're not very agreeable—in fact, you might be critical and grumpy or downright nasty.

♦ These differences in how agreeable or disagreeable you act are mostly due to differences in the situations you're in. You're probably less agreeable when other people are difficult to get along with, or when the situation is frustrating, or perhaps when you haven't been able to get enough sleep.

♦ Now imagine that this invisible researcher who's following you around gives you a rating from 1 to 10 in every situation to indicate how agreeable you are in that situation. If we plotted these ratings of your agreeableness across hundreds of situations on a graph, we'd find that they fall into a classic, normal, bell-shaped distribution.

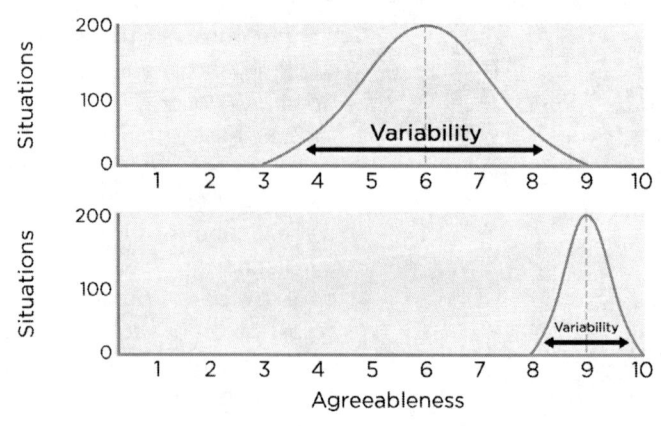

- Now imagine that the invisible researcher followed 100 people around for a few weeks and created a graph for each of these individuals. These graphs would show us 3 important things that are relevant to the question of consistency in personality:

  1. Different people's graphs peak at different places on the 1-to-10 agreeableness scale, reflecting differences in their personalities. People's general, or average, level of agreeableness differs.

  2. No matter where their peak is, everybody shows variability in their agreeableness. Even the people who are usually most agreeable sometimes behave disagreeably, and the people who are usually disagreeable sometimes act in a friendly and agreeable way. These differences are due to factors operating in those situations.

  3. People differ in the amount of variability they show in agreeableness across situations. Whatever their most common level of agreeableness—wherever their graph peaks—some people show more variability around their typical level of agreeableness than other people do. Psychologically, this means that agreeableness is a more influential part of some people's personality than it is for other people.

- This point applies to every personality characteristic, not just agreeableness. People differ not only in how they tend to behave on every personality dimension—in their average level of extraversion or anxiety or agreeableness—but they also differ in how consistently they behave on each dimension across situations.

- Researchers have found it challenging to deal with these differences in variability in their research. When we measure personality with a standard, self-report personality questionnaire, we do a pretty good job of assessing the person's dominant tendency, but we don't get information about how much the person's behavior varies around that tendency.

- In 1968, psychologist Walter Mischel started a firestorm of controversy when he noted that the average correlation between 2 measures of the same behavior taken at different times was rather low. This was explained by the notion that people have to adjust their behavior to fit the particular situation they're in.

- Mischel's commentary on personality inconsistency led some psychologists to question whether personality even exists. Mischel later offered an interesting resolution to the controversy about consistency that he started. He suggested that it's useful to think of personality as a very large set of conditional, if-then rules that guide our behavior.

- Personality is a system of if-then cognitive associations: If the situation is A, then do X, but if the situation is B, then do Y. Some of these if-then rules are shared by just about everybody. If the situation is a party, then be lively and funny; if the situation is a funeral, then be sedate and solemn. These mental rules automatically guide us to behave differently in different situations. But each of us also have our own, idiosyncratic if-then rules that may differ from other people's.

- The idea that personality operates according to if-then rules—which is known as the cognitive-affective processing system (CAPS) model—can explain both consistency and variability in behavior. The if-then rules that control your behavior are simply specific to each situation.

- Within the CAPS model, personality differences between people show up in how much of the time a person responds the same way across different situations. If your if-then rules for many different situations specify the same behavior, you will manifest a broad personality trait that transcends different situations.

- Aspects of your personality are situation-specific. You consistently behave the same way in the same kinds of situations, but you don't necessarily behave consistently across different situations because those situations have different if-then rules for you.

- Mischel's CAPS model was important in clarifying that personality consistency doesn't necessarily mean that you always act exactly the same way. It means that you tend to act roughly the same way when you are in the same situation on different occasions.

- Another factor that influences the consistency of our behavior is that we all have many aspects to our personality, and these different characteristics may push us to respond in competing ways. Any one trait by itself might exert a consistent influence on our behavior, but other tendencies might sometimes move us in other directions.

Personality characteristics can be thought of as tendencies to think, feel, or do certain things. Personality is related to the probability that people will respond in a particular way. As a result, people show a certain amount of consistency from situation to situation, but they also display variability and inconsistency.

STABILITY

- In addition to consistency across situations, a separate consideration involves how stable personality is over time. Usually, when we talk about whether something is stable over time, we're talking about absolute stability. For example, if you say that your weight has been stable for the last 5 years, it means that you weighed yourself 5 years ago and then today and there hasn't been much change.

- But personality isn't like weight because there aren't any absolute standards for quantifying most personality characteristics. If someone wanted to know how extraverted you are, they could have you complete self-report measures of extraversion, observe you in social interactions, or have other people who know you well rate how extraverted you are.

- For studying personality differences among people, we don't need an objective, standard criterion. All we need is a way to quantify differences in extraversion among people, and researchers have many ways to do that. But if we're trying to understand personality stability and change over time, the lack of a single absolute criterion that we can use across the life span creates problems and ambiguities.

- Consider a characteristic such as self-control. Let's say that we want to know whether self-control, as a personality trait, is stable over time. So, we get a sample of a few hundred 2-year-olds and measure their self-control in various ways. Then, we bring these same children back for retesting when they're 22 years old and measure their self-control again. How stable would their self-control be over that 20 years?

- There are a few problems. First, the tasks that we'd use to measure self-control in a 2-year-old are very different than we'd use to measure self-control in a 22-year-old. And if we can't use exactly the same measures, then how can we compare self-control at age 2 to self-control at age 22?

- In addition, even if we did have a single measure of self-control that worked on all ages, our data will certainly show that all of these children's self-control changed a great deal from age 2 to age 22. All of them would show much more self-control as young adults than they did as toddlers. So, in one sense, their personalities were very unstable when it came to self-control. They changed a lot.

- But this gigantic age-related change in self-control is obscuring the possibility that individuals' levels of self-control are actually highly stable when compared to people of their own age.

- Imagine that we rank-ordered all of the children when they were 2 years old from lowest to highest in self-control and we rank-ordered the participants again based on their self-control scores at age 22. We would find a high degree of stability in where each person ranked at age 2 and at age 22 compared to the rest of the sample.

- The children who were comparatively low in self-control when they were 2 will probably be comparatively low when they are 22. And those who were high in self-control compared to other 2-year-olds will tend to have high self-control when compared to other 22-year olds.

- Absolute stability in self-control would be very low: Everybody's self-control increased a lot. But rank-order stability would be high because people maintained their relative position in the sample; individual differences in self-control would be a rather stable trait across a 20-year span.

- To understand stability fully, we need to consider both rank-order stability, which involves how much people change relative to other people, as well as whether the average level of particular traits, such as self-control, changes over time.

People can change throughout their lives, but in general, personality becomes more stable with age, and stability peaks somewhere between age 55 and 65.

- In general, personality becomes more stable as people get older, both in terms of rank-order stability and absolute stability. This is partially because as we get older, we develop more and more habitual ways of responding to situations. In addition, our environment stabilizes more and more as we get older.

- As we get older, we also have fewer experiences that change us as dramatically than the extensive developmental changes that occur in childhood and adolescence. And these changes aren't as random or as dictated by other people as when we're younger. They're based on our own choices and behaviors, which means that the environments that we create, seek out, and end up in are based to a large extent on our personality.

- So, whatever our personality inclinations were to begin with, we gradually create a lifestyle and a life environment that supports and strengthens those characteristics. And that consistent lifestyle and environment makes our personality increasingly stable over time.

- Another reason that personality becomes more stable as we get older is that our identity stabilizes. Those certain stable views of ourselves provide a reference point for reacting to situations and making decisions. Because our identity has stabilized, our ways of responding become more consistent than they were when we were younger.

- Although we see greater stability in personality as people get older, people can and do change throughout life. There's never a point where your personality is etched in stone and has no chance of changing. New experiences, new life events, and new roles can always change the way we operate. Sometimes, people intentionally try to change themselves, such as working on anger management. But they typically change less because of the reasons just described.

> Across personality studies, we have data that includes people from birth up to 101 years old.

- Dozens of longitudinal studies have tracked people's personalities over extended periods of time, so we can see how the average level of certain personality characteristics changes with age. Some of this work has addressed the question of whether people become more well adjusted as they get older.

- Life experiences guide people into increasingly more adaptive and mature ways of dealing with life, so we see a general shift toward more functional personality profiles throughout life. For example, on average, neuroticism decreases with age. People also tend to become more conscientious and agreeable on average as they get older. Together, these seem to be positive changes, both for the individuals and the people around them.

- The picture for age-related changes in extraversion is a bit muddy. It looks like some aspects of extraversion change with age but others don't. In particular, people tend to become more dominant and assertive as they get older, but how outgoing or sociable they are on average doesn't change overall.

- The average level of openness doesn't seem to change with age. It's not that people don't change in how open they are, but there's no consistent pattern. Some people become more open as they get older, some become more set in their ways, and others don't change.

Suggested Reading

Dahl, "How Much Can You Really Change after You Turn 30?"

Mischel, "Toward an Integrative Science of the Person."

Roberts and Mroczek, "Personality Trait Change in Adulthood."

Questions to Consider

1. Think of a reaction that you have that varies a great deal across different situations. (Perhaps you're very calm in certain situations but easily upset in others, or maybe you're sometimes very generous but sometimes stingy or selfish.) Using Mischel's CAPS model, see if you can discern any if-then rules that might determine how you respond in different situations. These rules have the following form: If the situation is A, then do X, but if the situation is B, then do Y.

2. Do you have any traits, beliefs, motives, or values that regularly conflict with one another and thus lead you to behave differently depending on which one has precedence in a particular situation?

CONSISTENCY AND STABILITY OF PERSONALITY
LECTURE 13 TRANSCRIPT

The concept of personality implies that people show a certain degree of consistency in how they respond across different situations, and it also implies that their characteristic patterns of behavior are somewhat stable over time. The notion of personality would not make any sense at all if how people think, feel, and behave wasn't reasonably consistent over situations and stable over time. But people obviously don't act the same way all the time, and, of course, people's personalities do change over the course of their lives, at least within limits. This variability raises questions about the nature of personality, and it has led some behavioral scientists to question the importance of personality in understanding behavior. In fact, some have even questioned whether personality exists.

In this lecture, we're going to look into these questions, first by talking about the consistency of people's behaviors and emotions across different situations, and then by looking at the degree to which personality is stable over time. I mentioned earlier that to understand people's behavior fully, we have to consider both their personal psychological characteristics and the nature of the situation they are in at the moment—their environment. All thoughts, emotions, and behaviors are influenced to some extent both by people's internal, psychological characteristics and by the features of the situations in which they find themselves. To think about these 2 sets of influences, let's consider the trait of, let's say agreeableness; we could use any characteristic, but let's use agreeableness.

If we could send an invisible researcher to follow you around and record how agreeably you act in every situation that you're in for the next several weeks, we would find that your level of behavioral agreeableness varies a great deal across various situations. Sometimes you're exceptionally friendly, agreeable, and nice; sometimes, you're moderately friendly and agreeable; and sometimes you're not very agreeable at all. In fact, you may be critical and grumpy or downright nasty. These differences in how agreeable or disagreeable you act are mostly due to differences in the situations you're in. You're probably less agreeable when other people are hard to get along with, or when the situation is frustrating, or perhaps when you haven't been able to get enough sleep. We all vary in how agreeable we are across different situations.

Now, let's imagine that this invisible researcher who's following you around gives you a rating from, say, 1 to 10 in every situation to indicate how agreeable you are in that situation. If we plotted these ratings of your agreeableness across hundreds of situations on a graph, we'd find that they fall into one of those classic, normal, bell-shaped distributions. I'm talking here about a graph that shows how agreeably you personally tended to behave across many situations. This graph would show a peak somewhere along that 10-point rating scale from highly disagreeable to highly agreeable, and that peak would show the level of agreeableness that you tend to display more than any other level. But you didn't behave at that particular level of agreeableness in every situation. Sometimes you were more agreeable or less agreeable than your most common level of agreeableness.

Now, imagine that our invisible researcher followed a hundred people around for a few weeks and created a graph like this for each of these individuals. These graphs would show us 3 important things that are relevant to the question of consistency in personality.

First, different people's graphs would peak at different places on our 1 to 10 agreeableness scale. Some people's behaviors would tend to be mostly low in agreeableness; maybe they peak at about 3 on the scale. Other people would generally show a moderate level of agreeableness; maybe their peak on the graph is at 5 or 6. And some people might typically show a high level of agreeableness, with a peak at 8 or 9. These differences in where people's graphs peak reflect differences in their personalities. When we look at people's agreeableness across many situations, some people tend to behave more agreeably overall than other people do. People's general or average level of agreeableness differs.

The second thing these graphs would show us is that, no matter where their peak is, everybody shows variability in their agreeableness. Even the people who are usually most agreeable sometimes behave disagreeably, and the people who are usually disagreeable sometimes act in a friendly and agreeable way. These differences that we see in a given person's behavior across situations are due to factors operating in those situations.

Third, people differ in the amount of variability they show in agreeableness across situations. Whatever their most common level of agreeableness—wherever their graph peaks on the 1 to 10 scale—some people show more variability around their typical level of agreeableness than other people do. What does that mean?

Maybe you and I are both moderately high in agreeableness overall; maybe both of our graphs peak around a rating of 7 the 10-point scale. But if we look at the variability in our agreeableness around that point, your agreeableness across different situations might vary mostly from 6 to 8. You're almost always moderately high in agreeableness. But maybe my agreeableness varies mostly from 4 to 10 on the scale. I have the same average level of agreeableness that you do—we both peak at 7 on the graph—but I show more variability in how agreeable I am across situations than you do. Even though our general, most typical level of agreeableness is the same, I vary more than you do, even dipping down into the disagreeable range more often than you. Psychologically, what that means is that my agreeableness is affected more by situational factors than yours is. Or, to look at it the other way, you show more consistency in how agreeable you are across different situations than I do. Agreeableness is a more influential part of your personality than it is mine.

I used agreeableness as an example, but this point applies to every personality characteristic. People differ not only in how they tend to behave on every personality dimension—in their average level of extraversion or anxiety or agreeableness or whatever—but they also differ in how consistently they behave on each dimension across situations.

You can see these differences among people pretty easily. You can probably think of certain people who consistently behave in a particular way: They're pretty consistently extraverted, or neurotic, or closed-minded, or whatever. You're rarely surprised by how they behave on that dimension because they're so consistent. With other people, though, you don't quite know what to expect. Who's going to show up today: extraverted John or introverted John? Sometimes, Susan is emotionally stable and resilient, and at other times she's a neurotic mess. These people are harder to predict because their behavior varies more. Researchers have found it challenging to deal with these differences in variability in their research. When we measure personality with a standard, self-report personality questionnaire, we do a pretty good job of assessing the person's dominant tendency, but we don't get information about how much the person's behavior varies around that tendency.

In 1968, psychologist Walter Mischel started a firestorm of controversy when he noted that the average correlation between 2 measures of the same behavior taken at different times was rather low.

Imagine that we measure how moral or how outgoing a bunch of people are in one situation and then measure how moral or outgoing those same people are in another situation. Their level of morality or outgoingness in the first situation will be only weakly related to how moral or outgoing they are in the second situation. I'm not sure why that surprised anybody; people have to adjust their behavior to fit the particular situation they're in. Even so, Mischel's commentary on personality inconsistency led some psychologists to question whether personality even exists. They reasoned that if how people act in one situation isn't strongly related to how they act in another situation, then maybe there's no such thing as personality.

Mischel himself later offered an interesting resolution to the controversy about consistency that he started. He suggested that it's useful to think of personality as a very large set of conditional, if-then rules that guide our behavior. In his view, personality is a system of if-then cognitive associations. Let me explain what that means.

People obviously tailor their behavior to the situation that they're in, and they often do so pretty automatically. It's as if we have rules in our mind that say things like "If the Situation is A, then do X, but if the Situation is B, then do Y." Some of these if-then rules are shared by just about everybody: "If the situation is a party, then be lively and funny; if the situation is a funeral, then be sedate and solemn." These mental rules automatically guide us to behave differently in different situations. But each of us also have our own idiosyncratic if-then rules that may differ from other people's. You might have a rule that says, "If at first you don't succeed, try again." I might have a rule that says, "If at first you don't succeed, quit and do something else." You might have a rule that says "In a disagreement, look for a way to compromise;" I might have a rule that says "In a disagreement, stand your ground."

The idea that personality operates according to if-then rules—which is known as the cognitive-affective processing system, or CAPS, model—can explain both consistency and variability in behavior. If you have an if-then rule that says, "If you're at a party, then be lively and funny," you will probably be outgoing and humorous when you go to parties. So, you'll display a rather consistent pattern of behavior in that particular context, when you go to parties. But the fact that you have a different if-then rule about how you should behave at a funeral means that you won't act the same way at funerals as you do at parties. This might look like inconsistency—sometimes you're really funny, and sometimes you're not. You're not being consistent. But you're actually behaving very consistently at parties and very consistently at funerals. The if-then rules that control your behavior are simply specific to each situation.

Within the CAPS model, personality differences between people show up in how much of the time a person responds the same way across different situations. In how many different situations is your behavior guided by the same general if-then rule? If your if-then rules for many different situations specify the same behavior, you will manifest a broad personality trait that transcends different situations.

So, imagine that you have a rule that says "If you're at a party, then be humorous," and you have a rule that says "If you're in a meeting, then be humorous," and one that says "If you're on a date, then be humorous," and "If you're standing in line at the grocery store, then be humorous." If your if-then rules specify that the response to many situations is to be humorous, you'll be a pretty consistently humorous person. But if you have a rule that says, "If you're at a party, then be humorous," but have another rule that says, "If you're in a meeting, then be serious," and one says "If you're on a date, then be attentive," and "If you're standing in line, then be quiet," you won't be a globally humorous person overall. You won't show a broad personality trait that transcends many situations. But, again, you will be consistent within each of those situations: humorous at parties, serious in meetings, attentive on dates, and quiet in grocery lines.

So, aspects of your personality are situation-specific. You consistently behave the same way in the same sorts of situations, but you don't necessarily behave consistently across different situations because those situations have different if-then rules for you. Mischel's CAPS model was important in clarifying that personality consistency doesn't necessarily mean that you always act exactly the same way. It means that you tend to act roughly the same way when you are in the same situation on different occasions.

Another factor that influences the consistency of our behavior is that we all have many aspects to our personality, and these different characteristics may push us to respond in competing ways. Any one trait by itself might exert a consistent influence on our behavior, but other tendencies may sometimes move us in other directions.

Imagine a college student is studying for a test when his friends drop by to invite him to join them for drinks. Will he go out instead of studying? Let's set aside situational influences, such as how important the test is, how much studying he still has to do, and his relationships with these particular friends, and think just about his personality. If I tell you that this student is high in achievement motivation, you might predict that he'd decline the invitation to go out and keep studying. But what if I tell you that he's not only achievement-motivated, he's also highly extraverted. Now it's a little less clear. His extraversion will push him toward a different decision than his achievement motivation. And what about if he has a high need for acceptance and belonging, and he scores very high on a scale that measures FOMO—the fear of missing out? There really is such a scale.

Any one of these characteristics would lead us to make a reasonably confident prediction of what the student might do, but he has attributes that push his behavior in different directions. And we might imagine that, if faced with this choice between studying and going out with friends over many occasions, he might make a different decision each time. In each case, his choice would be consistent with certain aspects of his personality but inconsistent with others. But overall, it would look like he was behaving inconsistently.

So, people display consistencies in how they respond across different situations, but it's not as straightforward as people's personality characteristics manifesting all of the time, in all situations. The consistencies in people's personalities are more nuanced and probabilistic than that. That's why I usually refer to personality characteristics as tendencies to think, feel, or do certain things. Personality is related to the probability that people will respond in a particular way. Not only do situational forces affect behavior as people accommodate to norms, roles, other people's wishes, and other factors, but various aspects of our personalities may nudge us in opposing directions. As a result, people show a certain amount of consistency from situation to situation, but they display variability and inconsistency as well.

In addition to consistency across situations, a separate question involves how stable personality is over time. How much do people's personalities change?

Usually, when we talk about whether something is stable over time, we're talking about what's called absolute stability. So, if I say that my weight has been stable for the last 5 years, it means that I weighed myself 5 years ago and I weighed myself today, and there hasn't been much change in how much I weigh. But personality isn't like weight because there aren't any absolute standards for quantifying most personality characteristics. If I want to know how extraverted you are, for example, how do I find out? Well, I can have you complete self-report measures of extraversion, or I can observe you in social interactions, or I can have other people who know you well rate how extraverted you are. All sorts of ways. And for studying personality differences among people, that's fine. We're trying to understand psychological differences among people—what makes you different from the rest of us—so we don't need an objective, standard criterion like a bathroom scale that measures extraversion. All we need to do is to have a way to quantify differences in extraversion among people, and researchers have many ways to do that. But if we're trying to understand personality stability and change over time, the lack of a single absolute criterion that we can use across the lifespan creates problems and ambiguities. Let me explain.

Consider a characteristic such as self-control. Let's say we want to know whether self-control, as a personality trait, is stable over time. So we get a sample of a few hundred 2-year-olds and measure their self-control in various ways. Then, we bring these same kids back for retesting 20 years later, when they're 22 years old, and measure their self-control again. How stable would their self-control be over that 20 years? Well, we have a couple of problems. First, the tasks that we'd use to measure self-control in a 2-year-old are very different than we'd use to measure self-control in a 22-year-old. It's unavoidable. That's not like weight, where we can use the same scales to weigh 2-year-olds and 22-year-olds. And, if we can't use exactly the same measures, then how can we compare self-control at age 2 to self-control at age 22?

In addition, even if we did have a single measure of self-control that worked on all ages, our data will certainly show that all of these kids' self-control changed a great deal from age 2 to age 22. All of them would show much more self-control as young adults than they did as toddlers. So, in one sense their personalities were very unstable when it came to self-control. They changed a lot. But this gigantic age-related change in self-control is obscuring the possibility that individuals' levels of self-control are actually highly stable when compared to people of their own age.

Imagine that we rank-ordered all of the kids when they were 2-years-old from lowest to highest in self-control, and we rank-ordered the participants again based on their self-control scores at age 22. We would find a high degree of stability in where each person ranked at age 2 and age 22 compared to the rest of the sample. The children who were comparatively low in self-control when they were 2 will probably be comparatively low when they are 22. And those who were high in self-control compared to other 2-year-olds will tend to have high self-control when compared to other 22-year olds.

Again, absolute stability in self-control would be very low: everybody's self-control increased a lot. But rank-order stability would be high because people maintained their relative position in the sample. Sure, there would be some shifting around, but individual differences in self-control would be a rather stable trait across a 20-year span. So to understand stability fully, we need to consider both this rank-order stability that involves how much people change relative to other people, as well as whether the average level of particular traits, such as self-control, changes over time.

Personality becomes more stable as people get older, both in terms of rank-order stability and absolute stability. So, in the 10-year span between ages 5 and 15, we certainly see some stability in personality, but we see more stability in the 10 years between ages 15 and 25. And we see even more stability between, say, 45 and 55. Sure, people can change throughout their lives, but in general, personality becomes more stable with age, and stability peaks somewhere between age 55 and 65. But why? Why does personality become increasingly stable with age?

First, as we get older, we develop more and more habitual ways of responding to situations. When you were a child or teenager, you hadn't developed much of a personal style yet—you hadn't developed standard ways of dealing with life. But as you got older and had more experiences, you developed habits that you began to rely on without thinking much about them.

Second, your environment stabilized more and more as you got older. In childhood, adolescence, and even young adulthood, you probably wandered through a large assortment of classes, teachers, friends, groups, interests, relationships, and activities. So, your environment fluctuated a good deal over time, calling for a wide variety of reactions.

Compare that to how life is for people in their 30s, 40s, and older. By their 30s, life stabilizes some, and most people settle down a bit. They get a stable job, they develop a single close relationship, they pursue fewer new activities, and their days become more routine. Certainly, there are often big changes: people change jobs, move to a new town, have children, see their relationships break up. But most people go for longer periods of time without big changes compared to when they were children or teenagers.

So, not only does our environment stabilize more as we get older, but we also have fewer experiences that change us as dramatically than the extensive developmental changes that occur in childhood and adolescence. And, these changes aren't as random or as dictated by other people as when we're younger. They're based on our own choices and behaviors, which means that the environments that we create, and seek out, and end up in are based to a large extent on our personality. So, whatever our personality inclinations were to begin with, we gradually create a lifestyle and a life environment that supports and strengthens those characteristics. And that consistent lifestyle and environment makes our personality increasingly stable over time.

Another reason that personality becomes more stable as we get older is that our identity stabilizes. Our view of who we are and what we are like is pretty malleable in childhood and adolescence. When we're young, each new experience has the potential to change our views of ourselves, and thus, to change how we behave in the future. With age and experience, we come to see ourselves as a certain kind of person, with particular abilities and traits, with certain beliefs and values, and with certain ways of dealing with situations. Those views of ourselves provide a reference point for reacting to situations and making decisions. And because our identity has stabilized, our ways of responding become more consistent than they were when we were younger.

Although we see greater stability in personality as people get older, people can and do change throughout life. There's never a point where your personality is etched in stone and has no chance of changing. New experiences, new life events, and new roles can always change the way we operate. And sometimes, people intentionally try to change themselves as when someone decides to work on anger management or start meditating or write out a bucket list that leads them to behave in highly uncharacteristic ways. But they typically change less because of the reasons I just described.

Dozens of longitudinal studies have tracked people's personalities over extended periods of time, and across these studies, we have data that includes people from birth up until 101 years old! So, we can see how the average level of certain personality characteristics changes with age. Here we're talking about average, age-related changes in personality, and not whether people maintain their relative, rank-order position among others their age. Some of this work has addressed the question of whether people become more well-adjusted as they get older. You might expect that life experiences would guide people into increasingly more adaptive and mature ways of dealing with life, so we might see a general shift toward more functional personality profiles throughout life. Is that true?

The answer seems to be yes. For example, on average, neuroticism decreases with age. People seem to have fewer negative emotions and tend to cope better with the things that happen as they get older. People also tend to become more conscientious and responsible on average as they get older. Just compare the average 20-year-old with the average 40-year-old. You'll see big individual differences in both groups, but the 40-year-olds will be more conscientious on average.

Agreeableness also tends to increase with age. The average person tends to become kinder, friendlier, and more agreeable as they get older. Together, lower neuroticism, higher conscientiousness, and higher agreeableness seem to be positive changes, both for the individuals themselves and the people around them.

The picture for age-related changes in extraversion is a bit muddy. It looks like some aspects of extraversion change with age, but others don't. In particular, people tend to become more dominant and assertive as they get older, but how outgoing or sociable they are on average doesn't change overall. The average level of openness doesn't seem to change with age. It's not that people don't change in how open they are, but there's no consistent pattern. Some people become more open as they get older, some become more set in their ways, and others don't change.

So, personality shows an interesting mix of stability and change as people go through life. Certain things about your personality are quite similar to what you were like when you were younger. People who haven't seen you since you were a kid will probably detect certain tendencies that you displayed many years ago. Yet, you literally aren't the same person that you were earlier in life, and you're not exactly the same person now that you will be in the future.

EVOLUTION AND HUMAN NATURE

LECTURE 14

Personality reflects tendencies or regularities in people's thoughts, emotions, and behaviors—how a person generally tends to respond. And human beings as a whole show some of the same general tendencies. There are features of personality that can be seen in just about everybody, no matter where they live or what experiences they've had. There are ways in which your personality resembles everybody else's personality. There are regularities and tendencies in your emotions and behavior that can be seen in almost everybody else's personalities as well, and this lecture is about where those aspects of your personality came from.

EVOLUTION OF PSYCHOLOGICAL CHARACTERISTICS

◆ Physical characteristics evolve because animals who have them survive and reproduce at a higher rate than those who don't. Gradually, through the process of natural selection, animals with an adaptive characteristic have more offspring than those without the characteristic.

◆ Charles Darwin's *On the Origin of Species* was all about physical characteristics, but toward the end of the book, Darwin suggested that his ideas about natural selection could also be applied to psychological characteristics. After all, the brain is a physical organ, and just like every other organ of the body, it's subject to the process of natural selection.

◆ If an animal's brain is designed in such a way that it leads to behavior that increases survival and reproduction, then the genes for that more adaptive brain will get passed along at a higher rate, and the behavioral tendency will become part of the species' general personality.

◆ Anything that's part of human nature—just about any characteristic that we see in every normal person—is the result of natural selection. And that means that the aspects of your personality that you share with everybody else probably reflect evolutionary processes.

◆ The processes that produced human nature as it is today occurred over millions of years. This means that most of the processes that created human nature happened long before we became fully human only in the last 200,000 years or so, and these processes happened in an environment that was dramatically different from the one we live in today.

◆ Our prehuman ancestors lived in small bands that wandered across the plains of central Africa. They were hunters and gatherers and scavengers. The universal aspects of human personality evolved to meet the challenges of living in that sort of environment. This means that our personality includes some evolved tendencies that might have worked great 500,000 years ago but that aren't very helpful—and might even be problematic—in the 21st century.

- At the most basic level, the evolved characteristics that are relevant to understanding personality involve psychological processes that steered behavior in ways that promoted survival and reproduction during the course of evolution. So, it's helpful to think about the recurring problems that our prehistoric ancestors faced that had implications for the likelihood that they would survive and reproduce.

- As infants, they had to do things to get breast milk and to be protected by adults. Later, to survive, they had to get along with other people in a group context, avoid predators, secure an ongoing supply of food, avoid toxins and diseases, and avoid getting killed by other people. Then, to reproduce, they had to identify and attract desirable mates, fend off rivals who might pull their mate away, and be sure that whatever offspring they might have lived to reproductive age.

- The individuals who dealt with these and many other adaptive problems most successfully passed along their genes, and those genes contained the instructions for new brains that could also solve such problems.

- An example of why certain emotional and behavioral tendencies are part of your personality is judgments of physical attractiveness. Each of us finds certain people more attractive than other people, and each of us has certain personal preferences that other people might not agree with. But there are some notable consistencies in what people find attractive and unattractive that go deeper than personal preference. Some people are simply more attractive or unattractive than other people are to just about everybody.

- Most people—in every culture—show a clear and consistent preference for people without dark or bloodshot eyes, physical deformities, or open sores. This is because these physical features are often signs of disease; sometimes they indicate some problem that we might catch. So, natural selection favored individuals who kept their distance from people who showed signs of being sick.

- To look at it the other way, our prehistoric ancestors who found these features desirable and sought out people who showed signs of being infected or having a disease survived and reproduced at a lower rate than those who had negative reactions. So, now it's part of everybody's personality.

Acceptance and Belonging

Every normal person wants to be accepted and approved of by at least a few other people, even though people differ in the strength of this motive.

The need for acceptance and belonging can be traced to natural selection. Today, most people can survive without strong social connections, but for millions of years, survival depended on being integrated into a supportive social group.

Natural selection favored individuals who were drawn to live with other people and motivated to behave in ways that led those other people to accept and support them. This is how a strong desire for acceptance and belonging evolved to be part of the human personality.

SEX DIFFERENCES IN PERSONALITY

- Natural selection is also responsible for differences that we see in the personalities of men and women. There's been a good deal of controversy over the years—both among scholars and among the general public—regarding whether the differences that we see in the behavior of men and women is biological versus socialized. But now there's no scientific doubt that differences between men and women have both biological and social sources.

- All other species of mammals show clear differences in the behaviors of males and females, so we would be a very unusual species if none of the sex differences that we see in human beings were evolved. But socialization, culture, and learning also play a big role in how men and women act.

- The fundamental principle underlying natural selection is that organisms that are the most successful at reproducing contribute disproportionately to the gene pool. So, we are the descendants of prehistoric people who were most successful at reproducing. But throughout evolutionary history, men and women faced different reproductive challenges and evolved different strategies to meet those challenges.

- Men and woman faced different reproductive challenges because they differ biologically in their reproductive roles. First, men and women differ in reproductive constraint—the simple fact that, over a lifetime, women can potentially have a much smaller number of children than men can. Second, women invest much more biologically into their offspring than men do, including during pregnancy and breastfeeding.

- Biologists tell us that if an organism has a limited number of opportunities to reproduce and must invest more into each offspring, then it should be more careful with each of its mating opportunities than an organism that has more potential opportunities to have offspring and little biological investment. But an organism that can potentially have many offspring with a very low biological investment doesn't need to worry as much about any particular mating opportunity.

> Even if she works really hard at it, no woman can have more than, say, 20 children, and most women have many fewer. On the other hand, there's almost no limit to how many children a man could have. For example, Genghis Khan sired several hundred children.

- Research shows that, on average, women are more selective than men are when it comes to sex. This is a human universal: There's no society in which women are, as a group, less choosy and careful when it comes to sex than men are. It's part of the female personality to be more selective because, throughout evolution, females who were more selective made better mating decisions and had a larger number of viable offspring who lived to reproductive age.

- Evolution may also play a role in what men and women find attractive. We all have our personal tastes regarding who we find attractive, but we see some consistent differences between men and women that seem to be part of human nature.

- The most noticeable difference is that, on average, men prefer mates who are younger than they are. There are plenty of personal exceptions, but this preference shows up in every one of 37 cultures in which mating preferences have been studied. Scientists believe that the reason this preference is part of the male personality comes down to another difference in the reproductive challenges that men and women faced throughout evolution.

- From the standpoint of natural selection, the central reproductive task is finding a fertile mate with good genes. But finding a fertile mate has been much less of a challenge for women than for men. After all, men are potentially fertile from puberty until death, so almost no matter who women chose as a mate, chances are that he was fertile.

- But that wasn't the case for men, because women's reproductive years are limited. A man who preferred only 50- or 60-year-old women would not have passed along his genes, so natural selection would have favored men who preferred women who were younger than the age of menopause.

- In addition, a man was likely to have more offspring the younger his mate was because she had more child-bearing years ahead of her. This, too, would have given an evolutionary edge to men who preferred younger rather than older women.

- Men today are mostly the descendants of males who preferred younger, rather than older, females as mates. Whatever it was about the brains of those prehistoric men that led them to prefer younger women is still in the brains of men today.

If you look at the ages of heterosexual couples in the United States, women are, on average, 2.3 years younger than their male partner.

- This doesn't make sense in the modern world, in which people use contraception and often try to plan their families. In industrialized countries, most people who have children have only a few, and most people—men and women alike—stop having children by about age 40.

- But even though people today are virtually negating evolved dispositions to enhance reproduction, we're all walking around with a brain that evolved the way it did because it facilitated reproduction in prehistoric Africa hundreds of thousands of years ago.

EVOLVED PROCESSES THAT LEAD TO DIFFERENCES AMONG PEOPLE

- In the early days of evolutionary psychology, the focus was on the evolution of human nature—species-typical characteristics that can be seen, more or less, in every normal person. More recently, however, evolutionary psychologists have turned their attention to evolved processes that may contribute to differences among people.

- The general idea is that some evolved psychological adaptations may operate differently depending on different inputs from the individual's environment. If a single response is not adaptive under all circumstances, natural selection may create mechanisms that lead to different behaviors depending on environmental conditions.

- That means that people who live in one type of environment may respond differently from the way those who live in another environment respond. They would consistently differ from each other in terms of their typical reactions, but the source of the differences in their personalities would be an evolved conditional adaptation—one that appears only in certain environments.

- Throughout evolution, an adaptive problem that all children faced was to compete with their siblings for parental resources. Natural selection would have presumably favored children who were particularly successful at getting their share, if not more than their share, of food, protection, support, and other resources from their parents. And the notion that siblings compete for their parents' attention seems to be more or less universal.

- But the best strategy for getting one's share may differ depending on whether the child is the first-born child, the second-born child, or the third-born child, etc. The first-born child has an easy time of it at first, until the next brother or sister comes along. Then, suddenly, the first-born child has to share resources with a newcomer.

- One solution to this adaptive problem may be to identify with the parents and take on the responsibility of helping raise the younger sibling. First-born children often assume such a helper role, and this leads them to develop more responsible personalities—to be higher in conscientiousness, on average—than later-born children do.

- The second child in a family never has as much access to parents as the first one did because big brother or sister was there from the start. Then, when the third-born child comes along, he or she seems like an add-on.

- The youngest child, whatever number he or she is, is not going to have much authority or power in the family because everybody else is older. One solution to this problem is to get attention by being nonconforming and maybe even a bit rebellious.

- Evolutionary psychologists call this type of process strategic niche specialization. Although all children have faced the same general adaptive problem—how to get what they need in the context of the family—they may differ in how they pursue that goal, depending on the environment that they're born into based on their birth order. They essentially specialize in filling different niches within the family, and that difference in strategic niche specialization shows up as a difference in their personalities.

Suggested Reading

Buss, "Human Nature and Culture."

Geary, *Male, Female*.

Questions to Consider

1. Make a list of common human reactions that you think might be evolved features of human nature, both ones discussed in this lecture and others that you think might be universal. Which of these aspects of human nature continue to be beneficial in modern life, and which are no longer useful, or are even detrimental, now that we no longer live in small bands of hunter-gatherers?

2. Biologists believe that although the pace of evolution has slowed down, natural selection is probably still occurring. Consider the psychological traits that might be most adaptive under modern conditions and, thus, could become part of human nature over time if current conditions did not change over the next 500,000 years (which, of course, they will). Remember that these would be traits that enhance the probability of reproductive success (having many offspring who also survive to reproductive age) in the modern world.

EVOLUTION AND HUMAN NATURE
LECTURE 14 TRANSCRIPT

Most of the aspects of personality that we've covered already have dealt with ways in which people's personalities differ from one another. As we move into talking about where personality comes from, I want us to start in this lecture by looking at features of personality that you share with virtually everybody else. As we have seen, personality reflects tendencies or regularities in people's thoughts, emotions, and behaviors—how a person generally tends to respond. And when we step back and look at human beings as a whole, we find that they all show some of the same general tendencies. There are features of personality that can be seen in just about everybody, no matter where they live or what experiences they've had. There are ways in which your personality resembles everybody else's personality.

To show you what I mean, let me give you just a couple of examples of human psychological universals. I guarantee that you want to be accepted and approved of by at least a few other people in your life. There's no normal person anywhere, in any culture, who absolutely doesn't care whether anybody likes or accepts them. There's nobody who's not troubled at times by feeling ignored or disapproved of or rejected. People may differ in how concerned they are about rejection, but wanting to be accepted at least by a few people is part of human nature. And so, much of what you think, feel, and do reflects this universal desire for acceptance.

Here's another one: I bet that, all other things being equal, you don't find people with blemished or scarred or disfigured faces to be as physically attractive as people without blemishes, scars, and disfigurement. I'm not saying that you don't like them or reject them, just that there's something about facial blemishes and scars and skin infections that make people less attractive. Now, you might be thinking, "Well, sure! Of course, oozing sores are less attractive than clear skin!" But there's really not any of course to it. It wouldn't have to be that way. Why does everybody think clearer skin is more attractive than oozing skin?

One more: Imagine that you're walking into a room full of 15 strangers. And they're standing around clustered into 2 different groups. One group contains all people of your own ethnic group, and the other group is composed entirely of people of another ethnicity. Which group would you feel most comfortable walking up to and joining? I suspect that the vast majority of you are thinking, well I hate to admit it, but I'd feel a little more comfortable with my own group. That's a pretty universal reaction as well.

I could go on, but I think you get the idea. There are regularities and tendencies in your emotions and behavior that can be seen in almost everybody else's personalities as well, and we need to talk about where those aspects of your personality came from.

When you learned about evolution in school, you probably focused mostly on the evolution of animals' physical characteristics, like the giraffe's long neck or human beings' opposable thumbs. And you probably learned that these characteristics evolved because animals who had them survived and reproduced at a higher rate than those who didn't. There was an adaptive advantage for giraffes to have a long neck because they could reach more food, and there was an adaptive advantage to having an opposable thumb to grasp things. So, gradually through the process of natural selection, animals with an adaptive characteristic had more offspring than those without the characteristic. The descendants of giraffes with longer necks survived, and thus reproduced at a higher rate than those with short necks, so the giraffe gene pool became dominated by genes for long necks. You've heard that sort of thing before.

Charles Darwin's book, *The Origin of Species*, was all about these sorts of physical characteristics, but toward the end of the book, Darwin suggested that his ideas about natural selection could also be applied to psychological characteristics. I know that some people have a harder time seeing how psychological characteristics can evolve than seeing how physical characteristics evolve, but it's the same process. After all, the brain is a physical organ, and just like every other organ of the body, it's subject to the process of natural selection.

So, if an animal's brain is designed in such a way that it leads to behavior that increases survival and reproduction, then the genes for that more adaptive brain will get passed along at a higher rate, and the behavioral tendency will become part of the species' general personality. Anything that's part of human nature—just about any characteristic that we see in every normal person—is the result of natural selection. And that means that the aspects of your own personality that you share with everybody else probably reflect evolutionary processes.

When thinking about these characteristics, we have to keep in mind that the processes that produced human nature as it is today occurred over millions of years. After all, it's been over 6 million years since the branch of the family tree that led to modern human beings split from the branch that led to modern chimpanzees and bonobos, and many of these evolutionary processes were going on even long before then. What that means is that most of the processes that created human nature happened long before we became fully human only in the last 200,000 years or so, and these processes happened in an environment that was dramatically different from the one we live in today. We're talking about a period of several million years in which our pre-human ancestors lived in small bands that wandered across the plains of central Africa. They were hunters and gatherers and scavengers. They didn't have homes, didn't have jobs, no property except maybe a sharp rock or a stick. They didn't worry about getting an education or planning for retirement. The universal aspects of human personality evolved to meet the challenges of living in that sort of environment. That's important because it means that our personality includes some evolved tendencies that might have worked great 500,000 years ago but that aren't very helpful, and might even be problematic, in the 21st century.

At the most basic level, the evolved characteristics that are relevant to understanding personality involve psychological processes that steered behavior in ways that promoted survival and reproduction during the course of evolution. So it's helpful to think about the recurring problems that our prehistoric ancestors faced that had implications for the likelihood that they would survive and reproduce.

So as infants, they had to do things to get breast milk and to be protected by adults. Later, to survive, they had to get along with other people in a group context, they had to avoid predators, secure an ongoing supply of food, avoid toxins and diseases, and avoid getting killed by other people, to name just a few of their ongoing challenges. Then, in order to reproduce, they had to identify and attract desirable mates, fend off rivals who might pull their mate away, then be sure that whatever offspring they might have lived to reproductive age themselves. The individuals who dealt with these and many other adaptive problems most successfully passed along their genes, and those genes contained the instructions for new brains that could also solve such problems. So, let's look at just a few examples so that you'll start to get a sense of why certain emotional and behavioral tendencies are part of your own personality.

Let's start with judgments of physical attractiveness. Of course, each of us finds certain people more attractive than other people, and each of has certain personal preferences that other people might not agree with. But there are some notable consistencies in what people find attractive and unattractive that go deeper than personal preference. Some people are simply more attractive or unattractive than other people are to just about everybody. So, for example, we usually don't find people with really dark bags under their eyes to be as attractive as exactly the same people without bags under their eyes. Or people with bloodshot eyes—they're not as attractive. More obviously, people who have facial deformities—their face is crooked, or one eyelid droops—aren't as attractive. As I mentioned earlier, we also don't find people with open sores or obvious infections very attractive, and sometimes we are even viscerally repelled.

These reactions are part of your personality. Whether you like feeling this way or not—and we sometimes feel badly about having these kinds of reactions—something is affecting our judgment of other people' appearance and making us less likely to want to interact with them. Most people show a clear and consistent preference for people without dark or bloodshot eyes, or physical deformities, or open sores. And that's true of people in every culture. But why?

Because these are often signs of disease. It's not that everybody with these features is infectious or has something wrong with them, but sometimes these physical features do indicate some problem that we might catch. So, natural selection favored individuals who kept their distance from people who showed signs of being sick. Or to look at it the other way, our prehistoric ancestors who found these features desirable and who sought out people who showed signs of being infected or having a disease survived and reproduced at a lower rate than those who had negative reactions. So, now it's part of everybody's personality.

I said earlier that every normal person wants to be accepted and approved of by at least a few other people. People differ in the strength of this motive, but no one is as happy to be rejected as they are to be accepted. Again, we can trace the need for acceptance and belonging to natural selection. Today, most of us can survive without strong social connections: we can get our food at the store, go to the doctor when we're sick, count on our security system and the police to protect us, and hire people to do things that we need to have done. But for millions of years, we didn't have stores and doctors and police and hired hands to help us. Survival depended on being integrated into a supportive social group. How long would you last on the plains of Africa if you lived alone, armed only with a rock or a sharp stick? Natural selection favored individuals who were drawn to live with other people and motivated to behave in ways that led those other people to accept and support them. It was important to be concerned with how other members of the group viewed you and to avoid doing things that would get you kicked out. And that was a very adaptive strategy that increased the likelihood of survival and reproduction, not only for oneself but also for one's offspring because they were safer in the group as well. So, a strong desire for acceptance and belonging evolved to be part of the human personality.

Natural selection is also responsible for differences that we see in the personalities of men and women. There's been a good deal of controversy over the years, both among scholars and among the general public, regarding whether the differences that we see in the behavior of men and women is biological versus socialized. The pendulum has swung back and forth over the years, but there's not really any scientific doubt that differences between men and women have both biological and social sources. All other species of mammals show clear differences in the behaviors of males and females, so we would be a very unusual species if none of the sex differences that we see in human beings were evolved. But, of course, socialization and culture and learning also play a big role in how men and women act.

As we've seen, the fundamental principle underlying natural selection is that organisms that are the most successful at reproducing contribute disproportionately to the gene pool. So, we are the descendants of prehistoric people who were most successful at reproducing. But throughout evolutionary history, men and women faced different reproductive challenges and evolved different strategies to meet those challenges.

Men and woman faced different reproductive challenges because they differ biologically in their reproductive roles. First, men and women differ in reproductive constraint, the simple fact that, over a lifetime, women can potentially have a much smaller number of children than men can. Even if she works really hard at it, no woman can have more than, say, 20 children at most, and of course most women have had far fewer. On the other hand, there's almost no limit to how many children a man could have if he really wanted to. You've probably heard that Genghis Khan sired several hundred children.

Second, women invest much more into their offspring, biologically speaking, than men do both during 9 months of pregnancy and, if they're breastfeeding, for many months afterwards. They need to take in more food, they're more limited in what they can do physically, and they're at greater safety risk. Again, we're talking about life on the African savannah here. Biologically, men invest a teaspoon of semen, and that's about it. So, women potentially have fewer opportunities to have children than men, and they invest more of their biological resources into each child they have.

Now, let's think about the kinds of behaviors that natural selection would favor in order for women versus men to have a large number of healthy, genetically fit offspring, because that's the currency with which evolution operates.

Biologists tell us that if an organism has a limited number of opportunities to reproduce and must invest more into each offspring, then it should be more careful with each of its mating opportunities than an organism that has more potential opportunities to have offspring and little biological investment. With limited reproductive opportunities and greater investment, it can't afford to waste a reproductive opportunity on a bad choice, so it should be more selective in choosing mates. But an organism that can potentially have many offspring with a very low biological investment doesn't need to worry as much about any particular mating opportunity. Put differently, the greater one's reproductive constraint and biological investment, the more selective an animal should be.

You can probably see where this is going. You don't need a biologist or psychologist to tell you that women are more selective than men are when it comes to sex, although there is plenty of research that documents this difference. This is a human universal. There's no society in which women are, as a group, less choosy and careful when it comes to sex than men are. It's part of the female personality to be more selective because, throughout evolution, females who were more selective made better mating decisions and had a larger number of viable offspring who lived to reproductive age themselves. Of course that doesn't say that there aren't highly promiscuous women and highly selective men—other factors also affect people's sexual behavior—but on average, there's a difference.

Evolution may also play a role in what men and women find attractive. As I noted, we all have our personal preferences regarding who we find attractive, but we see some consistent differences between men and women that seem to be part of human nature. The most noticeable difference—and you can certainly see this in the people you know—is that, on average, men prefer mates who are younger than they are. There are plenty of personal exceptions of course. My wife is a couple of years older than I am, but this preference shows up in every one of 37 cultures in which mating preferences have been studied. You can see it starting in high school. Lots of senior guys dated sophomore and junior girls, but not many senior girls dated sophomore or junior guys, right? And, if you look at the ages of heterosexual couples in the United States, women are, on average, 2.3 years younger than their male partner. No one doubts that, all other things being equal, men prefer younger women. But why is that preference part of the male personality?

Scientists believe that it comes down to another difference in the reproductive challenges that men and women faced throughout evolution. From the standpoint of natural selection, the central reproductive task is finding a fertile mate with good genes. Anybody who mated only with someone unable to have children didn't contribute to the gene pool. So natural selection should have favored people who chose fertile mates. But finding a fertile mate has been far less of a challenge for women than for men. After all, men are potentially fertile from puberty until death; fertility certainly declines with age, but even 80-year-old men have fathered children. So, almost no matter who women chose as a mate, chances are that he was fertile. But that wasn't the case for men because women's reproductive years are limited. A woman might still have children with a 50- or 60-year-old man, but man who preferred only 50- or 60-year-old women would not have passed along his genes. So, natural selection would have favored men who preferred women who were younger than the age of menopause. Not only that, but a man was likely to have more offspring the younger his mate was because she had more child-bearing years ahead of her. And, this too would have given an evolutionary edge to men who preferred younger rather than older women. It would have been more advantageous for a 25-year-old man to have a 20-year-old mate than a 30-year-old mate because she would have more reproductive years.

So, men today are mostly the descendants of males who preferred younger, rather than older, females as mates. Whatever it was about the brains of those prehistoric men that led them to prefer younger women is still in the brains of men today. Strictly speaking, it's a little misleading to say that men's brains are designed to prefer younger women. Technically speaking, the important issue is fertility; natural selection favored men who preferred fertile women. But the male brain evolved to use cues of fertility, such as physical indicators of youthfulness, to steer men's mating choices in certain directions. Something was passed along that made the brain interpret certain signs of relative youthfulness as more pleasing and attractive than signs of old age.

This also explain why, the older a man gets, the younger his age preference is relative to his own age. A 30-year man might prefer a 28-year old woman—a 2-year difference. But if he had a choice, a 60-year old man probably prefers someone younger than 58. Let me stress that none of this makes any sense in the modern world in which people use contraception and often try to plan their families as best they can. In industrialized countries, most people who have children have only a couple. And most people, men and women alike, stop having kids by about age 40. But even though people today are virtually negating evolved dispositions to enhance reproduction, we're all walking around with a brain that evolved the way it did because it facilitated reproduction in prehistoric Africa hundreds-of-thousands of years ago.

In the early days of evolutionary psychology, the focus was on the evolution of human nature: species-typical characteristics that can be seen, more-or-less, in every normal person. More recently, however, evolutionary psychologists have turned their attention to evolved processes that may contribute to differences among people.

The general idea is that some evolved psychological adaptations may operate differently depending on different inputs from the individual's environment. If a single response is not adaptive under all circumstances, natural selection may create mechanisms that lead to different behaviors depending on environmental conditions. That means that people who live in one sort of environment may respond differently from the way those who live in another environment respond. They would consistently differ from each other in terms of their typical reactions, but the source of the differences in their personalities would be an evolved conditional adaptation, one that appears only in certain environments. Let me give a couple of examples of what I mean by conditional adaptation.

Throughout evolution, an adaptive problem that all children faced was to compete with their siblings for parental resources. Natural selection would have presumably favored children who were particularly successful at getting their share, if not more than their share, of food, protection, support, and other resources from their parents. And, if you have brothers or sisters, you know that siblings do seem to compete for their parents' attention. That seems to be more-or-less universal. But, the best strategy for getting one's share may differ depending on whether the child is the first-born child, the second-born child, third-born, or whatever. The first-born child has an easy time of it, at least until the next brother or sister comes along. Then suddenly, the first-born has to share resources with a newcomer.

One solution to this adaptive problem may be to identify with the parents and take on the responsibility of helping to raise the younger sibling. First-born children often assume such a helper role, and this leads them to develop more responsible personalities—to be higher in conscientiousness on average—than later-born kids do. The second child in a family never has as much access to parents as the first one did because big brother or sister was there from the start. Then, when the third-born child comes along, he or she seems like an add-on. What's a later-born child to do? The youngest child, whatever number he or she is, is not going to have much authority or power in the family because everybody else is older. One solution to this problem is to get attention by being nonconforming and strong-willed and maybe even a bit rebellious. Being responsible like older brother or sister isn't going to help that much.

Evolutionary psychologists talk about this sort of process as strategic niche specialization. Although all kids have faced the same general adaptive problem—how to get what they need in the context of the family—they may differ in how they pursue that goal depending on the environment that they're born into based on their birth order. They essentially specialize in filling different niches within the family, and that difference in strategic niche specialization shows up as a difference in their personalities.

Psychologists have been interested for many years in the effects of growing up in dangerous and stressful environments on personality development. No one questions that personality is affected when people grow up under very stressful conditions, whether that's a conflict-ridden family with constant fighting between the parents, or being physically abused, or growing up in a war zone. The question is: Why does stress affect personality as it does?

An evolutionary spin on this question is that the most effective strategies for dealing with common adaptive problems may differ depending on the stressfulness of the situation. If so, natural selection may have developed conditional adaptive strategies that are sensitive to the stressors in the environment. When the environment is relatively calm and stress-free, one set of strategies emerge, but when all hell is breaking loose, another set arises.

One provocative example involves the effects of childhood stress on the onset of puberty in girls. Central to this theory is the idea that human beings can potentially achieve reproductive success in one of 2 ways. When the environment is safe and predictable, the best strategy might have been to have fewer kids and invest more effort and resources in each one. But when the environment is dangerous and uncertain, the best strategy might be to pursue a faster, quantity-over-quality reproductive strategy. Under dangerous conditions, it's less certain that an individual can find a partner with whom to reproduce, and any offspring will be at greater risk as well. Interestingly, girls who grow up under more stressful conditions tend to start puberty earlier. They actually reach biological menarche, the start of menstruation, at an earlier age, and they also tend to become sexually active and start having children earlier. From an evolutionary perspective, this reflects an evolved conditional adaptation. For our purposes, it manifests as a difference in personality.

Let me stress that this explanation about the effect of stressful conditions is both speculative and controversial, but it does have a certain amount of research support. So, I mention it not as a confirmed fact but rather to show you the direction in which evolutionary analyses of personality and behavior are headed.

Let me wrap up by summarizing the 3 big take-home messages from this lecture:

1. Some aspects of your personality reflect evolved tendencies that you share with virtually everybody else. Because some ways of behaving were critical to survival and reproduction for millions of years, they became part of the shared human personality.

2. Other features of your personality evolved specifically for your sex. From the beginning, men and women have faced somewhat different reproductive problems, based mostly on the fact that they play different biological roles in reproduction. So, some sex differences in personality seem to reflect these sex-specific adaptations. And,

3. Evolutionary processes may also be responsible for certain differences among people. Because some evolved adaptations are conditional on the environment, people who live in different environments may develop different personalities.

PERSONALITY AND THE BRAIN

LECTURE 15

Everything that you think, feel, and do involves activity in the brain, so all differences in how people tend to think, feel, or behave must involve differences in their brain's anatomy or physiology. To give you a taste of the research being done on the psychophysiology of personality, this lecture will focus on 4 aspects of anatomy and physiology that involve brain regions, neurotransmitters, hormones, and bodily rhythms.

BRAIN REGIONS

- Many theorists have suggested that the most basic distinction that underlies virtually all behavior is the distinction between approach and avoidance. In other words, at the most basic level, virtually every behavioral reaction involves either approaching situations and activities and doing things or avoiding situations and activities and not doing things.

- Given the importance of this distinction for understanding behavior, researchers have worked to identify the systems in the brain that are responsible for approach and avoidance. Our current understanding of these 2 basic systems owes a debt to Jeffrey Gray, who first described them and mapped out the basic components. Researchers have extended Gray's work in many ways, including considering how these systems relate to personality.

- Approach and avoidance are controlled by 2 distinct systems: The approach system is called the behavioral activation system (BAS), and the avoidance system is called the behavioral inhibition system (BIS).

    - The BAS is the neurophysiological basis of behaviors and emotions that involve approach. The BAS is sensitive to possible rewards. Whenever rewards are salient, the BAS kicks on, orients you toward the rewarding activity, and motivates you toward doing the rewarding behavior. The BAS mediates reward-seeking behavior and the emotions that go along with seeking and getting rewards.

    - The BIS is involved in inhibition and avoidance. The BIS manages avoidance behaviors, including stopping behavior that's in progress, because the BIS is sensitive to possible punishments. Anxiety and fear and dread are the emotional language of the BIS.

- We all have activation and inhibition systems; we couldn't function and survive if we didn't have such systems. But people differ in how sensitive and active their BAS and BIS are. People differ in their overall reactions to possible rewards and punishments, which has many implications for how they feel and what they do.

- If you have a particularly active BAS, you're likely to be a bit on the impulsive side, because being impulsive reflects the fact that you find all kinds of things rewarding. If you have a more active BAS, you're also likely to be higher in extraversion than if your BAS activity is lower. The correlation between BAS and extraversion is rather high, which suggests that a sensitivity to rewards may contribute to extraversion. One reason why extraverts are out there doing extraverted things is because they find them rewarding.

- BAS scores are also related to people's tendency to experience positive emotions, which are reactions to real or anticipated rewards: The more sensitive you are to rewards, the more positive emotions you'll feel. This might also explain why people who are high in extraversion tend to have more positive emotions overall. The same brain system—the BAS—is related both to reward seeking and to positive emotions.

- Depression is associated with lower scores on measures of the BAS. It's not clear whether an underactive BAS predisposes people to depression (because they don't find things rewarding) or whether depression makes people less responsive to rewards—but it's probably both.

- On the other hand, the BIS—the avoidance system—is associated with the tendency to experience negative emotions because negative emotions are reactions to potential or actual punishments. So, the BIS is associated with the degree to which people experience anxiety, fear, frustration, sadness, disappointment, regret, dread, and just about every other emotion that occurs when bad things happen. If you have an active BIS, you probably score higher in neuroticism than if your BIS is less active.

- Whereas higher BAS is associated with impulsivity, higher BIS is associated with restraint—with inhibition and avoidance. People with a more active BIS are more risk averse; they're more focused on being sure that bad things don't happen than on seeking rewards.

- People who are higher in conscientiousness tend to be higher in both BAS and BIS than people who are lower in conscientiousness. One interpretation of this pattern is that people who are particularly conscientious and responsible are motivated both by the possible rewards they get from behaving conscientiously and also by the possible punishments of not being conscientious.

- Agreeableness is negatively associated with BAS and positively associated with BIS: Agreeableness is lower among reward-oriented people and higher among punishment-oriented people. This pattern suggests that agreeable people are more motivated by a concern with social punishments than by a desire for rewards.

- Curiously, openness isn't related to BAS one way or the other. However, openness is negatively related to BIS; people higher in openness tend to have a less active BIS. Openness seems to be higher when people don't fear punishment as much, so it looks like people are more open to new and different things when they aren't as afraid of having bad experiences.

- A good deal of research has explored ways in which brain activity differs for people who score low versus high on measures of BAS and BIS. As expected, the areas of the brain that seem to be related to the BAS are those that involve positive emotions, reactions to rewards, and the motivation to engage in behavior.

- While the neural substrates of the BAS are reasonably well established, the brain regions that mediate the BIS are less clear. The BIS does seem to involve neural structures that detect potential threats and violations of expectancies, but researchers have debated whether the BIS primarily manages avoidance or whether its purpose is to detect and manage conflicts between the impulses to approach and avoid.

NEUROTRANSMITTERS

- The nerve cells in your brain—the neurons—communicate with each other by releasing chemicals called neurotransmitters that stimulate, or sometimes inhibit, activity in other neurons. The concentration of neurotransmitters in various areas of the brain can influence people's reactions, making some responses more likely than others. And in affecting the tendency for neurons to fire, these neurotransmitters can affect people's personalities.

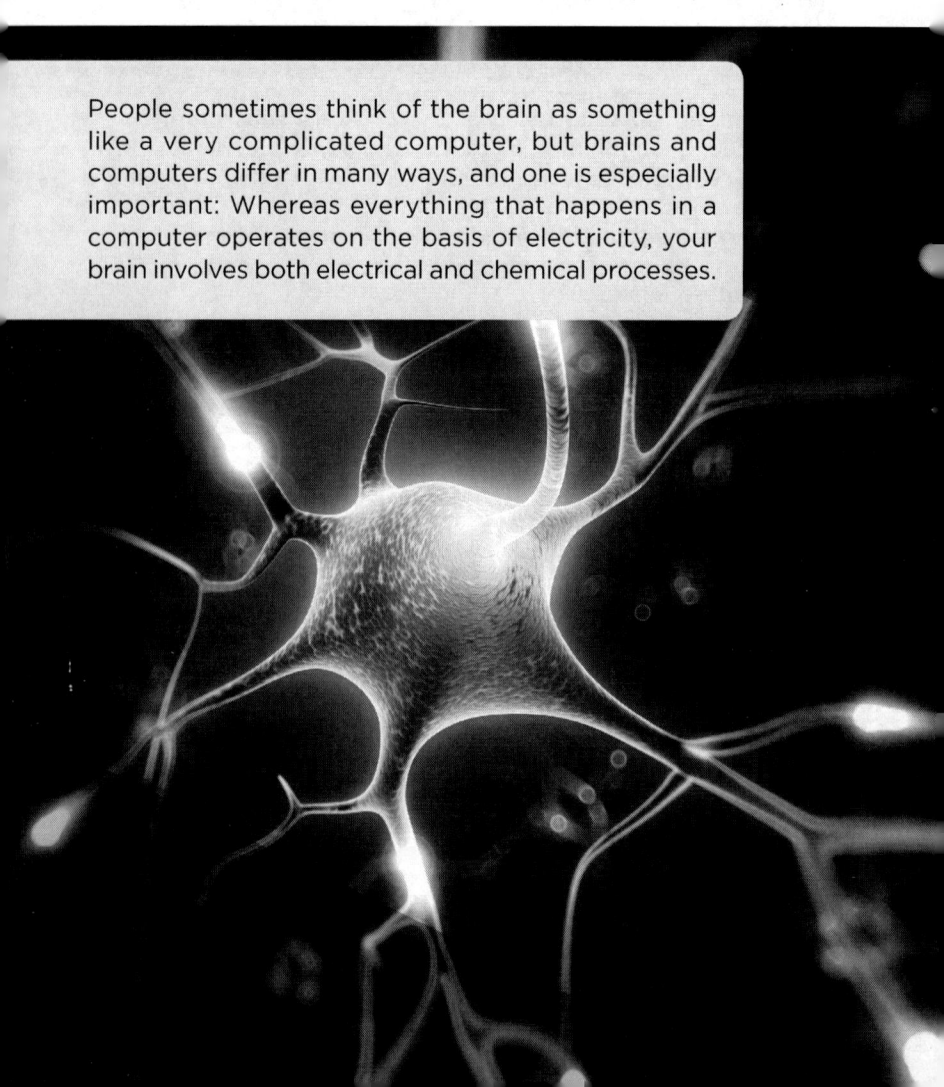

People sometimes think of the brain as something like a very complicated computer, but brains and computers differ in many ways, and one is especially important: Whereas everything that happens in a computer operates on the basis of electricity, your brain involves both electrical and chemical processes.

- Dozens of neurotransmitters have been identified, but a handful do the bulk of the work in neurotransmission, and these are the ones that have gotten the greatest research attention.

- To give just one example of how neurotransmitters relate to personality, let's consider the trait of sensation seeking, which was first identified during early research on the effects of stimulus deprivation.

- People differ a lot in how they respond to a low level of stimulation. Some people find lack of stimulation restful and relaxing, and other people find it very unpleasant, almost maddening. This led researcher Marvin Zuckerman to a life-long interest in personality differences in the degree to which people need stimulation—that is, to an interest in the trait of sensation seeking.

- People who are high in sensation seeking enjoy and seek out intense and exciting experiences. In everyday language, we might call them thrill seekers. They tend to like doing things that involve intense stimulation, such as skydiving and attending wild parties. They tend to drive faster than average and play their music louder. And they get bored easily when nothing exciting is going on.

- High sensation seekers also engage in more risky behaviors. For example, they're more likely to take illegal drugs, and they make more risky bets when they gamble.

- Sensation seeking is also related to people's job preferences. People who like a lot of stimulation go a little batty in quiet, unstimulating jobs. On the other hand, people who go into the military or who work in emergency rooms tend to score higher than average in sensation seeking.

- Sensation seeking is highly heritable. Part of the reason why some people crave stimulation, novelty, and intensity more than other people do involves neurotransmitters specifically, an enzyme called monoamine oxidase. Studies show that people who are higher in sensation seeking have lower levels of monoamine oxidase.

HORMONES

- Hormones are chemicals that the body produces that regulate the activity of certain cells or bodily organs, including helping bones and organs grow and regulating metabolism. And some of these hormones have a direct effect on the brain, increasing or decreasing the likelihood of certain emotions, motives, or behaviors.

- As an example, the hormone testosterone is responsible for male secondary sexual characteristics—all of the changes in appearance, body hair, muscle mass, and voice that boys experience at puberty. Overall, testosterone is not related to basic dimensions of personality, such as the big five, but it is clearly related to a narrow swath of behaviors that involve aggression and dominance.

Studies of men who are in prison show that prisoners with higher testosterone are more likely to have been incarcerated for violent crimes, such as murder and assault, whereas those with lower levels of testosterone are likely to be in prison for nonviolent crimes.

- For example, high levels of testosterone are related to getting into arguments and confrontations with people, and people who have higher concentrations of testosterone are more aggressive.

- Men have a much higher concentration of testosterone than women—8 to 10 times more, depending on their age—which might partly explain why men are much more likely to behave aggressively than women are. That's not to say that social factors don't also play a role in differences in aggression between men and women, but the males of almost all mammalian species are more aggressive than the females, and testosterone seems to be the reason.

- Researchers once interpreted these findings as reflecting a direct link between testosterone and aggressiveness, but the thinking now is that testosterone may not directly cause aggression. Instead, it predisposes people to be motivated to exert dominance and power over other people. Being angry and aggressive is one way to exert one's power and dominate others, but there are also other ways.

BODILY RHYTHMS

- Whether you are a morning person or an evening person involves the nature of your daily, circadian rhythm, which has a strong genetic basis and is relatively stable over long periods of time. Research has uncovered genetic differences between people who reported that they were morning or evening types, and those differences involved genes that are related to daily rhythms.

- Of course, we all have to conform to the schedules of daily life, but that doesn't mean that our body's natural rhythms necessarily go along with what society wants us to do.

- There is obviously some flexibility in these rhythms, particularly for people who aren't genetically programmed to be strong morning or evening types. In fact, we see general shifts in preferences across the life span. On average, people shift a little toward becoming more of an evening person around the age of 13, which reflects youth culture's preference for staying up late.

- Then, as people get jobs and have families, they usually have to start getting up earlier. But even then, many adults who have to drag themselves out of bed every morning haven't really become full-fledged morning people. Then, another shift tends to occur around age 50 toward becoming more of a morning person. We're not sure why.

- We usually talk about morningness and eveningness as if it's a dichotomy or a type. In fact, researchers call whether you are a morning person or an evening person your chronotype. But less than half of the population can be clearly classified as one type or the other, and most people fall in between. So, like most personality characteristics, this looks more like a continuous trait than a categorical type.

- Certainly, when we look at other indicators of chronotype than self-report—such as if we measure people's body temperature cycles or their ratings of how alert they feel at certain times during the day—morningness and eveningness look more like a continuum than like a dichotomy. But people do differ along this continuum, and people at the extremes—the true morning people (called larks by researchers) and the true evening people (called owls)—differ in ways that are reflected in their personalities.

- For example, morning people tend to be more conscientious than evening people are, and they also tend to be less impulsive. Larks also have a more proactive approach to life than owls in the sense that they show a greater ability to take action to change situations to their advantage.

- Larks tend to do better in school than owls. On the other hand, owls tend to score higher in extraversion than morning people do, and they seem to be more creative. They're also higher in their desire to have fun. Evening people also tend to consume more addictive substances, both legal substances (such as nicotine and caffeine) and illegal drugs.

Suggested Reading

Siever, "The Frontiers of Pharmacology."

Sullivan, "The He Hormone."

Questions to Consider

1. Looking at your own behaviors and emotional reactions, do you think that your personality is dominated by the behavioral activation system (approach) or the behavioral inhibition system (avoidance), or do these systems seem to be equally strong for you? What evidence supports your answer?

2. Do you think that you are low, average, or high in sensation seeking? How has your life been affected by your level of sensation seeking, and how might your life be better or worse if you had a different level of sensation seeking?

PERSONALITY AND THE BRAIN
LECTURE 15 TRANSCRIPT

Everything that you think, feel, and do involves activity in the brain, so all differences in how people tend to think, feel, or behave must involve differences in their brain's anatomy or physiology. Let me say that again: All differences that we see in people's personalities—and I literally mean all—are based on differences in what's happening somewhere in their brains. All psychological traits are rooted in biology. Where else would personality come from? Some of those biological differences are due to genetic influences, how our brains were designed from the start. And some of those differences are due to changes in the brain that are the result of what we experience and learn in the course of our lives. But at the moment that we have a thought or feel an emotion or behave in a particular way, something is happening in the brain.

Researchers have been interested for many years in understanding how differences among people's personalities correspond to differences in their brains, and in exploring exactly how activity in various parts of the brain relates to personality. What regions of the brain are active when a particular aspect of personality manifests? What neurotransmitters or hormones are involved? How do the processes work? Until recently, these were difficult questions to answer because researchers lacked the ability to examine the brains of living people at a high level of resolution, but technological advances in neuroscience over the past 20 years have created an explosion of research on this topic. We now have ways to scan the brain and measure neurotransmitters and conduct genetic analyses that give us much greater insight into what's happening inside the brain.

Now, you might ask, "Well, if all of human behavior and all of personality come down to what's happening in the brain, why don't we just study the brain? Why have we been talking about all of this other stuff in this course?" I addressed this question briefly at the outset of our discussions, but let me answer it in greater depth by giving you 3 answers to why understanding behavior and personality requires much more than just knowing what's going on in the brain.

First, knowing what's happening in the brain, what region is involved or what neurotransmitters are responsible, doesn't address most interesting and important questions about the causes of behavior. Even if we knew exactly what's happening in people's brains when, say, their feelings are hurt or they have a prejudiced attitude or they procrastinate, we still wouldn't understand what causes the brain to respond in a way that causes hurt feelings, prejudice, or procrastination. Answering the question only at the level of biological processes in the brain misses the big psychological and social influences.

Second, the fact is that we don't understand the brain well enough to identify the necessary and sufficient biological processes that create most emotional, cognitive, and behavioral reactions. We can talk in general terms about the anatomical structures and physiological processes, but we don't know enough about the details.

And, third, biological explanations don't provide enough information to help us change people's personalities. Without understanding the psychological and social factors that are involved in hurt feelings or prejudice or procrastination, we couldn't help people reduce how much their feelings are hurt, how prejudiced they feel, or how much they procrastinate. Yes, pharmaceutical companies are finding ways to change our brain activity through drugs, which is fine when some biochemical problem is involved. But, in general, I don't think that we want to start writing prescriptions to change people's personalities. So, a biological level of analysis by itself isn't sufficient for understanding the complexities of personality, but it's certainly very important. To give you just a taste of the research being done on the psychophysiology of personality, I want to focus on 4 aspects of anatomy and physiology that involve brain regions, neurotransmitters, hormones, and bodily rhythms.

Many theorists have suggested that the most basic distinction that underlies virtually all behavior is the distinction between approach and avoidance. That is, at the most basic level, virtually every behavioral reaction involves either approaching situations and activities and doing things, or else avoiding situations and activities and not doing things. Your life is a never-ending journey through the land of approach and avoidance.

Given the importance of this distinction for understanding behavior, researchers have worked to identify the systems in the brain that are responsible for approach and avoidance. Our current understanding of these 2 basic systems owes a debt to Jeffrey Gray, who first described them and mapped out the basic components. Researchers have extended Gray's work in many ways, including considering how these systems relate to personality.

Approach and avoidance are controlled by 2 distinct systems. The approach system is called the behavioral activation system, and the avoidance system is called the behavioral inhibition system. Let me tell you about what these 2 systems do and then talk about how they relate to personality.

The behavioral activation system, which neuroscientists usually call BAS—B-A-S for behavioral activation system—is the neurophysiological basis of behaviors and emotions that involve approach. Think for a moment about why you approach and engage in certain activities. Generally, it's because you expect that the behavior will bring about a reward, or at least that it will be more rewarding than something else that you might do instead. So, the behavioral activation system is sensitive to possible rewards, whether you're approaching an enjoyable activity, an attractive person, or a piece of cake. Whenever rewards are salient, the BAS kicks on, orients you toward the rewarding activity, and motivates you toward doing the rewarding behavior. BAS mediates reward-seeking behavior and the emotions that go along with seeking and getting rewards. So when you experience hope, for example, that's your BAS orienting you toward a future reward. When you feel happiness or joy, BAS is responding to an actual reward. When something is fun, that's BAS talking.

The behavioral inhibition system, or BIS—B-I-S—is involved in inhibition and avoidance. BIS manages avoidance behaviors, including stopping behavior that's in progress, because BIS is sensitive to possible punishments. So, if you're reluctant to introduce yourself to someone because you're afraid of rejection, your BIS is active. Or when you stop suddenly because you see a snake on the path ahead of you, that's BIS. When you procrastinate because you don't want to do something unpleasant, the behavioral inhibition system is operating. Anxiety and fear and dread are the emotional language of the BIS.

Now, we all have activation and inhibition systems; we couldn't function and survive if we didn't have systems that activate behavior and pull us toward certain things and systems that stop behavior and push us away from other things. But, for purposes of understanding personality, the important thing is that people differ in how sensitive and active their BAS and BIS are. People differ in their overall reactions to possible rewards and punishments, which has many implications for how they feel and what they do.

First, if you have a particularly active behavioral activation system, you're likely to be a bit on the impulsive side. Why? Because being impulsive reflects the fact that you find all sorts of thing rewarding. So, you sit down to do one thing, and then some other rewarding thing pops up, and off you go. And when you get an idea of something rewarding or fun to do, you often do it without a great deal of thought because your BAS is motivating you to seek rewards.

If you have a more active BAS, you're also likely to be higher in extraversion than if your BAS activity is lower. The correlation between BAS and extraversion is rather high, which suggests that a sensitivity to rewards may contribute to extraversion. One reason why extraverts are out there doing extraverted things is because they find them rewarding. BAS scores are also related to people's tendency to experience positive emotions. Positive emotions are reactions to real or anticipated rewards, so the more sensitive you are to rewards, the more positive emotions you'll feel.

This might also help explain why people high in extraversion tend to have more positive emotions overall. The same brain system, BAS, is related both to reward-seeking and to positive emotions. And, we know that depression is associated with lower scores on measures of BAS. It's not clear whether an underactive BAS predisposes people to depression because they don't find things rewarding, or whether depression makes people less responsive to rewards. Probably both. So, overall, people who have a more active behavioral activation system are more influenced by the possibility of rewards than people with a less active BAS.

On the other hand, the behavioral inhibition system—the avoidance system—is associated with the tendency to experience negative emotions because negative emotions are reactions to potential or actual punishments. So, BIS is associated with the degree to which people experience anxiety, fear, frustration, sadness, disappointment, regret, dread, and just about every other emotion that occurs when bad things happen. If you have an active BIS, you probably score higher in neuroticism than if your BIS is less active. Whereas higher BAS is associated with impulsivity, higher BIS is associated with restraint, with inhibition and avoidance. People with a more active behavioral inhibition system are more risk-averse; they're more focused on being sure that bad things don't happen than on seeking rewards.

So, extraversion is associated with an active BAS, and neuroticism is associated with an active BIS. But what about the other 3 big five traits? Well, people higher in conscientiousness tend to be higher in both BAS and BIS than people who are lower in conscientiousness. One interpretation of this pattern is that people who are particularly conscientious and responsible are motivated both by the possible rewards they get from behaving conscientiously, and also by the possible punishments of not being conscientious.

On the other hand, agreeableness is negatively associated with BAS and positively associated with BIS. Think about that for a moment: agreeableness is lower among people who are reward-oriented and higher among people who are punishment-oriented. That pattern suggests that agreeable people are more motivated by a concern with social punishments than by a desire for rewards.

And finally, what about the trait of openness? Is openness related to approach or avoidance? Is it related to BAS or to BIS? You might think that open people are especially drawn by the rewards of new and different things so they'd be high in BAS. But curiously, openness isn't related to BAS one way or the other! That is, people's scores on measures of openness don't correlate with scores on measures of BAS. However, openness is negatively related to BIS. People higher in openness tend to have a less active behavioral inhibition system. Openness seems to be higher when people don't fear punishment as much. So, it looks like people are more open to new and different things when they aren't as afraid of having bad experiences. Here's a case where considering the neurological underpinnings of personality revealed information about openness that was different than we might have expected.

A good deal of research has explored ways in which brain activity differs for people who score low versus high on BAS and BIS. As we would expect, the areas of the brain that seem to be related to the behavioral activation system are those that involve positive emotions, reactions to rewards, and the motivation to engage in behavior. I won't go into details about the specific brain regions and neurotransmitters that are involved, which would require a long lecture on brain anatomy and physiology, but the neural substrates of the behavioral activation system are reasonably well-established. However, the brain regions that mediate the behavioral inhibition system are less clear. BIS does seem to involve neural structures that detect potential threats and violations of expectancies. But researchers have debated whether BIS primarily manages avoidance, or whether its purpose is to detect and manage conflicts between the impulse to avoid and the impulse to approach

In other words, rather than simply causing people to avoid things, BIS might function to detect situations in which tendencies to approach and to avoid are in conflict with each other. When your urges to approach and avoid something are competing, BIS may lead you to analyze the situation to decide how to respond. So, BIS might be designed to stop behavior when it's not clear whether one should approach or avoid a stimulus. In any case, neuroscientific studies have helped to clarify exactly how people with tendencies to be low or high in BIS and BAS differ from each other.

People sometimes think of the brain as something like a very complicated computer, but brains and computers differ in many ways, and one is especially important: Whereas everything that happens in a computer operates on the basis of electricity, your brain involves both electrical and chemical processes. In particular, the nerve cells in your brain—the neurons—communicate with each other by releasing chemicals called neurotransmitters that stimulate or sometimes inhibit activity in other neurons.

You might have learned somewhere along the way that neurons aren't directly connected to each other. Instead, they're separated from one another by a small gap—the synapse—and a nerve impulse has to cross this gap to continue on its way along a nerve. And the impulse crosses this gap when one neuron releases a chemical—a neurotransmitter—that then stimulates the next neuron or set of neurons. So, the transmission of a signal in the brain isn't like electricity going from one wire to another; the transmission between neurons involves chemicals. Importantly, the concentration of the chemicals in the synapse—the space between the neurons—has to be just right. If there's not enough neurotransmitter, the next neuron might not fire. If there's too much neurotransmitter, the next neuron might continue to fire even though it shouldn't.

What that means is that the concentration of neurotransmitters in various areas of the brain can influence people's reactions, making some responses more likely than others. And, in affecting the tendency for neurons to fire, these neurotransmitters can affect people's personalities. Dozens of neurotransmitters have been identified, but a handful do the bulk of the work in neurotransmission, and these are the ones that have gotten the greatest research attention.

To give just one example of how neurotransmitters relate to personality, let's consider the trait of sensation-seeking. Sensation-seeking was first identified during early research on the effects of stimulus deprivation. The question was: What happens to people when they're deprived of ordinary stimulation for a while, such as having to sit alone in an empty, silent room for hours? Would that bother you? Well, people differ a lot in how they respond to a low level of stimulation. Some people find lack of stimulation restful and relaxing, and other people find it very unpleasant, almost maddening. This led researcher Marvin Zuckerman to a life-long interest in personality differences in the degree to which people need stimulation—that is, to an interest in the trait of sensation-seeking.

People who are high in sensation-seeking enjoy and seek out intense and exciting experiences. In everyday language, we might call them thrill-seekers. They tend to like doing things that involve intense stimulation: roller coaster rides, sky diving, bungee jumping, scuba diving, mountain climbing, wild parties, those sorts of things. They tend to drive faster than average, and play their music louder as well. And not surprisingly, they get bored easily when nothing exciting is going on. High sensation-seekers also engage in more risky behaviors: they're more likely to speed and to get traffic tickets, they practice safe sex less regularly, they're more likely to take illicit drugs, and they make more risky bets when they gamble. It's not that they necessarily want to do dangerous things, but taking risks is a way to have intense, arousing experiences. And high sensation-seekers like that.

And, sensation seeking is related to people's job preferences. People who like a lot of stimulation go a little batty in quiet, unstimulating jobs. So, it's not surprising that people who go into the military and into police work or who work in emergency rooms tend to score higher than average in sensation-seeking. Sensation-seeking is highly heritable. In fact, its heritability is higher than almost any other trait that we'll talk about. But what's being inherited? Why do some people crave stimulation and novelty and intensity more than other people do?

Part of the answer to that question involves neurotransmitters. It's a complicated picture, and I'm not going to go into all of the details, but it comes down to an enzyme called monoamine oxidase, often called M-A-O, that maintains a proper level of neurotransmitters in the synapses between neurons. Studies show that people who are higher in sensation-seeking have lower levels of monoamine oxidase. One study even showed that professional bullfighters, who could be the poster children for high sensation-seeking, have abnormally low MAO.

Monoamine oxidase helps to break down neurotransmitters after they've been released into the synapse, so having too little monoamine oxidase results in too much neurotransmitter hanging around in the synapse. So, if your level of monoamine oxidase is low, certain neurons will continue to fire and you will have excessive activity in certain areas of the brain. And many researchers believe that having this high level of activity in certain brain regions causes people to have a higher desire for stimulation and sensations. It's not as simple a process as one enzyme affecting one neurotransmitter that causes sensation-seeking, but researchers are convinced that monoamine oxidase and neurotransmitters are part of the story behind high sensation-seeking.

You might never have thought much about hormones being involved in personality because they don't seem to be part of the brain. But in fact, certain hormones do act on the brain in ways that affect emotion and behavior. Hormones are chemicals that the body produces that regulate the activity of certain cells or bodily organs. So, there are hormones that help bones and organs grow, control the menstrual cycle, regulate metabolism, maintain proper levels of blood sugar, and so on. And some of these hormones have a direct effect on the brain, increasing or decreasing the likelihood of certain emotions, motives, or behaviors.

Let's consider the hormone, testosterone, for example. As you know, testosterone is responsible for male secondary sexual characteristics—all of the changes in appearance, body hair, muscle mass, and voice that boys experience at puberty. Testosterone can be reliably measured in saliva, so researchers have looked at the relationship between testosterone concentrations and various aspects of personality. Overall, testosterone is not related to basic dimensions of personality, such as the big five, but it is clearly related to a narrow swath of behaviors that involve aggression and dominance. For example, high levels of testosterone are related to getting into arguments and confrontations with people, and people who have higher concentrations of testosterone are more aggressive. Studies of men who are in prison show that prisoners with higher testosterone are more likely to have been incarcerated for violent crimes, such as murder and assault, whereas those with lower levels of testosterone are likely to be in prison for nonviolent crimes.

Of course, men have a much higher concentration of testosterone than women—8 to 10 times more depending on their age—which might partly explain why men are much more likely to behave aggressively than women are. That's not to say that social factors don't also play a role in sex differences in aggression between men and women, but the males of almost all mammalian species are more aggressive than the females, and testosterone seems to be the reason.

Researchers once interpreted these findings as reflecting a direct link between testosterone and aggressiveness, but the thinking now is that testosterone may not directly cause aggression. Instead it predisposes people to be motivated to exert dominance and power over other people. Of course, being angry and aggressive is one way to exert one's power and dominate others, but there are other ways as well. Whatever the connection, testosterone contributes to personality differences in dominance and aggression.

Let me wrap up our discussion of biological influences on personality with a variable that you might not think of as a personality characteristic at all. And that's whether you are a morning person or an evening person.

When you aren't being controlled by schedules that are imposed on you by work or school or other people, do you tend to get up early, often without an alarm clock, feel most energetic early in the day, and then go to bed relatively early in the evening? Or do you sleep later, feel most energetic in the afternoon and evening, and then go to bed late? Some of you will fall in between these extremes and say that neither one perfectly describes you, but many of you will say that you are clearly and consistently either a morning person or an evening person. Researchers who study this difference call you morning people "larks" and you evening people "owls."

Whether you are a morning person or an evening person involves the nature of your daily, circadian rhythm, which has a strong genetic basis and is relatively stable over long periods of time. Research has uncovered genetic differences between people who reported that they were morning or evening types, and those differences involved genes that are related to daily rhythms. Of course, we all have to conform to the schedules of daily life, but that doesn't mean that our body's natural rhythms necessarily go along with what society wants us to do.

There is obviously some flexibility in these rhythms, particularly for people who aren't genetically programmed to be strong morning or evening types. In fact, we see general 2 shifts in preferences across the life span. On average, people shift a little toward becoming more of an evening person around the age of 13, which reflects youth culture's preference for staying up late. Then, as people get jobs and have families, they usually have to start getting up earlier. But even then, many adults who have to drag themselves out of bed every morning haven't really become full-fledged morning people. Then another shift tends to occur around age 50 toward becoming a more morning person. We're not sure why.

We usually talk about morning-ness and evening-ness as if it's a dichotomy or a type. In fact, researchers call whether you are a morning person or an evening person your chronotype. But, less than half of the population can be clearly classified as one type or the other, and most of us fall in between. We wake up at some midrange time that's neither really early nor really late, and go to bed at a reasonable, but not too early, hour. So, like most personality characteristics, this looks more like a continuous trait rather than a categorical type. Certainly when we look at other indicators of chronotype than self-report, such as if we measure people's body temperature cycles or their ratings of how alert they feel at certain times during the day, morning-ness and evening-ness look more like a continuum than like a dichotomy. But, regardless, people do differ along this continuum, and people at the extremes—the true larks and true owls—differ in ways that are reflected in their personalities. For example, morning people tend to be more conscientious than evening people are, and going along with that, they also tend to be less impulsive. Larks also have a more proactive approach to life than owls in the sense that they show a greater ability to take action to change situations to their advantage. Larks tend to do better in school than owls. Whether that's due to their greater conscientiousness and proactivity or to the fact that they're more likely to be alert during morning classes isn't clear.

On the other hand, owls, the evening people, tend to score higher in extraversion than morning people do, and they seem to be more creative. They're also higher in their desire to have fun, so perhaps they have a more active behavioral activation system. Since more fun things tend to happen at night than in the early morning, maybe owls stay up later partly because their BAS leads them to seek rewarding experiences. Evening people also tend to consume more addictive substances, both legal substances—such as nicotine and caffeine—and illegal drugs. But what's not clear is whether owls have a more addictive personality or whether this is simply due to the fact they stay up and socialize later at night. Morning and evening people spend different amounts of time in different social environments during the day. Whatever the connection between personality and morning-ness or evening-ness, it's clear that biological rhythms play a role in our lifestyle, when we're at our best, and when we prefer to say goodnight.

I've touched on just a few topics from work in neuroscience to give you a sense of the ways in which biological factors can influence personality. I wanted you to see that that personality differences arise not only from differences in the structure and activity of the brain, but also from neurotransmitters, hormones, and the body's natural rhythms.

While we still have a lot to learn about how biological and other factors combine to make us who we are, the pace of research suggests that many important discoveries are just around the corner.

GENETIC INFLUENCES ON PERSONALITY

LECTURE 16

One of psychology's longest-standing controversies is the nature-nurture debate: the genetic factors that influence who we are (nature) versus the environmental variables that influence who were are (nurture)—not only how we were raised, but also our personal experiences, our social relationships, and the influence of the surrounding culture. Today, there is no doubt that personality—almost every major characteristic that has been studied—is influenced by both nature and nurture. This lecture addresses how strong the effect of genes versus the environment is for particular traits, how genes and environment interact to affect personality, and how genetic influences can affect people's environments.

GENES AND PERSONALITY

- Most of the work on genetic influences on personality has been conducted by researchers in behavioral genetics, which is an interdisciplinary field that studies the genetic and environmental influences on personality and behavior. It's essentially the field that studies questions about nature and nurture.

- The goal of behavioral genetics is to document how much genetic and environmental factors influence behavior and to study the ways in which genes and environment operate, both individually and together, to produce differences in personality.

- The central concept that we need to understand to make sense out of research findings in behavioral genetics is the concept of heritability, which is defined as the proportion of phenotypic variance in a trait that is attributable to genetic variance.

- Phenotypic variance is simply the observed variability in some characteristic. Normally, biologists think about variability in an animal's physical characteristics, but for behavioral geneticists, phenotypic variance is the variability that we observe in some behavior or psychological characteristic across people.

- As a proportion, the heritability of a trait can range from 0—indicating that none of the phenotypic variance in a trait is due to genetics—to 1—indicating that all of the variance in the trait is due to genetics. In between 0 and 1, the heritability tells us the proportion of variability in the trait that's due to genetic influences.

- Although certain physical characteristics, such as eye color, have heritabilities of 1, no personality trait seems to be completely determined by genes, so we never see heritabilities of 1 in behavioral genetics. We also rarely see a heritability of 0, as most behavior has at least some small genetic component.

- When it comes to the 5 basic dimensions of personality—extraversion, neuroticism, agreeableness, conscientiousness, and openness—somewhere between about 40% and 60% of the variability we observe in these traits is due to genetic factors. Genes play a big role in why we are the way we are with respect to the big five traits.

> Research shows that the heritability of height for Americans is 0.87, which means that 87% of the variability we observe in height is due to differences in genes. Only 13% of the variability in height is due to nongenetic influences—mostly nutritional factors.

- Heritability is a population-based statistic, which means that it tells us the proportion of the variability in a trait that is genetic when we consider everyone in a particular population. But heritability does not tell us how much of your personality, or any individual's personality, is due to genetics.

- There's no way to know what proportion of a given individual's personality is due to genetic versus environmental influences. But even though heritability is based on population-level analyses, it does give us a ballpark idea of how much genes versus environment have influenced any one of us.

- Virtually every personality characteristic shows evidence of being influenced by genes. Of course, their heritabilities differ: Some traits are more strongly influenced by genes than other traits are. But most traits have a genetic basis, and the heritability for most of them falls between about 0.3 and 0.6. About 30% to 60% of the variability in most traits is due to genetic factors.

- Researchers in behavioral genetics use a number of approaches to estimate the heritability of a trait, but most of them come down to comparing the personalities of people who share genes and/or environments. Statistical analyses are conducted to estimate heritability for whatever trait is being studied.

- Some studies compare the personalities of adopted children to the personalities of both their biological parents and their adoptive parents. If the personalities of children who were adopted early in life resemble those of their biological parents more than those of their adoptive parents, then genetic influences appear to be operating. If they resemble their adoptive parents more than their natural parents, the environment seems to have an effect.

- Other studies compare monozygotic (or identical) to dizygotic (or fraternal) twins to see the degree to which monozygotic twins are more similar in their personalities than dizygotic twins are. If monozygotic twins are more similar than dizygotic twins, then genetic factors may be responsible because monozygotic twins are more similar genetically. This kind of comparison is enhanced when the twins have been either raised together—in the same family—or raised apart, which permits a more nuanced analysis of genetic and environmental effects.

- Many genetic influences on personality begin to reveal themselves soon after birth. Personality traits that are obvious soon after birth—inborn personality characteristics—are called temperaments by psychologists. Researchers have identified a number of characteristics that can be observed soon after birth, although they disagree about how many temperaments there actually are.

> The heritability of intelligence, as measured by standard IQ tests, is about 0.5, which means that 50% of the variability that we see in intelligence across people is due to genetic differences among them. This also means that environmental factors affect intelligence about the same amount.

- Perhaps the most obvious temperament in newborns is activity level. Babies show a good deal of consistency in activity across situations and time: Active babies tend to stay active as they get older, and less active babies remain less active. So, differences in activity that exist at birth persist as features of personality.

- Fearfulness is also considered a temperament. Interestingly, research shows that the degree to which children react fearfully as young infants predicts their scores on measures of neuroticism as they get older. Furthermore, some babies are easier to soothe when they're upset, whereas for others, there's not much you can do to make them feel better. The basis of low and high neuroticism is present at birth, which makes sense given that neuroticism is partly heritable.

- We should be careful not to conclude that all differences that we see among newborns are necessarily genetic. After all, a developing fetus is exposed to environmental influences even before birth. The mother's emotions, nutrition, drug use, and other factors during pregnancy can affect the fetus's developing brain in ways that have implications for personality later on. Even so, most of the differences that we see in personality at birth are probably due to genes.

GENES AND ATTITUDE

◆ In addition to influencing personality traits, genes can play a role in people's attitudes. We usually think of attitudes as something we learn from other people—from our parents or peers or culture at large—but research shows that a wide variety of attitudes have sizable heritabilities.

◆ For example, the heritability of attitudes toward the death penalty is 0.5—just as high as for major personality characteristics. In other words, 50% of the variability in people's attitudes toward the death penalty is due to genetic differences. Not all attitudes have a genetic component, though. For example, the heritability for attitudes toward playing organized sports is 0.

The heritability of identifying as politically liberal or conservative is 0.43.

Attitudes toward organized religion have a heritability of 0.45.

The heritability of attitudes about exercise is 0.36.

Attitudes toward reading have a heritability of 0.37.

- Even when the heritability of a trait or attitude is high, it's misleading to say that people are inheriting their personality or attitudes except in a very loose sense. You don't actually inherit your traits or attitudes or behaviors; rather, you inherit a nervous system that tends to respond in particular ways. Genes influence the development of our physical body, including the brain and other parts of the nervous system, and that's what you actually inherit.

- Just as genes can cause people to be tall or have bad eyesight, genes also influence the structure of our brains. And differences in how the brain operates can lead people to respond in different ways.

- For example, the limbic system is the part of the brain that's directly involved in responding to threatening and stressful events. If your genes led you to have a limbic system that is unusually responsive to threats, you'll probably score high in neuroticism. Technically, you didn't actually inherit neuroticism—you inherited a brain that has an active limbic system. Likewise, if you inherited a limbic system that's less responsive than average, you'll probably be lower in neuroticism.

- Researchers have only started to explore the genetically determined differences in people's brains that underlie various personality characteristics, but whatever personality differences among people are due to genetic influences must be due to differences in how their brains operate.

- The same thing holds for attitudes. People whose brains respond in certain ways will find certain attitudes more agreeable to them than people whose brains respond in other ways. For example, if your genes designed your brain in such a way that you happen to find highly stimulating activities enjoyable, you'll have more positive attitudes toward stimulating activities, and you'll be high in sensation seeking.

- Similarly, if your genes designed your brain in such a way that makes you prefer stability and dislike change, you're likely to be more traditional and maybe lean toward conservative ideas. But if your brain leads you to like novelty and to be open to change and new ideas, you might be more likely to be liberal.

- Your environment, upbringing, and experiences also played a role in your political views, and your environment might even have overridden your inherited inclinations. But by creating a brain that responds in a particular way, your genes probably played a role in your political attitudes. Keep in mind that it's also possible to develop an attitude that has no apparent genetic basis.

Think about the link between genes and attitudes when you deal with people whose attitudes are so different from yours that you can't fathom how someone could hold such views. Remind yourself that your difficulty in understanding these people might lie in the fact that your brain is designed so differently from theirs that you can't even begin to resonate with their attitude. And, of course, they don't understand your views either.

GENES AND ENVIRONMENT

- Genes can influence our personality not only by designing our brain in a particular way, but also by changing our environment in ways that then affect our personality. Genes can influence personality in 3 distinct ways, some of which make it difficult to disentangle the separate influences of genes and environment:

    1. Most obviously, genes can affect personality and behavior more or less directly by influencing the brain and other parts of the nervous system.

    2. A second way that genes affect personality arises when genes create a brain that leads people to behave in ways that affect their environment and then the environment affects the person's personality. This process is called a reactive, or evocative, gene-environment correlation, in which a person's genes directly affect the nervous system and lead to certain patterns of behavior, which lead to certain reactions from other people, which affect the person's personality.

    3. A third way that genes can influence personality is known as an active gene-environment correlation, in which genes create a brain that is associated with certain motives, interests, preferences, or behaviors, and these genetically influenced inclinations lead the person to gravitate toward certain environments and activities. Then, spending time in those particular environments affects the person's personality.

A Psychological Puzzle

In studying personality development during the 1960s and 1970s, researchers initially found evidence suggesting that parents have little or no effect on their children's personalities.

Studies showed that 2 adopted children raised in the same home by the same parents are no more similar, on average, than any 2 random people.

As researchers dug deeper into this puzzle, they found that parents do indeed affect their children's personalities, but those effects differ across their children. In other words, parents affect their children, but they affect different children in different ways.

- In both the reactive and active gene-environment correlation, what starts out as a genetic effect on the nervous system creates different environments either by affecting how other people treat the person or by leading the person to select different environments and activities. In both cases, the environment created by the person's own actions then influences his or her personality.

Suggested Reading

Holmes, "How Dogs Are Helping Decode the Genetic Roots of Personality."

Pinker, "My Genome, My Self."

Plomin, "Behavioral Genetics."

Questions to Consider

1. Imagine 2 cultures: In culture A, every child is raised in exactly the same way, and parents are allowed no latitude in how they treat their children. In culture B, children are raised in many different ways, and parents can treat their children however they wish. If we calculated the heritability of a trait separately in culture A and in culture B, would you expect the heritability to differ in the 2 cultures? Why or why not? To answer this question, keep in mind how heritability is defined and calculated.

2. Explain the 2 ways in which people's genes can affect their environment, which then influences their personality. Although there's no way to know for certain, can you think of ways in which one or both of these processes might have occurred in your life?

GENETIC INFLUENCES ON PERSONALITY
LECTURE 16 TRANSCRIPT

Many forces have combined over a number of years to make you who you are today: the way you were raised by your parents and other caregivers, the relationships that you've had with various people—your family, friends, lovers, teachers, coaches, and others—what you've learned, the experiences that you've had, even seemingly trivial things such as the TV shows that you've watched and the books that you've read. But the very first influences that have affected who you are began much earlier, literally at the moment of conception. At that moment, when the genetic material provided by your mother and your father combined, processes were set in motion that have guided your development all along.

On several previous occasions, I have mentioned, more-or-less in passing, that a particular trait has a genetic component, but perhaps it's time to take a close look at what that means and the ways in which the genes that you inherited from your parents have contributed to your personality. The field of psychology has been roiled by many debates over the years, but one of the most long-standing controversies is the classic nature-nurture debate. By nature, of course, we're talking about the genetic factors that influence who we are—what we're born with. By nurture, we mean all of the environmental variables that influence who we are; not only how we were raised—which is what most people think about when they hear the word, nurture—but also our personal experiences, our social relationships, and the influence of the surrounding culture.

Psychology inherited the nature-nurture debate from philosophy, where philosophers such as René Descartes argued in favor of nature, and philosophers such as Thomas Hobbes and John Locke argued for nurture. Without the research tools needed to resolve the question, the debate dragged on for hundreds of years, but with advances in research designs, statistical methods, and our understanding of genetics, we have made substantial progress over the past 50 years, and I'm happy to announce that the war is over and the nature-nurture debate is dead. There is no doubt whatsoever that personality is influenced by both nature and nurture, by both genes and the environment. And this is true of almost every major personality characteristic that has been studied.

In retrospect, the nature-nurture controversy was a silly debate, and it's hard to understand why anyone would have ever thought that personality was due only to nature or only to nurture. But with the debate laid to rest, we've moved beyond asking whether personality is affected by nature or by nurture to more nuanced questions such as how strong the effect of genes versus the environment is for particular traits. Some traits are more strongly affected by genes than other traits are, and we can examine the relative influence of genes and environment for particular characteristics. We can also ask questions about how genes and environment interact to affect personality. For example, we now know that certain genes affect people's personalities only if the person grows up in a particular kind of environment. And we can ask interesting questions about ways in which genetic influences can affect people's environments, which really complicates the picture. The idea that genes can affect the environment might initially sound nonsensical to you, but we'll take a look at how it works a little later.

Most of the work on genetic influences on personality has been conducted by researchers in behavioral genetics, which is an interdisciplinary field that studies the genetic and environmental influences on personality and behavior. It's essentially the field that studies questions about nature and nurture. The goal of behavioral genetics is to document how much genetic and environmental factors influence behavior and to study the ways in which genes and environment operate, both individually and together, to produce differences in personality.

The label behavioral genetics is a bit of a misnomer, because it implies that the field focuses only on behavior and genes. In reality, researchers in behavioral genetics study the influence of both genes and the environment on behavior. In fact, it's essentially impossible to study the influence of genes without studying the environment as well.

The central concept that we need to understand in order to make sense out of research findings in behavioral genetics is the concept of heritability. I'll be referring to heritability every time that I mention genetic influences on particular traits, so let's start there. Heritability is a concept in genetics that is defined as the proportion of phenotypic variance in a trait that is attributable to genetic variance. Unless you're a biologist or a geneticist, that definition might sound unnecessarily complex and filled with jargon, so let me unpack it.

Again: Heritability is the proportion of phenotypic variance in a trait that is attributable to genetic variance. What does that mean? Phenotypic variance is simply the observed variability in some characteristic. Normally, biologists think about variability in an animal's physical characteristics, but for behavioral geneticists, phenotypic variance is the variability that we observe in some behavior or in some psychological characteristic across people.

Consider the trait of extraversion. People vary a great deal in how extraverted they are, from people who are very low in extraversion to those who are very high. For example, scores on one measure of extraversion can range from 12 to 60. A behavioral geneticist would say that there is phenotypic variance in extraversion. And if we had extraversion scores from a large sample of people, we could calculate a statistic that expresses how much variance in extraversion there is among people. That is, we could get a number that tells us how much phenotypic variance exists in extraversion.

The question for behavioral geneticists is this: How much of that variability—how much of the phenotypic variance—is due to genetic differences among people? Specifically, they want to know what proportion of the phenotypic variance in extraversion is due to genetic variance. This is the heritability: the proportion of phenotypic variance in a trait that is attributable to genetic variance.

As a proportion, the heritability of a trait can range from 0 to 1. A heritability of 0 would indicate that none of the phenotypic variance in a trait is due to genetics; genes play no role in this trait. At the upper extreme, a heritability of 1 would indicate that all of the variance in the trait is due to genetics. Although certain physical characteristics, such as eye color, have heritabilities of 1, I'm not aware of any personality trait that is completely determined by genes. So, we never see heritabilities of 1 in behavioral genetics. We also rarely see a heritability of 0, as most behavior has at least some small genetic component. In between 0 and 1, the heritability tells us the proportion of variability in the trait that's due to genetic influences. Let me give you a couple of examples.

Let's start with the heritability of a physical characteristic: a person's height. We all know that height is inherited; taller parents tend to have taller children. But how much of the variability that we see in people's height—what proportion of the phenotypic variance in height—is due to genetic variability? Research shows that the heritability of height for Americans is 0.87, which means that 87% of the variability we observe in height is due to differences in genes. That's a pretty strong genetic influence. Only 13% of the variability in height is due to non-genetic influences, mostly nutritional factors.

The heritability of intelligence, as measured by standard IQ tests, is about 0.5. So, 50% of the variability that we see in intelligence across people is due to genetic differences among them. On average, genes account for about half of the phenotypic differences we see in intelligence across people. And, if the heritability is about 0.5, that means that environmental factors affect intelligence about the same amount.

But what about personality? Let's start with the big five personality traits. Of course, different studies get slightly different estimates of heritability based on the samples and the specific measures that they use, so what I'm going to give you are average heritabilities across many separate studies, most of which have been conducted in the North America, Europe, and Australia.

Let's start with extraversion. Extraversion has a heritability of 0.54, which tells us that just over half of the variance we observe in extraversion—54%—is due to genetic differences among people. Neuroticism is similar. The heritability for neuroticism is 0.49. Again, about half of the variability we see in neuroticism across people is due to genetic factors. The heritability for agreeableness is a bit lower but still substantial. Its heritability is 0.42. The heritability of conscientiousness is 0.49, and the heritability for openness is highest of the big five, coming in at 0.57.

Now, for our purposes, these specific numbers aren't particularly important. The take-away message here is that, when it comes to the 5 basic dimensions of personality, somewhere between about 40% and 60% of the variability we observe in these traits is due to genetic factors. Genes play a big role in why we are the way we are with respect to the big five traits. But let me make something clear about these numbers: Heritability is a population-based statistic. That means that heritability tells us the proportion of the variability in a trait that is genetic when we consider everyone in a particular population. But heritability does not tell us how much of your personality or my personality is due to genetics. In other words, knowing that the heritability of extraversion is 0.54 does not mean that 54% of your level of extraversion is caused by your genes. It means that 54% of the variability in extraversion that we see across people is due to genetic differences.

In fact, there's no way to know what proportion of a given individual's personality is due to genetic versus environmental influences. That would require measuring all of the genetic and environmental factors that might have affected a person's personality from conception to the present and then estimating the role that each factor played in the person's personality. It just can't be done.

But even though heritability is based on population-level analyses, it does give us a ballpark idea of how much genes versus environment have influenced any one of us. For example, chances are that your standing on the big five traits was influenced about equally by your genes and your environment. But again, for any individual, we don't know exactly. The bottom line is that virtually every personality characteristic shows evidence of being influenced by genes. Of course, their heritabilities differ: Some traits are more strongly influenced by genes than other traits are. But most traits have a genetic basis, and the heritability for most of them falls between about 0.3 and 0.6. About 30% to 60% of the variability in most traits is due to genetic factors.

You might be wondering how we estimate the heritability of a trait. Researchers in behavioral genetics use a number of approaches, but most of them come down to comparing the personalities of people who share genes and/or share environments. For example, some studies compare the personalities of adopted children to the personalities of both their biological parents and their adoptive parents. If the personalities of children who were adopted early in life resemble those of their biological parents more than those of their adoptive parents, then genetic influences appear to be operating. If they resemble their adoptive parents more than their natural parents, the environment seems to have an effect.

Other studies compare monozygotic twins—that is, identical twins—to dizygotic, or fraternal, twins to see the degree to which monozygotic twins are more similar in their personalities than dizygotic twins are. If monozygotic twins are more similar than dizygotic twins, then genetic factors may be responsible because monozygotic twins are more similar genetically. This kind of comparison is enhanced when the twins have been either raised together in the same family, or raised apart, which permits a more nuanced analysis of genetic and environmental effects. In all of these studies, statistical analyses are conducted to estimate heritability for whatever trait is being studied.

Many genetic influences on personality begin to reveal themselves soon after birth. Personality traits that are obvious soon after birth are often called temperaments. In everyday language, we sometimes use the word temperament to refer to personality characteristics that involve people's way of handling problems and stressful events. We talk about someone having the right temperament for a particular job, for example. But psychologists tend to reserve use of the term temperament for inborn personality characteristics. Researchers have identified a number of characteristics that can be observed soon after birth, although they disagree about how many temperaments there actually are.

Perhaps the most obvious temperament in newborns is activity level. Once babies have recovered from their journey into the world, newborns vary a great deal in their level of activity. Some babies squirm, wiggle, and flail around, whereas others don't move around very much. And they show a good deal of consistency in activity across situations and time: squirming babies tend to stay squirmy as they get older, and less active babies remain less active. So, differences in activity exist at birth that persist as features of personality.

Fearfulness is also considered a temperament. Some babies are more afraid of things from the beginning than other babies are. Researchers have designed some rather diabolical studies in which they present scary things to babies and measure the babies' reactions. Interestingly, the degree to which children react fearfully as young infants predicts their scores on measures of neuroticism as they get older.

And not only do some babies get upset more easily, but some babies are easier to soothe when they're upset, whereas for others, there's not much you can do to make them feel better. Clearly, the basis of low and high neuroticism is present at birth, which makes sense given that neuroticism is partly heritable.

We should be careful not to conclude that all differences that we see among newborns are necessarily genetic. After all, a developing fetus is exposed to environmental influences even before birth. The mother's emotions, nutrition, drug use, and other factors during pregnancy can affect the fetus's developing brain in ways that have implications for personality later on. Even so, most of the differences that we see in personality at birth are probably due to genes.

I've been talking about genetic influences on personality traits, but you might be surprised to learn that genes can also play a role in people's attitudes. We usually think of attitudes as something we learn from other people, from our parents or peers or culture at large, but research shows that a wide variety of attitudes have sizable heritabilities. For example, are you for or against the death penalty? Research shows that the heritability of attitudes toward the death penalty is 0.5, just as high as for major personality characteristics. Fifty percent of the variability in people's attitudes toward the death penalty is due to genetic differences. Do you identify yourself as politically liberal or conservative? That's partly inherited too. The heritability of liberalism/conservativism is 0.43. Or, how about your attitude toward organized religion? Its heritability is 0.45. Do you like or dislike exercising? The heritability of attitudes about exercise is 0.36. How much do you like to read? Attitudes toward reading have a heritability of 0.37.

Not all attitudes have a genetic component, though. For example, the heritability for attitudes toward playing organized sports is perfectly 0. And, the heritability of attitudes toward doing crossword puzzles is only 0.02. Only 2% of the variance in liking crossword puzzles is genetic. But what's going on here? How can genes affect our attitudes toward things as diverse as capital punishment, reading, religion, and exercising? To answer that question, let's think more deeply about inherited characteristics.

Strictly speaking, even when the heritability of a trait or attitude is high, it's misleading to say that people are inheriting their personality or attitudes except in a very loose sense. You don't actually inherit your traits or attitudes or behaviors. Rather, what you're actually inheriting is a nervous system that tends to respond in particular ways. Genes influence the development of our physical body, including the brain and other parts of the nervous system, and that's what you actually inherit.

Just as genes can cause people to be tall or to have bad eyesight or have flat feet, genes also influence the structure of our brains. And differences in how the brain operates can lead people to respond in different ways. So for example, the limbic system is the part of the brain that's directly involved in responding to threatening and stressful events. If your genes led you to have a limbic system that is unusually responsive to threats, you'll probably score high in neuroticism. You'll experience more negative emotions, get upset more easily, and take longer to return to baseline when negative events occur. Strictly speaking, you didn't actually inherit neuroticism—you inherited a brain that has an active limbic system. And likewise, if you inherited a limbic system that's less responsive than average, you'll probably be lower in neuroticism.

Researchers have only started to explore the genetically-determined differences in people's brains that underlie various personality characteristics, but whatever personality differences among people are due to genetic influences must be due to differences in how their brains operate. The same thing holds for attitudes. People whose brains respond in certain ways will find certain attitudes more agreeable to them than people whose brains respond in other ways. For example, if your genes designed your brain in such a way that you happen to find highly stimulating activities enjoyable, you'll have more positive attitudes toward stimulating activities, and you'll be high in sensation-seeking.

The heritability of positive attitudes toward riding roller coasters is 0.37! Of course, your attitude toward roller coasters is also based on your experiences—perhaps you had particularly good or bad experiences on roller coasters when you were a child—but genes play a role. Similarly, if your genes designed your brain in such a way that makes you prefer stability and dislike change, you're likely to be more traditional and maybe lean toward conservative ideas. But if your brain leads you to like novelty and to be open to change and new ideas, you might be more likely to be liberal.

Again, your environment, upbringing, and experiences also played a role in your political views, and your environment might even have overridden your inherited inclinations. But by creating a brain that responds in a particular way, your genes probably played a role in your political attitudes.

I think about this link between genes and attitudes when I deal with people whose attitudes are so different from mine that I can't begin to fathom how someone could hold such views. I remind myself that my difficulty in understanding this person might lie in the fact that my brain is designed so differently from theirs that I can't even begin to resonate with their attitude. And, of course, they don't understand my views either. But keep in mind that it's also possible to develop an attitude that has no apparent genetic basis. If you love doing crossword puzzles, research suggests that the pleasure you take in them comes almost entirely from your experiences and not from your genes.

So far, I have been talking about direct genetic effects on brain anatomy and physiology that cause people to respond in particular ways or to have particular attitudes. But, genes can influence our personality not only by designing our brain in a particular way but also by changing our environment in ways that then affect our personality. Now this may sound absurd. How could my genes possibly affect my environment? But stay with me for a minute.

Genes can influence personality in 3 distinct ways, some of which make it difficult to disentangle the separate influences of genes and environment. Most obviously, genes can affect personality and behavior more-or-less directly by influencing the brain and other parts of the nervous system. This is the path we've been discussing. A second way that genes affect personality arises when genes create a brain that leads people to behave in ways that affect their environment, and then the environment affects the person's personality. This process is called a reactive or evocative gene-environment correlation.

In a reactive gene-environment correlation, genes influence the person's behavioral tendencies as we just discussed. But then, those behavioral tendencies cause other people to react to the person in a particular way. When lots of other people treat the person in this way, it can have a lasting effect on the person's personality. So, the person's genes directly affected the nervous system and led to certain patterns of behavior, which led to certain reactions from other people, which affected the person's personality.

Imagine that genes create a brain that leads a child to be more responsible and mature than most of his classmates in school. Seeing this, parents and teachers give the child extra responsibilities and more freedoms than they give other kids, and giving him more responsibility affects his personality over time. Maybe these experiences lead him to develop leadership skills that he wouldn't have developed otherwise. Or, let's say that genes create a brain that leads a child to be obstinate and disobedient. Parents and teachers will often respond to his antics negatively, or even punitively, and they'll probably try extra hard to control the kid. All of that negative attention and control by adults will probably affect the child's personality development in one way or another.

In these examples, are these effects genetic or environmental? I guess they're both, but the picture is complicated by the fact that the genes fostered an environment that then affected personality.

A third way that genes can influence personality is known as an active gene-environment correlation. In an active gene-environment correlation, genes create a brain that is associated with certain motives, interests, preferences, or behaviors, and these genetically-influenced inclinations lead the person to gravitate toward certain environments and activities. Then, spending time in those particular environments affects the person's personality.

Imagine 2 7-year-old children. One is sociable and confident and likes speaking in public, and the other one is reserved and dislikes being the center of attention. We might expect that these children will gravitate toward somewhat different activities and interests. The first child may spend more time in social interactions and start volunteering for things in which she can be in charge. The other might gravitate toward more introverted kinds of activities. Over time, their experiences in these different kinds of settings will have cumulative effects on their personalities. Spending time in the spotlight, taking leadership roles, and being in charge promote different interests and skills than staying in the background and being a follower.

In both the reactive and active gene-environment correlation, what starts out as a genetic effect on the nervous system creates different environments either by affecting how other people treat the person or by leading the person to select different environments and activities. In both cases, the environment created by the person's own actions then influences his or her personality.

Let me conclude by describing a puzzle that emerged from research on genetic and environmental effects on personality, and once befuddled psychologists. In studying personality development during the 1960s and 70s, researchers initially found evidence suggesting that parents have little or no effect on their children's personalities.

That's right: The studies showed that, although parents clearly affected children's beliefs, attitudes, and habits to some degree, they didn't seem to have much of an effect on kids' personality traits. Of course, children's personalities often resemble those of their parents as well as their brothers' and sisters', but those similarities appeared to be mostly a genetic effect and not an effect of the home environment. To make this point clear, consider adoptive siblings—children who have different biological parents but are raised by the same adoptive parents. Many researchers reasoned that, if parents affect their children's personalities, we should find that adopted kids raised by the same, non-biological parents should be somewhat similar to each other.

But they aren't. Studies showed that 2 adopted children raised in the same home by the same parents are no more similar, on average, than any 2 random people! Such findings seemed to suggest that parents don't have any effect on their children's personalities. Of course, that seems ridiculous. It certainly seems that parents affect how their kids turn out.

Well, to make a long story short, as researchers dug deeper into this puzzle, what they found was that parents do indeed affect their children's personalities, but those effects differ across their kids. In other words, parents affect their children, but they affect different children in different ways. To understand why, consider 2 things: First, parents tailor their parenting practices to particular children, as they should, which creates differences in how kids grow up. Not only that, but even when parents treat their children the same, the kids may respond differently to exactly the same treatment. Given that siblings differ from each other genetically, they often don't respond the same way even when the parents treat them the same. So, parents do influence their children's personalities, but they don't affect all of their children in the same way.

So, once again, the bottom line is that genes play an important role in personality, but so do a variety of environmental influences, including what parents do. We'll be talking more about some of these environmental influences in the future.

LEARNING TO BE WHO YOU ARE

LECTURE 17

This lecture will focus on 4 simple but powerful processes that involve learning: classical conditioning, operant conditioning, observational learning, and experiential learning. These processes lead us to develop tendencies to respond in certain ways and, thus, influence our personalities. And although the foundations of our personalities are laid in childhood, these processes occur throughout life, so new aspects of people's personalities can emerge or disappear at any point, depending on what they learn along the way.

CLASSICAL CONDITIONING

- Ivan Pavlov was a Russian physiologist who discovered classical conditioning. He found that the dogs that he used in his research would often start salivating even before they were fed and that he could condition dogs to salivate to almost anything that he presented to them in connection with food. All he had to do was introduce the stimulus just before feeding the dog.

- In each case, after they learned to associate a sound or an image with food, the dogs' digestive systems would start working when the stimulus was presented, even if no food came. This phenomenon came to be known as classical conditioning.

- In the language of classical conditioning, the sound or image was a conditioned stimulus. It was a previously neutral stimulus that gained the power to influence the dogs' reactions by being paired with an unconditioned stimulus—the food—that naturally produces the reaction—salivation—without conditioning.

- Many of our emotional and visceral reactions are conditioned in exactly the same way that Pavlov's dogs were conditioned to salivate to other stimuli. When a previously neutral stimulus becomes paired with an unconditioned stimulus, the neutral stimulus may begin to elicit the same reaction.

- You probably have reactions to particular kinds of people, events, and other stimuli that were classically conditioned sometime in your past. These conditioned associations lead you to respond in particular ways and thus contribute to your personality.

- In some cases, you might remember exactly what it was that created this conditioned response. For example, you may know that your fear of bees started the day you were stung at a picnic. In other cases, the memory of the original event is lost, or you may have never realized that the reaction was conditioned. But if you have certain stable patterns of reactions to things that themselves wouldn't be expected to produce that reaction, those patterns might have been classically conditioned.

- The best examples of this phenomenon are emotional reactions, particularly fears and aversions. For example, most animals don't naturally produce fear unless we've either had a scary experience with one or other people have scared us by telling us how bad they are. And while the sight of most food isn't inherently nauseating, many people have aversions to certain foods so that simply the sight or smell—or maybe even just the thought—of that food makes you feel queasy because you got sick after eating it in the past.

- Positive reactions can also be classically conditioned. Some people have unusual sexual reactions to what would seem to be neutral, nonsexual stimuli, such as certain articles of clothing, people's feet, or tattoos. One answer to why people become aroused to neutral things is classical conditioning. If neutral stimuli become associated with sexual arousal, even accidentally, people may begin to become aroused by the neutral thing.

OPERANT CONDITIONING

- While some parts of your personality were classically conditioned, other aspects of your personality arose through a second type of learning, operant conditioning.

- In 1905, Edward Thorndike was the first psychologist to describe the law of effect—the idea that behaviors that produce a satisfying, pleasant effect become more likely to occur and behaviors that produce a discomforting, unpleasant effect become less likely.

- A few years later, John Watson, the founder of behaviorism, claimed that he could use the law of effect to turn any infant into whatever he wanted, such as a doctor or even a thief, regardless of the child's genes. Of course, people's abilities, personalities, and ways of thinking are strongly affected by genetics, so you can't turn people into absolutely anything you want, but you can influence the development of people's personalities within limits.

- As an example, about half of the variability that we see in conscientiousness across people is due to genetic factors. But the other half is due to other things, and operant conditioning probably ranks high among them. Many people are strongly reinforced their whole lives for behaving in conscientious ways, such as planning and being organized, because such characteristics are valued by society in general.

- But some people received much more encouragement and reinforcement for being conscientious than others over a period of many years. And some people were punished—reprimanded or deprived of privileges or even physically punished—when they showed a lack of conscientiousness, such as when they were irresponsible and slacked off. Over time, all of that reinforcement and punishment led you to behave conscientiously, sometimes when it doesn't really matter.

For operant conditioning to occur, it doesn't matter whether the behavior actually caused the reinforcement or punishment. All that matters is that a particular reinforcing or punishing event followed the behavior.

- So, to some extent, you are the way you are because of operant conditioning: You were reinforced for certain behaviors and possibly punished when you did other things. Reinforcement and punishment are important determinants of behavior.

- In everyday language, we think of reinforcement as a positive thing—a reward—and punishment as something negative. But this way of thinking about reinforcement and punishment can sometimes be misleading because people differ so much in what they find rewarding.

- In psychology, reinforcement and punishment are defined by their consequences, so we don't know whether something is reinforcing or punishing in a particular instance until we see what effect it has on the person's behavior.

- Reinforcement is an event that increases the likelihood of behavior that preceded it. If you do something and get attention and then you keep doing the behavior, then attention was reinforcing.

- Punishment is an event that decreases the likelihood of behavior that preceded it. If you get attention for something and then never do that thing again, it would appear that attention is punishing for you.

OBSERVATIONAL LEARNING

- For many years, psychologists assumed that people had to be reinforced or punished personally to affect the likelihood that they would repeat or refrain from a given behavior in the future. But this is not correct, because that's not the only way we learn.

- We learn a great deal, for example, by watching what other people do—and what happens to them afterward. In other words, we learn a great deal through purely observational learning. Watching other people receive rewards and punishments can serve as incentives that then influence our behavior.

♦ We learn 3 distinct kinds of things by observing other people: how to perform behaviors, what consequences may occur, and how likely various consequences will be.

EXPERIENTIAL LEARNING

♦ One other process by which we acquire parts of our personality through learning is personal experience. Through their personal experiences, people learn new ways of seeing themselves and the world. And what they learn then provides guidelines for how they should behave in the future.

♦ Our views of ourselves are based on many things, but our personal experiences play an important role in how we think about ourselves. To some extent, you figure out what you're like from the things that happen to you. We sometimes draw the wrong conclusion, and our views of ourselves are often based on just a handful of particularly memorable experiences rather than on a careful analysis of all the evidence. Still, whether your conclusions are correct or incorrect, your experiences teach you things about yourself.

♦ These kinds of experience-based effects on personality have been widely discussed in the context of how people react to traumatic events, such as physical attacks, catastrophic injuries, life-threatening illnesses, natural disasters, or losses of loved ones. These kinds of traumatic events can have a dramatic effect on people's personalities. Many people are not the same person after the event as they were before.

♦ But what's interesting is that the effects of traumatic events can be either negative or positive in the long run. In the aftermath of a traumatic event, some people return to normal, some show chronic post-traumatic stress and depression, and some show post-traumatic growth.

Imagine that a person grows up in an environment in which parents and other adults are distant, selfish, and not available when needed. That type of personal experience might lead the person to develop the belief that other people really can't be counted on and that people have to look out for themselves.

But a person who grew up with a great deal of support from other people might conclude, based on personal experiences, that most people will come through when you need them, and they'll learn to trust and count on others.

By creating different sets of guiding beliefs, these different personal experiences would result in quite different personalities: The first person would be distrusting and make every effort to be self-sufficient while the second person would be trusting and willing to rely on other people.

- The difference seems to depend, at least in part, on what they learned from the experience. When these changes in perspective are beneficial in helping them deal with life, people get back to normal or even experience post-traumatic growth. But when what they learned—or think they learned—from the event is not beneficial, people experience post-traumatic stress.

- Research on post-traumatic reactions suggests that traumatic events can change people's views in several major areas—people's sense of their future opportunities, people's views of their relationships with others, people's views of themselves, and people's views of life in general—and those changes can be either beneficial and lead to growth or detrimental and lead to disintegration.

- Each of these post-traumatic changes involves learning; people's experiences have changed their beliefs about the world and about themselves. It's interesting that precisely the same traumatic event can lead to positive post-traumatic changes for some people but to negative changes for other people, and we don't know a great deal about why people come away from traumatic events having learned different things.

- But some of it has to do with what their personalities were like before the trauma. People who, before the traumatic event, were optimistic and high in openness to experience, perceived that they had greater control over their lives, and believed that they coped well with negative events are more resilient in the face of crises and traumas than people without these characteristics. So, people who don't cope well even with ordinary daily problems get even worse when they experience traumatic events.

- Some research shows that people who cope better with traumatic events are more flexible in the coping strategies that they use. Traditionally, clinical psychologists have suggested that people need to confront the bad things that happen to them and that they shouldn't suppress or deny what happened or their feelings about it.

♦ But research has suggested that there are times when confronting trauma is more beneficial, and there are times when it's better not to dwell on it and to ignore it or push it aside instead. And the people who cope best are those who flexibly move back and forth in how they deal with what's happened to them—sometimes thinking about and confronting it and sometimes putting it on the shelf. We don't know much about what makes these flexible people's personalities different from people who use a single coping strategy, but it seems to work for them.

Suggested Reading

Collier, "Growth after Trauma."

Layton, "How Fear Works."

Questions to Consider

1. Do you see any common emotional reactions you have that you think might be the result of classical conditioning?

2. Looking back at your childhood, what behaviors did your parents or guardians tend to reinforce, and what behaviors did they tend to punish? Do you now have behavioral tendencies that may reflect these patterns of reinforcement and punishment? Perhaps more interestingly, do you have behavioral tendencies today that your parents or guardians clearly did not reinforce, and perhaps even punished, when you were young? If so, where do you think those tendencies came from?

LEARNING TO BE WHO YOU ARE
LECTURE 17 TRANSCRIPT

Some people are a bit unsettled by the notion that they partly had to learn to be who they are. They have the sense "I am who I am, and I've always been me from the day I was born, so how could I have ever become somebody else?" But, once you think about it, it's obvious that you could have easily ended up being someone else, somebody quite different from how you are now, in terms of how you think, what you believe, what you feel, and how you behave.

Of course, your genes would have been the same, so you would have been somewhat similar to how you are now no matter what. But, as we saw earlier, genes generally account for only about 30% to 60% of the variability we see in people's personalities. The rest reflects the impact of the environment, which really comes down to what you have experienced along the way, all of the things that have happened to you as you moved through life. And, a lot's happened, hasn't it? Many of the things that you've experienced have affected your personality in a wide variety of ways.

We're going to take a look at 4 processes that involve the effects of experiences on personality. What all of these processes have in common is that they involve learning in one way or another. We often think of learning in terms of somebody teaching us something, but learning is involved anytime something that we experience creates an intellectual or psychological or behavioral change. When you learn something, it means that you experienced something that changed you in some way. As I talk about these 4 processes, I hope that you'll be thinking about the ways in which your own experiences might have affected your personality and helped to make you who you are. Of course, it's impossible to know for certain what effect any particular experience had on us, but it's interesting to consider the possibilities.

If you've ever had a class in introductory psychology, you probably learned about Ivan Pavlov. Pavlov was a Russian physiologist who was interested in the digestive system. In fact, he received a Nobel Prize for his work on the physiology of digestion. But today, Pavlov's better known as the scientist who discovered classical conditioning.

While he was studying digestion in dogs, Pavlov noticed something odd about the way they salivated. Now, many animals salivate when they eat, but Pavlov found that the dogs that he used in his research would often start salivating even before they were fed. Just the sight of the research assistant who brought their food or the sound of the laboratory door opening could start the dogs salivating. This made it difficult for him to study the physiology of digestion, and it messed up parts of his research program. But Pavlov realized that this was an interesting phenomenon in its own right, so he began to focus on it.

Pavlov found that he could condition dogs to salivate to almost anything that he presented to them in connection with food. All he had to do was introduce the stimulus just before feeding the dog. Most psychology books talk about Pavlov conditioning his dogs to salivate to the sound of a bell, but he used many other sounds as well, including whistles, tuning forks, and metronomes, and he also conditioned them to salivate to visual stimuli. In each case, after they learned to associate a sound or an image with food, the dogs' digestive systems would start working when the stimulus was presented, even if no food came. This phenomenon came to be known as classical conditioning.

In the language of classical conditioning, the sound or image was a conditioned stimulus. It was a previously neutral stimulus that gained the power to influence the dogs' reactions by being paired with an unconditioned stimulus—the food—that naturally produces the reaction—that is, salivation—without conditioning. Many of our emotional and visceral reactions are conditioned in exactly the same way that Pavlov's dogs were conditioned to salivate to other stimuli. When a previously neutral stimulus becomes paired with an unconditioned stimulus, the neutral stimulus may begin to elicit the same reaction. So you probably have reactions to particular kinds of people, events, and other stimuli that were classically conditioned sometime in your past. These conditioned associations lead you respond in particular ways, and thus contribute to your personality.

In some cases, you might remember exactly what it was that created this conditioned response. You may know that your fear of bees started the day you were stung at the picnic, or that certain smells—maybe those you smelled during vacations at your grandparents' house—now evoke certain feelings. Originally, seeing a bee or smelling that odor didn't have any effect, but after these stimuli were paired with a bee sting or experiences at your grandparents' house, they started to evoke emotional responses. In other cases, the memory of the original event is lost, or you may have never realized that the reaction was conditioned. But if you have certain stable patterns of reactions to things that, in-and-of-themselves wouldn't be expected to produce that reaction, those patterns might have been classically conditioned.

The best examples of this phenomenon are emotional reactions—particularly fears and aversions—although positive reactions can be classically conditioned as well. Do you have any fears or aversions? Things that evoke negative emotions, that might have been classically conditioned? Are you now afraid of a particular kind of animal? Most animals don't naturally produce fear unless we've either had a scary experience with one, or other people have scared us by telling us how bad they are.

Phobias of all kinds are often classically conditioned. When I worked in my mom's day care center as a high school student, we had a preschooler who was petrified by thunder. Even just a distant rumble of thunder would make him panic. Why would a kid be so afraid of distant thunder? When we mentioned his fear to his mother, she said, "Oh, I know, but I don't understand why he's so afraid. From the time he was very little, whenever I heard thunder, I'd hurry him down to the basement and have him sit on a wooden stool in case the house got struck by lightning. So, he's never had a bad experience with thunderstorms. I don't know why he's so afraid." This mother had classically conditioned fear of thunder in her son, scaring the I-don't-know-what out of him by anxiously rushing him to the basement whenever they heard thunder. So, a neutral sound—the distant rumble of thunder—became associated in his mind with his mom's panicked reactions and the kid's feelings of fear about being struck by lightning, so distant thunder began to evoke fear by itself. I suspect that somewhere, there's some 50-year-old man who still feels extremely uneasy when he hears thunder, and he might not even know why.

Many of you may have aversions to certain foods, so that simply the sight or smell or maybe even just the thought of that food makes you feel queasy because you got sick after eating it in the past. The sight of most food isn't inherently nauseating; you have to be conditioned to be nauseated looking at or thinking about a particular food. Or, maybe there's a particular alcoholic drink that you used to like but never touch anymore because of an unfortunate time that you drank too and paid the price. Just the thought or smell of it is enough to make you gag.

Positive reactions can be classically conditioned as well. Some of you might have some, shall we say, unusual sexual reactions to what would seem to be neutral, nonsexual stimuli. It makes sense that people become sexually aroused when they see sexually explicit stimuli or receive certain kinds of sexual stimulation. But, many people are aroused by objects and parts of the body that aren't inherently sexual: certain articles of clothing, boots and shoes, leather, people's feet, tattoos, people wearing glasses, all sorts of things, some of which can get pretty kinky.

All that's fine. But it's interesting to consider why people become aroused to neutral things. And one answer is classical conditioning. If neutral stimuli become associated with sexual arousal, even accidentally, people may begin to become aroused by the neutral thing. It's just like Pavlov's dogs, but the unconditioned response is sexual arousal rather than salivation. There have been a few experiments in which researchers showed that they could classically condition participants to become aroused to neutral stimuli by pairing erotic pictures, which are naturally arousing, with things like a pair of boots and, in one study, a jar of pennies. It works. We can actually classically condition people to be turned on by a penny-jar. So, parts of your personality were classically conditioned when some previously neutral stimulus was associated with particular reactions. Now that stimulus reliably elicits those responses, and you might not even know why.

Other aspects of your personality arose through a second type of learning, operant conditioning. In 1905, Edward Thorndike was the first psychologist to describe what he called the law of effect: the idea that behaviors that produce a satisfying, pleasant effect become more likely to occur, and behaviors that produce a discomforting, unpleasant effect become less likely. This might seem pretty obvious, but it wasn't widely recognized at the time that Thorndike did his work.

A few years later, John Watson, the founder of behaviorism, claimed that he could use the law of effect to turn any child into whatever he wanted. Watson said, and I'm quoting:

> Give me a dozen healthy infants, well-formed, and my own specified world to bring them up in, and I'll guarantee to take any one at random and train him to become any type of specialist I might select—doctor, lawyer, artist, merchant, chief and, yes, even beggar-man and thief, regardless of his talents, penchants, tendencies, abilities, vocations, and race of his ancestors.

Of course, Watson was overstating the case. As we've seen, people's abilities, personalities, and ways of thinking are strongly affected by genetics, so you can't turn people into absolutely anything you want. But if Watson had said, give me a bunch of infants and I will influence the development of their personalities within limits, he would have certainly been entirely correct.

Let's take a particular personality trait—let's say conscientiousness. We already saw that conscientiousness has a heritability of about 0.49, which means that about half of the variability that we see in conscientiousness across people is due to genetic factors. But that means that the other half is due to other things, and operant conditioning probably ranks high among them. Many of you have been strongly reinforced your whole life for behaving in conscientious ways: for planning and being organized and keeping things clean and doing what you're supposed to do. Of course, such characteristics are valued by society in general, so all of us have been reinforced for these actions to some extent. But some of us received much more encouragement and reinforcement for being conscientious than others over a period of many years.

And, I suspect that some of you were also punished when you showed a lack of conscientiousness, when you were irresponsible and slacked off. You may have been reprimanded or deprived of privileges or maybe even physically punished. And over time, all of that reinforcement and punishment led you to behave conscientiously, sometimes when it doesn't really matter.

Or, think about the things that motivate you the most. If you're really high in achievement motivation, why is that? Well, like for most traits, there's a genetic influence—the heritability of achievement motivation is about 0.4—but it's probably also because you were consistently reinforced for working hard and achieving. If you had been criticized, reprimanded, and punished every time you did something well, I suspect that your motivation to achieve would be much lower.

Or what about your interests? By and large, we're interested in whatever we're interested in—sports, reading, music, volunteering, golf, family activities, whatever—because we find it rewarding somehow. That doesn't necessarily mean that somebody else reinforced us when we did the activity previously, though in many cases they did. It may have been rewarding for many reasons. Whatever the case, you keep doing the things you do because you have been reinforced for doing them along the way.

Keep in mind that for operant conditioning to occur, it doesn't matter whether the behavior actually caused the reinforcement or punishment. All that matters is that a particular reinforcing or punishing event followed the behavior. So, to some extent, you are the way you are because of operant conditioning; you were reinforced for certain behaviors, and possibly punished when you did other things. Reinforcement and punishment are important determinants of behavior.

Now, to dig into this a little deeper, I want to say a few things about the concepts of reinforcement and punishment. In everyday language, we think of reinforcement as a positive thing, a reward; and punishment as something negative. But although that way of thinking about reinforcement and punishment works fine much of the time, it can sometimes be misleading because people differ so much in what they find rewarding. For example, one person might really like attention, and do all sorts of things to get it. But another person might really dislike getting attention and avoid doing things that bring attention to him or her at all costs. So, is attention a reinforcement or a punishment? In the abstract, we really can't say. In psychology, reinforcement and punishment are defined by their consequences, so we don't know whether something is reinforcing or punishing in a particular instance until we see what effect it has on the person's behavior.

Reinforcement is an event that increases the likelihood of behavior that preceded it. If you do something and get attention, and then you keep doing the behavior, we'd say that attention was reinforcing for you. Punishment is an event that decreases the likelihood of behavior that preceded it. If you get attention for something and then never do that thing again, it would appear that attention is punishing for you.

Let's say that a parent wants their teenager to keep their room clean and takes away some privilege—the car keys, for example—when the teenager's room is a mess. In everyday language, we might say that the kid is being punished. But if taking away the car keys doesn't affect whether or not the kid cleans his room, then strictly speaking, it's not punishment at all, and it's certainly not reinforcement either.

For many years, psychologists assumed that people had to be reinforced or punished personally in order to affect the likelihood that they would repeat or refrain from a given behavior in the future. But this is obviously not correct, because that's not the only way we learn. We learn a great deal, for example, by watching what other people do and what happens to them afterward. So, I don't have to put my hand in the fire and be burned to learn not to put my hand in the fire. I only need to see what happens when you put your hand in the fire. We learn a great deal through purely observational learning. Watching other people receive rewards and punishments can serve as incentives that then influence our behavior.

We learn 3 distinct sorts of things by observing other people. As I talk about these 3 processes, think about how they might apply to your personality. What did you learn from watching other people that made you the way that you are?

The first thing we can learn from observation is simply how to do a behavior. When you're in an argument with someone, do you generally argue in a calm, rational, and unemotional manner, or do you become angry and emotional? Where did you learn to argue that way? Did you learn it from observing other people? Of course, we observe many behaviors that we never perform ourselves. Just seeing someone model a behavior doesn't make it part of our behavioral repertoire. So, we have to distinguish between learning a behavior and actually performing the behavior. We generally perform a behavior that we observed only if we believe that doing so will result in reinforcement for us. That means that we observe not just how to do a behavior, but also the consequences that are likely to occur if we do it ourselves. We watch what happens to other people when they act in certain ways: How was their behavior received by others? Positively or negatively? If I do the behavior, am I likely to get my way? Will people like me or make fun of me? Will this behavior result in punishment or reinforcement? And we not only learn about the consequences that might result from the behavior, but also about the likelihood that certain consequences will occur. What's the likelihood that doing this thing will result in reinforcement or punishment?

By observing what happens with other people, we learn how to perform behaviors, we learn what consequences may occur, and we may get an idea about how likely various consequences will be. So, our personality can be affected by classical conditioning, operant conditioning, and observational learning. Let me mention one other process by which we acquire parts of our personality through learning, and that's personal experience.

Through their personal experiences, people learn new ways of seeing themselves and the world. And what they learn then provides guidelines for how they should behave in the future. There's no direct conditioning going on here, just changes in how we perceive and think about the world based on things that happen to us. Those effects of personal experience on people's beliefs then lead them to respond a certain way in the future. So, imagine that a person grows up in an environment in which parents and other adults are distant, selfish, and not available when needed. That sort of personal experience might lead the person to develop the belief that other people really can't be counted on and that people have to look out for themselves.

But, a person who grew up with a great deal of support from other people might conclude, based on personal experiences, that most people will come through when you need them, and they'll learn to trust and count on others. By creating different sets of guiding beliefs, these different personal experiences would result in quite different personalities. The first person would be distrusting and make every effort to be self-sufficient, while the second would be trusting and willing to rely on other people.

Similarly, our personal experiences teach us things about ourselves. How competent versus incompetent are you as a person in general? How much do other people like you? Where do you fall on a continuum from being a very bad person to a very good person? How well do you deal with stress? Our views of ourselves are based on many things, but our personal experiences play an important role in how we think about ourselves. To some extent, you figure out what you're like from the things that happen to you and how you react. Of course, we sometimes draw the wrong conclusion, and our views of ourselves are often based on just a handful of particularly memorable experiences rather than on a careful analysis of all the evidence. Still, whether your conclusions are correct or incorrect, your experiences teach you things about yourself.

These kinds of experience-based effects on personality have been widely discussed in the context of how people react to traumatic events. People can experience a lot of pretty awful things: physical attacks, sexual assaults, catastrophic injuries, life-threatening illnesses, natural disasters, traumatic losses of loved ones, financial ruin, and on and on. And these kinds of traumatic events can have a dramatic effect on people's personalities. Many people are not the same person afterwards as they were before. But what's interesting is that the effects of traumatic events can be either negative or positive in the long run. That is, after the initial acute reaction to the event has faded over weeks or months, some people adjust and get back to where they were before, some people are permanently worse off, and some come away with a personality that is even more adaptive and resilient than they had beforehand.

In the aftermath of a traumatic event, some people return to normal, some show chronic post-traumatic stress and depression, and some show post-traumatic growth. And the difference seems to depend, at least in part, on what they learned from the experience. When these changes in perspective are beneficial in helping them deal with life, people get back to normal or even experience post-traumatic growth; but when what they learned or think they learned from the event is not beneficial, people experience post-traumatic stress. Research on post-traumatic reactions suggests that traumatic events can change people's views in several major areas, and those changes can be either beneficial and lead to growth or detrimental and lead to disintegration.

First, major crises can change people's sense of their future opportunities. Sometimes a traumatic event, such as a debilitating injury, seems to take away opportunities, and the person has difficulty dealing with the loss. But sometimes, people find that new opportunities emerge from their traumatic experience, opening up possibilities that were not present before. For example, a person might conclude that they now have a purpose in life that energizes and uplifts them. Traumatic events can also change people's views of their relationships with others. People may believe that their relationships with specific people, or even people in general, are irreparably damaged by the traumatic event. Or they may experience closer relationships with certain people, or develop a greater sense of connection to others who have suffered similar misfortunes.

People's views of themselves can also change. Some people feel diminished by the experience, permanently damaged, whereas other people gain the belief that they are stronger than they had previously thought. Traumatic experiences can also change people's views of life in general. After experiencing a personal catastrophe, some people feel that life is random and meaningless, and become cynical. Other people gain a greater appreciation for life.

Each of these post-traumatic changes involves learning. People's experiences have changed their beliefs about the world and about themselves. It's interesting that precisely the same traumatic event can lead to positive post-traumatic changes for some people but to negative changes for other people, and we don't know a great deal about why people come away from traumatic events having learned different things. But some of it has to do with what their personalities were like before the trauma. We know that people who, before the traumatic event, were optimistic and high in openness to experience, who perceived that they had greater control over their lives, and believed that they coped well with negative events are more resilient in the face of crises and traumas than people without these characteristics. So, sadly, people who don't cope well even with ordinary daily problems get even worse when they experience traumatic events.

And, some research shows that people who cope better with traumatic events are more flexible in the coping strategies that they use. Traditionally, clinical psychologists have suggested that people need to confront the bad things that happen to them, that they need to work through them, come to an understanding of what happened, express their feelings to themselves and others, and even try find meaning in the events. And psychologists usually say that people shouldn't suppress or deny what happened or their feelings about it. The idea has been that just pushing it aside never helps anything. But research has suggested that there are times when confronting trauma is more beneficial, and there are times when it's better not to dwell on it and to ignore or push it aside instead. And the people who cope best are those who flexibly move back and forth in how they deal with what's happened to them, sometimes thinking about and confronting it, and sometimes putting it on the shelf. We don't know much about what makes these flexible people's personalities different from people who use a single coping strategy, but it seems to work for them.

This lecture has focused on 4 simple, but powerful processes that involve learning: A neutral stimulus, such as the bell Pavlov rang for his dogs, will eventually begin to elicit the same response as an unconditioned stimulus with which it is paired, such as the food for which the dogs salivated; behaviors that are followed by a pleasant outcome tend to be repeated, whereas behaviors that are followed by an unpleasant outcome tend to stop; simply observing other people's actions and the consequences of those actions can lead to psychological and behavioral changes; and people develop beliefs about themselves and the world from personal experiences that then influence their behavior in the future.

These simple, but powerful processes involving classical conditioning, operant conditioning, observational learning, and experiential learning lead each of us to develop tendencies to respond in certain ways and, thus, influence our personalities. And although the foundations of our personalities are laid in childhood, these processes that I've described occur throughout life, so that new aspects of people's personalities can emerge or disappear at any point, depending on what they learn along the way.

HOW CULTURE INFLUENCES PERSONALITY

LECTURE 18

Culture has been defined in many ways, but it fundamentally comes down to a set of beliefs that are shared by a large group of people—beliefs about what's important, what's right and wrong, how things should be done, and how people should behave. And the beliefs that people adopt from their culture influence their tendency to behave in certain ways. As a result, people from different cultures show systematic differences in their thoughts, behaviors, and even emotions.

TIGHT VERSUS LOOSE CULTURES

- Personality doesn't manifest as much in strong situations that pressure people to act in certain ways as it does in weak situations, and cultures differ in the degree to which they generally exert a strong or a weak effect on people's behavior. So, cultures differ in the degree to which people's behavior reflects their individual personalities.

- Some cultures put more pressure on people to behave in certain ways—to be a certain kind of person—than other cultures do. And the more that cultural pressures require people to act in culturally prescribed ways, the less people's individuality comes through and the less variability we see among people.

- For example, the dominant culture of the United States permits a great deal of individual choice in how people behave, including what they do for a living, who they live with, what they wear, how they spend their free time, and whether they practice a religion. In fact, American culture not only permits a great deal of latitude in behavior, but it values and actively encourages individuality.

- There are still social norms and pressures to conform in certain ways—that's true of every society—but people's personalities are given more freedom to operate when cultural pressures are relatively weak.

- Contrast that with cultures that limit people's discretion to choose their lifestyle or occupation or religion or spouse. In those cultures, which researchers sometimes call tight cultures, how people behave is more heavily scripted by the culture and less influenced by personality. These cultures allow less personal discretion than so-called loose, or weak, cultures.

- Tight cultures are more common in homogeneous societies, where just about everyone shares the same basic racial and ethnic background, cultural beliefs, religion, and social values. Those societies have many norms and rules about how people should behave, and they punish those who deviate from the rules, even in minor ways.

- In contrast, heterogeneous societies tend to be looser and more tolerant of individuality because many different cultural belief systems are present. People are permitted to make their own choices of what to believe and how to live.

- Growing up in a tight culture creates a different orientation to rules, authority, and one's place in the society than growing up in a loose culture. And when rules are strict, people have fewer opportunities for autonomy, and their behavior is less likely to express their individual personalities.

INDIVIDUALISM VERSUS COLLECTIVISM

- Comparing the personalities of people from different cultures presents a number of challenges. Most notably, when the people in the cultures being studied speak different languages, it's difficult to be certain that the translations of the measures being used are equivalent. Typically, researchers translate a measure from one language to another and then translate it back to the original language to be sure that the words mean the same thing in both directions. This often requires several efforts, back and forth, before they get it right.

- But even then, exactly the same word or phrase may have different connotations in different cultures, which may affect how people answer the question. And sometimes questions on a personality measure contain concepts or situations that don't even make sense in another culture.

- The other big challenge for researchers has been identifying the characteristics of cultures that affect personality. Cultures differ in many ways—some quite important and some very trivial. And it's been a challenge to identify and measure the aspects of culture that might have psychological consequences.

- To do this, researchers have tried to identify the basic dimensions on which cultures differ from each other. Just as we can describe people's personal characteristics in terms of basic personality dimensions, we can also describe the characteristics of cultures along basic dimensions.

- Cultures differ along many dimensions, but the one that has attracted the most research attention is individualism versus collectivism. One of the big challenges of life involves managing the tension between looking out for yourself versus looking out for other people. But there's no clear answer to the question of how you should balance your focus on yourself as an individual with your focus on the other people in your life.

- Cultures differ in their beliefs about how people should balance this tension between self and other, and those differences are captured by a dimension that has individualism at one end and collectivism at the other end. Individualist cultures give greater priority to the individual, and collectivist cultures give higher priority to the collective, or the group.

- Individualist cultures are based on the idea that each person's life ultimately belongs to that person, so people have a right to select their own beliefs and values and can live almost any way they please. Collectivist cultures are based on the belief that a person's life belongs mostly to a group or society, so people often have to sacrifice their personal goals and interests for the benefit of the group.

> The most individualist countries tend to be the most Westernized; the United States, Australia, Canada, Great Britain, and the Netherlands top the list.
>
> It's common for people from Western cultures to assume that the most collectivist cultures are countries in East Asia, such as Japan, but in fact, the most collectivist countries are places such as Ecuador, Peru, Columbia, and Venezuela. Pakistan is also on that list.
>
> Japan actually falls in the middle of the individualist-collectivist continuum, along with countries such as Spain, India, Israel, and Austria. They're the most balanced between individualism and collectivism.

- All cultures have individualist and collectivist features, as well as individuals who depart from the cultural norm. But as a whole, cultures differ markedly in the degree to which they are individualist or collectivist, and those differences have implications for the personalities of the people who live or operate within those cultures.

- For example, individualist cultures encourage behaviors that are more extraverted in the sense of being assertive and dominant and attracting attention to oneself, whereas collectivist cultures encourage a less extraverted and more introverted style.

- People raised in individualist cultures also tend to be higher in openness than people from collectivist cultures, possibly because collectivist cultures encourage people to adopt the norms of their groups and don't allow as much individual freedom in choosing what to believe and how to behave.

- People from individualist cultures are not as good at taking other people's perspectives as people from collectivist cultures are. It's not that individualists can't do it; they just don't take other people's perspectives as automatically or as quickly as people from collectivist cultures do.

CULTURAL VALUES AND PERSONALITY

♦ Values are one route by which cultures influence people's personalities. For example, a culture that values toughness and aggression will presumably have a higher proportion of tough, aggressive people than a culture that values being gentle and kind. In helping people prioritize what's important, a culture's values change how people tend to behave.

♦ Given the large number and diversity of values around the world, researchers have looked for broad themes in the values that cultures promote. A leader in this area has been Geert Hofstede, who has studied the basic dimensions of cultural values across more than 50 countries.

♦ Hofstede's research identifies 4 basic dimensions of values on which cultures differ and, thus, dimensions that might affect the personalities of the people in a given culture. Not surprisingly, one of the values that he identified is the value placed on individualism versus collectivism.

♦ A second value that he identified is called power distance, which refers to the degree to which people should recognize and accept an uneven distribution of power among people. At one end of this value dimension are cultures that are very hierarchical—cultures in which people generally relate to one another in terms of their relative status and power and in which everyone accepts where they are in the hierarchy and the hierarchical status quo. Middle Eastern countries are particularly high in power distance, as are countries with a caste system, such as India.

♦ At the other end of the power distance dimension are cultures in which people generally interact with one another as equals and hierarchies are used only when necessary, such as in the military. Countries with the lowest power distance include New Zealand, Austria, Israel, Ireland, and the Scandinavian countries. The United States is also relatively low in power distance—in the bottom quarter of countries—but it's not as low as you might expect for a country founded on the idea that all people are created equal.

- In most status hierarchies, there are many more people toward the bottom of the hierarchy than there are at the top. As a result, most people in high-power-distance cultures have low status and power. And research shows that most people in a high-power-distance culture are socialized to be subservient—to follow the rules and stay in their place.

- People from cultures that are high in power distance also tend to score higher in conscientiousness. They follow the rules and do what they're supposed to—that is, they do what people higher up the hierarchy tell them to do.

> Researchers who looked at the relationship between cultural personality fit and well-being across 28 countries found that immigrants whose personality characteristics were more consistent with cultural norms in the new country had greater psychological well-being.

- They are also lower in extraversion, so they're less dominant and assertive. They're also lower in openness; they're less likely to entertain new ways of thinking and doing things. That would go against the status quo.

- A third dimension of cultural values is usually called masculinity-femininity. At the high end of this dimension—the so-called masculine end—are cultures that emphasize ambition, achievement, success, competition, and acquiring wealth. At the low end of this dimension—the so-called feminine end—are cultures that emphasize caring, cooperation, nurturance, and valuing the quality of life.

- A better name for this dimension might be agentic versus communal orientation. Cultures that value an agentic orientation stress getting things done, succeeding, and focusing on oneself, including focusing on making money. Cultures that value a communal orientation emphasize helping other people and fostering good relationships.

- Most industrialized countries, including the United States, lean toward the agentic, achievement-oriented side of this dimension. After all, becoming an industrialized country requires people to generally value achievement, success, and making money. Japan scores highest in terms of valuing this agentic orientation.

- The 4 countries that emphasize the communal, supportive orientation the most in the world, by far, are the Scandinavian countries: Finland, Sweden, Norway, and Denmark. Costa Rica and Portugal are also relatively communal, along with some countries in central Africa.

- People in agentic, achievement-oriented, so-called masculine cultures score higher in neuroticism than people in cultures that value a communal orientation. People in agentic cultures are notably more likely to be unhappy, distressed, angry, upset, and stressed out than those in communal cultures.

- People in agentic cultures also score higher in openness. It's not completely clear why, but it might be that people who value achievement and success have to be willing to be open and flexible in their beliefs and behaviors to succeed. Success requires novelty and innovation, which are valued more by people high in openness.

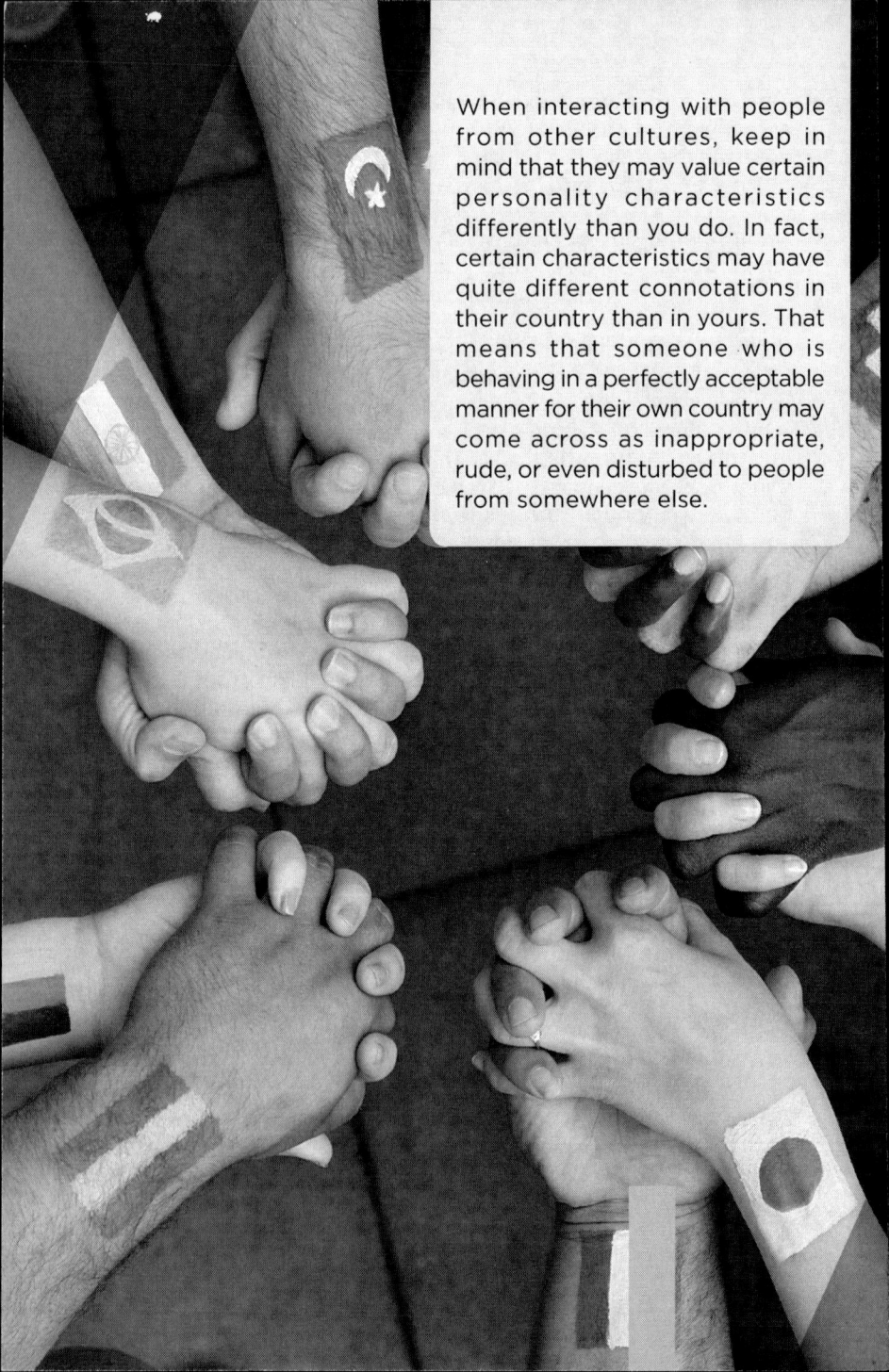

When interacting with people from other cultures, keep in mind that they may value certain personality characteristics differently than you do. In fact, certain characteristics may have quite different connotations in their country than in yours. That means that someone who is behaving in a perfectly acceptable manner for their own country may come across as inappropriate, rude, or even disturbed to people from somewhere else.

- Hofstede's fourth dimension of cultural values involves uncertainty avoidance, which refers to the degree to which a culture leads its members to feel either uncomfortable or comfortable in unstructured and ambiguous situations.

- Cultures that are high in uncertainty avoidance don't like situations that are novel, unstructured, surprising, or different than usual. So, such cultures minimize uncertainty by having stricter rules, laws, and regulations that specify how things should be done and how people should behave. They also emphasize safety and security. Cultures that are high in uncertainty avoidance don't like innovation and change, and they can feel repressive compared to cultures that are low in uncertainty avoidance.

- Cultures that are low in uncertainty avoidance are more tolerant of different beliefs and opinions, including being comfortable with a variety of religions. They try to have as few rules as possible and allow people the freedom to live as they wish.

- In general, uncertainty avoidance is higher in Latin countries, Japan, and Germany, and it's lower in Scandinavia, English-speaking countries, Jamaica, China, Hong Kong, and Singapore.

- People in cultures that value accepting uncertainty score significantly lower in neuroticism. Normally, uncertainty, novelty, and change worry people, but if your culture values those things and says that uncertainty is not really a problem, you'll probably be more accepting of it all.

- Greater acceptance of uncertainty is also associated with higher agreeableness. When a culture promotes a live-and-let-live philosophy, people are nicer to each other.

- We can interpret these relationships between cultural values and personality in 2 ways: We could conclude that growing up in cultures that value particular orientations leads people to develop certain personalities, but perhaps people in different cultures have different genetic predispositions that influence their personalities, and over time, people with different kinds of personalities create different kinds of cultures.

Suggested Reading

Hofstede, "Dimensionalizing Cultures."

Jarrett, "Different Nationalities Really Have Different Personalities."

Triandis and Suh, "Cultural Influences on Personality."

Questions to Consider

1. Individualist and collectivist cultures each have benefits and liabilities in terms of people's personality development and psychological well-being. What do you see as the advantages and disadvantages of each?

2. In what ways does your personality fit and not fit the culture in which you live? In other words, compare the primary characteristics that your culture values to your own configuration of personal characteristics and think about how well your personality matches your culture's ideal.

HOW CULTURE INFLUENCES PERSONALITY
LECTURE 18 TRANSCRIPT

For many years, most research in psychology was conducted in just a handful of Western countries: the United States, Canada, Great Britain, Australia, Germany, the Netherlands, and a few others. And, almost all participants in psychological studies were from that same group of countries. That's not a very diverse sample of people, and it certainly didn't allow much research on how personality might be influenced by culture. Well, those same countries still dominate scientific psychology, but the number of behavioral scientists in other countries has grown exponentially. Not only that, but Western psychologists have taken more seriously the idea that they need to consider cultural differences in the phenomena they study.

Many researchers regularly conduct studies in other areas of the world, often in collaboration with researchers from places that have typically been underrepresented in psychological research. So, we know much more about the effects of culture on personality than we did not too long ago. Think for a moment: How might you have turned out differently, in terms of your personality, if you had grown up in a culture that was different in important respects from the one you grew up in? You would certainly not be the person you turned out to be, but in what ways might you have been different? To explore this question, let's start by making it clear what we mean when we talk about culture.

Culture has been defined in many ways, but it fundamentally comes down to a set of beliefs that are shared by a large group of people. Although the term culture is usually used to refer to the beliefs of people in a particular country or ethnic group, it can also be applied to other groups such as a particular company, or area of the country, or even a sports team. We often think about culture in terms of how people act—their traditions, how they dress, what they eat, how they interact with each other, and so on—and culture involves all those things. But cultures are fundamentally based on beliefs; beliefs about what's important, beliefs about what's right and wrong, beliefs about how things should be done and how people ought to behave.

So, when we say that culture influences personality, we mean that the beliefs that people adopt from their culture influence their tendency to behave in certain ways. As a result, people from different cultures show systematic differences in their thoughts, behaviors, and even emotions. Before talking about how cultural factors influence particular personality characteristics, I want to make a general point about cultural influences on personality. We talked previously about the fact that personality doesn't manifest as much in strong situations that pressure people to act in certain ways as it does in weak situations. Well, cultures differ in the degree to which they generally exert a strong or a weak effect on people's behavior. So, cultures differ in the degree to which people's behavior reflects their individual personalities.

Some cultures put more pressure on people to behave in certain ways, to be a certain kind of person, than other cultures do. And the more that cultural pressures require people to act in culturally prescribed ways, the less people's individuality comes through, and the less variability we see among people. For example, the dominant culture of the United States permits a great deal of individual choice in how people behave. People can choose what they do for a living, who they live with, what they wear, how they spend their free time, whether they practice a religion, and so on. In fact, American culture not only permits a great deal of latitude in behavior, but it values and actively encourages individuality. Be yourself! March to your own drummer! There are still social norms and pressures to conform in certain ways—that's true of every society—but people's personalities are given more freedom to operate when cultural pressures are relatively weak.

Contrast that with cultures that limit people's discretion to choose their lifestyle or their occupation or their religion or their spouse or how they spend their free time. In those cultures, which researchers sometimes call tight cultures, how people behave is more heavily scripted by the culture and less influenced by personality. These cultures allow less personal discretion than so-called loose or weak cultures. Tight cultures are more common in homogeneous societies where just about everyone shares the same basic racial and ethnic background, cultural beliefs, religion, and social values. Those societies have many norms and rules about how people should behave, and they punish those who deviate from the rules, even in minor ways.

In contrast, heterogeneous societies tend to be looser and more tolerant of individuality because many different cultural belief systems are present. People are permitted to make their own choices of what to believe and how to live. Clearly, growing up in a tight culture creates a different orientation to rules, authority, and one's place in the society than growing up in a loose culture. And when rules are strict, people have fewer opportunities for autonomy, and their behavior is less likely to express their individual personalities.

Psychologists have been interested in cultural differences in personality for many years, but comparing the personalities of people from different cultures presents a number of challenges. Most notably, when the people in the cultures being studied speak different languages, it's difficult to be certain that the translations of the measures being used are equivalent. Typically, researchers translate a measure from one language to another and then back-translate the translation back to the original language to be sure that the words mean the same thing in both directions. This often requires several efforts, back-and-forth, before they get it right. But, even then, exactly the same word or phrase may have different connotations in different cultures, which may affect how people answer the question. And, sometimes, questions on a personality measure contain concepts or situations that don't even make sense in another culture. An item such as "I like to start new fads and fashions" would make absolutely no sense in most tight cultures.

The other big challenge for researchers has been identifying the characteristics of cultures that affect personality. Cultures differ in many, many ways, some quite important and some very trivial. And it's been a challenge to identify and measure the aspects of culture that might have psychological consequences. To do this, researchers have tried to identify the basic dimensions on which cultures differ from each other. Just as we can describe people's personal characteristics in terms of basic personality dimensions, we can describe the characteristics of cultures along basic dimensions as well. Cultures differ along many dimensions, but the one that has attracted the most research attention is individualism versus collectivism, so let's start there.

One of the big challenges of life involves managing the tension between looking out for yourself versus looking out for other people. To get by in life, we can't just focus totally on ourselves, but we also can't just focus on other people. There's has to be some blend or balance. But there's no clear answer to the question of how you should balance your focus on yourself as an individual with your focus on the other people in your life. Cultures differ in their beliefs about how people should balance this tension between self and other, and those differences are captured by a dimension that has individualism at one end and collectivism at the other end.

As the labels indicate, individualist cultures give greater priority to the individual, and collectivist cultures give higher priority to the collective or the group. Individualist cultures are based on the idea that each person's life ultimately belongs to that person, so people have a right to select their own beliefs and values, and can live almost any way they please. Collectivist cultures are based on the belief that a person's life belongs mostly to group or society, so people often have to sacrifice their personal goals and interests for the benefit of the group.

The most individualist countries tend to be the most Westernized: the United States, Australia, Canada, Great Britain, and the Netherlands top the list of individualist countries. But which are the most collectivist? It's common for people from Western cultures to assume that the most collectivist cultures are countries in east Asia, such as Japan, but in fact, the most collectivist countries are actually places such as Ecuador, Peru, Columbia, and Venezuela. Pakistan is also on that list. Japan actually falls about in the middle of the individualist-collectivist continuum, along with countries such as Spain, India, Israel, and Austria. They're the most balanced between individualism and collectivism.

Now, this distinction is clearly an overgeneralization; all cultures have individualist and collectivist features, as well as individuals who depart from the cultural norm. But as a whole, cultures differ markedly in the degree to which they are individualist or collectivist, and those differences have implications for the personalities of the people who live or operate within those cultures. For example, individualist cultures encourage people to be themselves, to figure out what they personally want in life, and to pursue it. So people who grow up in individualist cultures are, well, more individualistic. They're more focused on their own goals and desires.

In an individualist culture, people are encouraged to do things that make them stand out, to be better than other people, to get noticed. But in collectivist cultures, the emphasis is on fitting in and not drawing too much attention to yourself. Why? Because standing out and outperforming other people isn't good for harmony within the group. It's not about you; it's about the collective.

In individualist cultures, people are allowed, or even encouraged, to speak their minds and give their opinions, even if they disagree with other people. But in collectivist cultures disagreement and conflict are avoided when possible because they interfere with group harmony. In conflict situations, collectivists are primarily concerned with maintaining their relationships with other people, so they prefer to resolve conflicts in way that protects relationships. Individualists, on the other hand, are more concerned with being right and achieving justice, and they're sometimes willing to sacrifice relationships as long as justice is served. So, these 2 cultural approaches differ in the emphasis they place on asserting one's own views and protecting relationships.

Furthermore, in individualist societies, the connections between individuals are looser than they are in collectivist societies. Everybody is expected to look after themselves and their immediate family, but whether you worry much about your extended family or neighbors or strangers is up to you. But in collectivist societies, people tend to be integrated into strong, cohesive groups, which often include extended families, clans, and even villages. Although collectivist cultures might sound less selfish, less conflict-ridden, and more peaceful than individualist cultures, keep in mind that collectivist norms that encourage getting along with other people are reserved primarily for members of one's own group, however that's defined. So, in a collectivist culture, we're all supposed to get along with others in our group, but it's not uncommon to have conflicts, fights, and even wars with people outside our group.

The individualism or collectivism of a culture can affect personality. For example, individualist cultures encourage behaviors that are more extraverted in the sense of being assertive and dominant, and attracting attention to oneself, whereas collectivist cultures encourage a less extraverted and more introverted style. People raised in individualist cultures also tend to be higher in openness than people from collectivist cultures, possibly because collectivist cultures encourage people to adopt the norms of their groups and don't allow as much individual freedom in choosing what to believe and how to behave.

One interesting implication of individualism's emphasis on focusing on oneself and one's own goals is that people from individualist cultures are not as good at taking other people's perspectives as people from collectivist cultures are. It's not that individualists can't do it; they just don't take other people's perspectives as automatically or as quickly as people from collectivist cultures do.

We talked about the relationship between values and personality previously, but I want to say a few more things about values here, because values are one route by which cultures influence people's personalities. For example, a culture that values toughness and aggression will presumably have a higher proportion of tough, aggressive people than a culture that values being gentle and kind. In helping people to prioritize what's important, a culture's values change how people tend to behave.

Given the large number and diversity of values around the world, researchers have looked for broad themes in the values that cultures promote. A leader in this area has been Geert Hofstede, who has studied the basic dimensions of cultural values across more than

50 countries. His research identifies 4 basic dimensions of values on which cultures differ, and thus, dimensions that might affect the personalities of the people in a given culture. There are others, but let's focus on these 4.

Not surprisingly, one of the values that Hofstede identified is the value placed on individualism versus collectivism, but we've already talked about that. A second value that he identified is called power distance, which refers to the degree to which people should recognize and accept an uneven distribution of power among people. At one end of this value dimension are cultures that are very hierarchical; cultures in which people generally relate to one another in terms of their relative status and power, and in which everyone accepts where they are in the hierarchy and accepts the hierarchical status quo. Middle Eastern countries are particularly high in power distance, as are countries with a caste system, such as India.

At the other end of the power distance dimension are cultures in which people generally interact with one another as equals, and hierarchies are used only when necessary such as in the military. Countries with the lowest power distance include New Zealand, Austria, Israel, Ireland, and the Scandinavian countries. The United States is also relatively low in power distance—in the bottom quarter of countries—but it's not as low as you might expect for a country founded on the idea that all people are created equal.

Well, what difference might the degree to which a culture values power distance make for personality? Consider the fact that in most status hierarchies, there are many more people toward the bottom of the hierarchy than there are at the top. As a result, most people in high power-distance cultures have low status and power. So, we might expect to find that most people in a high power distance culture would be socialized to be subservient, to follow the rules, stay in their place, and not rock the boat. And that's what research shows.

People from cultures that are high in power distance also tend to score higher in conscientiousness—they follow the rules and do what they're supposed to—that is, they do what people higher up the hierarchy tell them to. They are also lower in extraversion, so they're less dominant and assertive, and they're lower in openness—they're less likely to entertain new ways of thinking and doing things. That would go against the status quo. So living in a hierarchical culture in which authority and status are valued is associated with being less assertive, more conforming, and more dutiful.

A third dimension of cultural values is usually called masculinity-femininity, but I don't like that label because masculinity and femininity connote all sorts of things that don't have anything to do with this dimension. Let me describe it, and we'll come up with a better label. At the high end of this dimension—the so-called masculine end—are cultures that emphasize ambition, achievement, success, competition, and acquiring wealth. At the low end of this dimension—the so-called feminine dimension—are cultures that emphasize caring, cooperation, nurturance, and valuing the quality of life.

A better name for this dimension might be agentic versus communal orientation. Cultures that value an agentic orientation stress getting things done, succeeding, and focusing on oneself, including focusing on making money. Cultures that value a communal orientation emphasize helping other people and fostering good relationships. Most industrialized countries, including the United States, lean toward the agentic, achievement-oriented side of this dimension. After all, becoming an industrialized country requires people to generally value achievement and success and making money. Japan scores highest in terms of valuing this agentic orientation. The 4 countries that emphasize the communal, supportive orientation the most in the entire world, by far, are the Scandinavian countries: Finland, Sweden, Norway, and Denmark. Costa Rica and Portugal are also relatively communal, along with some countries in central Africa.

For me, one of the most interesting findings is that people in agentic, achievement-oriented, so-called "masculine" cultures score higher in neuroticism than people in cultures that value a communal orientation. And it's a fairly good-sized correlation! People in agentic cultures are notably more likely to be unhappy, distressed, angry, upset, and stressed-out than those in communal cultures. I suppose this is consistent with research showing that those 4 communal Scandinavian countries are always among the top 10 happiest countries in the world.

People in agentic cultures also score higher in openness. It's not completely clear why, but it might be that people who value achievement and success have to be willing to be open and flexible in their beliefs and behaviors to succeed. Success requires novelty and innovation, which are valued more by people high in openness.

Hofstede's fourth dimension of cultural values involves uncertainty avoidance. That's a strange label, I know, but it refers to the degree to which a culture leads its members to feel either uncomfortable or comfortable in unstructured and ambiguous situations.

Cultures that are high in uncertainty avoidance don't like situations that are novel, unstructured, surprising, or different than usual. So, such cultures minimize uncertainty by having stricter rules, laws, and regulations that specify how things should be done and how people ought to behave. They also emphasize safety and security. Cultures that are high in uncertainty avoidance don't like innovation and change, and they can feel repressive compared to cultures that are low in uncertainty avoidance. Cultures that are low in uncertainty avoidance—we can think of them as uncertainty-accepting cultures—are more tolerant of different beliefs and opinions, including being comfortable with a variety of religions. They try to have as few rules as possible, and allow people the freedom to live as they wish. In general, uncertainty avoidance is higher in Latin countries, in Japan, and in Germany; and it's lower in Scandinavia; English-speaking countries such as the United States, England, Ireland, and Australia; and in Jamaica, China, Hong Kong, and Singapore.

Think about the ways in which uncertainty-avoiding and uncertainty-accepting cultures might influence the personalities of the people in those cultures. The biggest effect, which was found in a study of 33 countries, is that people in cultures that value accepting uncertainty score significantly lower in neuroticism, which makes sense. Normally, uncertainty, novelty, and change worry people, but if your culture values those things and says that uncertainty is not really a problem, you'll probably be more accepting of it all. Greater acceptance of uncertainty is also associated with higher agreeableness. When a culture promotes a live-and-let-live philosophy, people are nicer to each other.

We can interpret these relationships between cultural values and personality in 2 ways. On one hand, we could conclude that growing up in cultures that value particular orientations leads people to develop certain personalities. If my culture values individualism or power distance or communal traits or accepting uncertainty, I'm more likely to develop a personality that's consistent with those values. But some researchers have suggested that the direction of causality might go the other way. Perhaps people in different cultures have different genetic predispositions that influence their personalities, and over time, people with different kinds of personalities create different kinds of cultures. For example, over many generations, a population that is genetically predisposed to be less extraverted, less open, and more conscientious may develop a culture that's high in power distance in which hierarchy and authority are important.

Separating these 2 causal directions between cultural values and personality is difficult, but studies of immigrants can help. Consider a study that compared these 3 groups:

- People whose parents immigrated from China to Canada before they were born, so that the people were raised solely in a Western culture;

- People who immigrated from China to Canada many years ago, and so have had a fairly long time to adapt to Canadian culture; and

- People who immigrated from China to Canada quite recently, and so have had little time to adapt.

If culture affects personality, we should find that the 3 groups' personalities differ because they spent different lengths of time immersed in Canadian culture. But if culture plays little or no role in personality, the 3 groups should not differ much. The results showed that the 3 groups did differ. The people who were born in Canada of Chinese parents—and thus lived in Canada their whole lives—had the most Westernized profile of personality traits. And the most recent immigrants to Canada had the least Westernized profile, with the long-term immigrants falling in between. So, people who were born in Canada were more extraverted, open, and agreeable than those who immigrated later, even though they all had Chinese parents.

Such a pattern supports the idea that culture influences personality, but another interpretation is possible. What if people in these 3 groups started out with different genetic predispositions? Many years ago, immigration from China to Canada was much less common than it is today, so people who took that leap may have been more extraverted and open and less neurotic than average. But those who immigrated more recently, now that it's fairly common, may not need to be as extraverted, open, and emotionally secure to decide to move to another country. Perhaps immigrants who came to Canada many years ago were genetically predisposed to have more Western personalities even before they got here, whereas people who immigrated more recently had no such predisposition.

Although that's possible, research shows that immigrants to a new country change in the direction of the prototypical personality for that country the more acculturated they become, which shows that the culture itself has an effect on their personality. For example, one study showed that the more that Japanese immigrants to the United States became involved in American culture through friendships with Americans, the amount of time they spoke English, and adopting American lifestyles, the more their personalities changed away from a typical Japanese profile and toward a typical European-American profile. The more they became immersed in American culture, the more American they became with respect to openness, neuroticism, and conscientiousness. In any case, you can see why it's hard for researchers to answer the chicken-and-the-egg question when it comes to cultural values and personality.

While I'm talking about immigrants, let me make another point. Immigrants obviously face many challenges as they adjust to a new culture, but one challenge that isn't discussed much is the mismatch between the immigrant's personality as it developed in his or her home country and the dominant, valued personality in the new country. The more an immigrant's personality matches the normative personality for a new culture, the easier the transition to the new culture should be. But if an immigrant's personality doesn't match how people are supposed to be in the new culture, more stress is likely.

Along these lines, researchers looked at the relationship between cultural personality fit and well-being across 28 countries. They found that immigrants whose personality characteristics were more consistent with cultural norms in the new country had greater psychological well-being. Having a personality that's consistent with a culture's values helps people fit in and gives them validation and support from other people, which enhances their well-being. But having a personality that doesn't quite fit the culture creates stress, interferes with the person's social life, and undermines happiness.

Whatever type of culture we're from, we each value certain attributes more than others and have stereotypes about people who have certain psychological characteristics. So, when we meet and interact with people from a culture that values different characteristics, misunderstandings can arise. One of the hurdles in getting to know and to get along with people from other places is not just that they may speak different languages or practice different religions or have different traditions. One challenge is that we sometimes have different ways of being a person and interacting with other people.

In interacting with people from other cultures, it's helpful to keep in mind that they may value certain personal characteristics differently than you do. In fact, certain characteristics may have quite different connotations in their country than in yours. That means that someone who is behaving in a perfectly acceptable manner for their own country may come across as inappropriate or rude or even disturbed to people from somewhere else. Just being aware of the fact that cultures value and socialize different personality characteristics in their members, may help us to be more understanding when interacting with people from different cultural backgrounds.

NONCONSCIOUS ASPECTS OF PERSONALITY

LECTURE 19

The focus of this lecture is that much of what influences people's emotions and behavior occurs outside of their conscious awareness and that to understand people's personalities, we have to consider nonconscious processes. At any given moment, you are aware of only a small portion of what's actually going on around you and only a small portion of what's happening in your own mind. And that's a good thing. Your brain has a limited capacity to think consciously about things, so it handles most tasks without you having to think consciously about what you're doing.

NONCONSCIOUS PROCESSES

- Imagine yourself at a large party. There's a lot of noise, so when you're talking with people, you have to focus very carefully on what they are saying and ignore everything else. In fact, if someone asked you what the other people around you were talking about while you were carrying on a conversation with someone, you probably couldn't tell them. Even though they are within hearing distance, you're totally oblivious to what they are saying. Until, out of the hubbub, you hear someone say your name, and your ears perk up.

- This tells us that you've actually been monitoring all of those other conversations all along, or at least your brain has been—it's doing so nonconsciously, without you thinking consciously about it. Only if it picks up something that might be important to you, such as your name, does your brain bother you by bringing it to conscious awareness so that you can figure out what's going on.

- This so-called cocktail party phenomenon tells us not only that your brain is monitoring things nonconsciously, but also that it's using information stored in your memory to make nonconscious decisions about how to respond. After all, your brain recognized your name—nonconsciously—so it was pulling information from memory as it monitored the situation.

- At the broadest level, human beings possess 2 distinct systems that process information, influence emotion, and guide behavior. In other words, there are 2 basic types of thinking, and they go by a variety of names: nonconscious versus conscious, automatic versus controlled, and system 1 versus system 2.

Researchers have studied nonconscious effects by putting headphones on people and playing different messages to each of their ears. They tell people to listen carefully to one of the messages and then ask participants about the message in the other ear, the one that they were not consciously monitoring. People would claim not to know anything about what was said, yet certain kinds of words would pop out and get their attention—not only their own name, but also words pertaining to sex and curse words.

- You're already pretty familiar with the conscious system, system 2, because you're consciously aware of the way that it works. If you're trying to make a decision, whether about something important or something trivial, you're consciously aware of what you're thinking about. You can make lists of what the considerations are, and you can articulate what your thought processes are. And afterward, you can explain the basis of your decision—or at least the conscious basis of your decision.

- Conscious thought is important, but it has some drawbacks. You can think consciously about only one thing at a time—in spite of what habitual multitaskers may say. Conscious thought is also rather slow and deliberate, so you often can't make instantaneous judgments consciously.

- Fortunately, we also have system 1, the nonconscious system, which can process lots of information simultaneously and very rapidly. But you're not aware of anything that's going on inside the system until an answer or a reaction pops out. You engage in many behaviors all day, many of them very complicated behaviors, using the nonconscious system.

- Talking is usually completely nonconscious. As you are chatting with someone, you usually aren't choosing your words consciously. Of course, sometimes people try to manage their speech consciously; when you want to be careful of what you're saying, some conscious thought might be involved. But usually it's not.

- This means that many manifestations of your personality—ways in which you tend to feel or behave—are not mediated by conscious thought. You often don't deliberately and consciously decide to act the way you do, have the reactions that you have, or be the person that you are.

- Sometimes you do make deliberate, conscious decisions that reflect aspects of your personality. If you're a highly conscientious person, you might plan things out and purposefully get organized and talk to yourself in ways that keep you on task.

- So, sometimes conscious thought can reflect aspects of our personality and create our typical ways of responding. But much of what determines your personality is entirely nonconscious.

NONCONSCIOUS CONTENT

- The processes that occur nonconsciously involve brain mechanisms that process information in ways that you aren't aware of. There's nothing particularly mysterious about this, although it is terribly complicated. Computers can process lots of information all at once to make decisions, and they do so presumably without any conscious awareness of what they are doing. They are nonconscious information-processing devices.

- Your brain isn't exactly like a computer, but it's similar to the extent that it's also an information-processing device. And the analogy helps us see that mechanisms can process information and make decisions without conscious awareness. So, the fact that you can process information and make decisions nonconsciously isn't too difficult to grasp.

- The more challenging part is to explain the content of the information that's being processed nonconsciously, because that's what makes people's personalities different. Your brain's nonconscious processes are using somewhat different nonconscious content from the content that another person's brain uses.

- What's actually in your nonconscious? That question is misleading because it implies that the nonconscious is a place in your mind. In fact, nonconscious processes take place in many different parts of the brain. But the internal content that influences your nonconscious reactions is just stored in memory like other information in your brain.

- Consider this question: What color do you associate with the word "stop?" When the answer popped up in your mind—"red"—where did that information come from? And did you have to think consciously about it, or did the answer just come out of nowhere? Most likely, you associated "red" with "stop" very quickly without having to think about it consciously.

- And when you're driving, you probably respond very quickly and automatically when the light turns red without thinking consciously, "Oh, the light turned red, and red means stop." The association between "stop" and "red" is stored in the memory that your conscious mind uses, but your nonconscious processes also have ready access to it.

- That's a very simple association, one that doesn't have much relevance or impact outside of driving, and just about everybody has that same association. But some of our nonconscious associations are idiosyncratic. One person might have developed a very different set of automatic associations to certain situations, events, or kinds of people from the associations that another person has. These 2 people might respond differently in a particular situation because they have different nonconscious associations to stimuli that are present.

MOTIVES

- Two people also might respond differently because they have different motives. Modern research shows that people have motives that they aren't aware of. These nonconscious motives are called implicit—to distinguish them from explicit motives that people are aware of and can think about.

- The idea that people have motives that they aren't aware of creates a problem for researchers in psychology, who depend a great deal on questionnaires and interviews to ask people about themselves. Psychologists have well-designed and highly valid self-report measures of people's motives, but people can report only on their explicit, or conscious, motives, which leaves us in a bind.

- One solution to the problem of determining what people's implicit motives might be is to use projective tests, which provide people with an ambiguous stimulus or unstructured task of some kind, such as an ambiguous picture or a task that can be accomplished in many different ways. The idea is that people's motives will come out in how they interpret the ambiguous picture or deal with the unstructured task even if they can't identify or verbalize what their motives are.

- The most popular measures of implicit motives have been variations of tests modeled on the Thematic Apperception Test (TAT), which involves a set of drawings of ambiguous situations. For example, one picture shows a woman lying in bed with a man standing by the bedside shielding his eyes or grasping his forehead—it's not clear. And the respondent is asked to tell a story about the scene.

> Research has shown that a projective measure of power motivation predicts long-term success as a business manager better than a self-report measure of power motivation.

- The kinds of stories that people tell differ a great deal in who respondents think the people in the picture are and what their relationship is. Some think the woman's asleep; others think she's dead. Sometimes the man is her husband or lover; sometimes he's a guy who picked her up in a bar the previous night. Respondents even describe the people's emotions differently. Some think that the man is covering his eyes out of guilt; others think that he is rubbing his eyes as he gets up to go to work early.

- You can't tell too much about someone from the story he or she tells about any particular picture. But after coding a person's stories about several of these ambiguous pictures, certain themes often emerge. You can begin to get a sense of how people interpret the world, thereby shining some light on their concerns and motives, even if they can't consciously identify or explain what those motives are.

- If you measure a particular motive using this kind of projective technique and you also administer standard self-report personality scales on which people answer questions about their motives, the scores on the 2 measures often don't correlate very highly. In other words, the nonconscious, implicit motives reflected in the stories people tell on projective tests don't necessarily relate to the explicit motives that they report on questionnaires.

- Researchers have spent a lot of time trying to understand why implicit, projective measures and explicit, self-report measures don't seem to be getting at the same thing. The best conclusion is that people have 2 sets of motives—one nonconscious, implicit set; and one conscious, explicit set—that may or may not converge, but both sets manifest in people's personalities.

- Given what we know about nonconscious versus conscious processing—about system 1 versus system 2 thinking—it's not surprising that people can have nonconscious motives that don't necessarily line up with their conscious motives.

- Sometimes we have automatic, gut-level desires to do something, and sometimes we think carefully about what we should do. And there's no reason that these 2 processes will necessarily lead to the same motivation. In fact, we are sometimes motivated to do something that we consciously tell ourselves we shouldn't be doing, which shows that we can have competing motivational influences.

- Another thing we've learned is that implicit, nonconscious motives predict people's long-term outcomes in life better than explicit, conscious motives do, whereas explicit motives predict people's specific choices on particular tasks better than nonconscious motives.

- When we're confronted with an explicit decision—something specific that we have to decide right now—we tend to think about it consciously, so our conscious motives figure prominently in our reactions. But as life unfolds, there are many subtle, seemingly unimportant decisions and choices that we don't think about consciously, and in those unimportant situations, our nonconscious motives are likely to be operating.

HABITS

- Another example of how nonconscious processes can influence behavior in ways that make people different from each other is habits. A habit forms when people are cued to perform a behavior automatically without making a conscious decision to do so.

- Many people have the habit of following a certain routine as they get ready for work each morning. A certain contextual cue—getting out of bed—cues an automatic pattern of behavior. If you have a habit for this kind of thing, you don't sit on the edge of the bed each morning and ponder what to do to get ready for work. You just start your day, without any conscious thought or deliberation. Your day is filled with habitual responses, and they help make you who you are.

The fact that much of our personality operates outside of our awareness has a few important implications: First, given that nonconscious processes affect our reactions, we can't know for sure why we do certain things. Second, the fact that we aren't privy to nonconscious influences helps explain why it's often so difficult to change our behavior.

- Habits are exceptionally efficient because they allow us to perform certain actions without devoting time or energy to figuring out what to do or how to do it. The downside is that, because they're automatic, habits sometimes unfold even though they aren't the best responses in a particular situation—and even when they conflict with our intentions.

- Neuroscience research shows that as habits form and strengthen, control of the behavior shifts from areas of the brain that are associated with conscious thinking and goal-directed control to brain areas that are involved in perceiving stimuli and initiating actions—that react automatically and nonconsciously.

Suggested Reading

Bargh, *Before You Know It*.

Wilson, *Strangers to Ourselves*.

Questions to Consider

1. Compare Freud's view of the unconscious to the view of nonconscious processes endorsed by many modern personality psychologists. In what ways are the 2 views similar, and in what ways are they different?

2. Automatic, habitual reactions lead to consistencies in our behavior even without us thinking about them. What automatic, habitual responses can you see in your own behavior?

NONCONSCIOUS ASPECTS OF PERSONALITY
LECTURE 19 TRANSCRIPT

If I asked just about anyone to write down the names of the most famous psychologists of all time, I have no doubt that the name Sigmund Freud would be on almost everybody's list. That would be wrong. As we've discussed, Freud wasn't a psychologist, but virtually everybody's heard of him. Although he was a physician, a neurologist, rather than a psychologist, Freud had a dramatic impact not only on psychology but on other intellectual domains as well. Most people also have at least a vague notion of some of Freud's ideas. For example, it's commonly known that Freud stressed the importance of unconscious processes in human behavior. It's also widely known that he thought a person can get stuck or fixated at certain stages of childhood development; that interpreting people's dreams can give us insight into their problems; and that little kids want to have sex with their parents.

Now, most contemporary psychologists don't agree with much of what Freud said, but they still give him a lot of credit for getting us to think about the human mind and personality and psychological problems in a different way. One of Freud's primary insights—the one I want to focus on in this lecture—was that much of what influences people's emotions and behavior occurs outside of their conscious awareness. Freud would say that to understand people's personalities, we have to consider unconscious processes.

At any given moment, we are aware of only a small portion of what's actually going on around us, and we are also aware of only a small portion of what's happening in our own mind. At this moment, you are conscious of only a small fraction of the external stimuli and internal processing that are going on. And that's a good thing. Your brain has a limited capacity to think consciously about things, so it handles most tasks without you having to think consciously about what you're doing. Right now, your brain is making sense out of all of these sounds coming out of my mouth, without you having to think about the process or to be aware of how it's interpreting what I'm saying. But if I suddenly use an unfamiliar word, you might start to think consciously about what I mean.

The idea that most of our behaviors and emotions are mediated by processes that occur below the level of our conscious awareness is taken for granted by modern psychologists, but it wasn't at the time that Freud started talking about it. Freud went a step further than just suggesting that much of our behavior results from processes that we're not consciously aware of. Freud believed that the unconscious mind contains primitive desires and urges that influence our actions without our awareness. He saw the unconscious mind as a cauldron of primitive impulses, most of them involving sex and aggression, that are unconscious because they would be too disturbing or frightening for us to be aware of. So, these dark motives are kept locked away in an unconscious repository.

He also suggested that people's psychological problems stem mostly from things that are going on in their unconscious mind. The essential problem is that we have dark, animalistic impulses that need to be satisfied, but the rational, decision-making part of our brain knows that we can't go around satisfying our urges like a wild animal. And if unfulfilled, this tension between the demands of our animal nature and the rules of society creates psychological problems. Freud developed a method of psychotherapy called psychoanalysis to help make these unconscious tensions conscious because he thought that was the only way to expose and deal with this mess.

Not many modern psychologists believe the details of this aspect of Freud's theory, although some do adopt offshoots and modifications of it. But they do believe his central premise that nonconscious processes influence behavior in ways that people don't realize. You might have noticed that I just used the word nonconscious, whereas I had been using the word unconscious when talking about Freud's ideas. Because Freud's ideas about the unconscious mind have fallen out of favor and carry so much conceptual baggage, most researchers in psychology use the word nonconscious instead to distinguish modern scientific ideas about nonconscious processes from Freud's conjectures about the unconscious mind. So, as I talk about aspects of your personality that you are not aware of, I'm generally going to use the word nonconscious.

Because many of Freud's ideas seemed pretty weird, and researchers didn't have a good way to study things that people aren't aware of in their own minds, scientific psychologists lost interest in nonconscious processes for several years. But then in the 1950s and 60s, interest was renewed, initially within cognitive psychology, by the discovery of the cocktail party phenomenon.

Imagine yourself at a large party. There's a lot of noise, a lot of hubbub, so when you're talking with people you have to focus very carefully on what they are saying and ignore everything else. There are other conversations all around, but you're focusing only on the one in which you are engaged and pretty much screening out everything else that's going on. In fact, if I asked you what the other people around you were talking about while you were carrying on a conversation with someone, you probably couldn't tell me. Even though they are within hearing distance, you're totally oblivious to what they are saying. Until, out of the hubbub, you hear someone say your name, and your ears perk up. Huh? You've had that happen right?

Well, what's that tell us? It tells us that you've actually been monitoring all of those other conversations all along, or at least you brain has been. While you're thinking about the conversations in which you're engaged, your brain is keeping track of what else is going on around you. Only it's doing so nonconsciously, without you thinking consciously about it. Only if it picks up something that might be important to you, like your name, does your brain bother you by bringing it to conscious awareness so that you can figure out what's going on.

The cocktail party phenomenon tells us not only that you brain is monitoring things nonconsciously, but also that it's using information stored in your memory to make nonconscious decisions about how to respond. After all, your brain recognized your name nonconsciously, so it was pulling information from memory as it monitored the situation. It might have also gotten your attention if someone had mentioned your hometown or your occupation or some other personally relevant topic. Nonconsciously, your brain knew what might be important to you.

Researchers were able to study this sort of nonconscious effect by putting headphones on people and playing different messages to each of their ears. They'd tell people to listen carefully to one of the messages—they'd be tested on it later—and then ask participants about the message in the other ear, the one that they were not consciously monitoring. People would claim not to know anything about what it said, yet certain kinds of words would pop out and get their attention: not only their own name but also words pertaining to sex and curse words.

These findings led researchers to realize that, at the broadest level, human beings possess 2 distinct systems that process information, influence emotion, and guide behavior. To say it differently, there are 2 basic types of thinking, and they go by a variety of names: nonconscious versus conscious, automatic versus controlled, and System 1 versus System 2.

You're already pretty familiar with the conscious system—System 2—because, well, you're consciously aware of the way that it works. If you're trying to make a decision, whether about something important such as where to live or what job to take, or something trivial like what to have for dinner or what present to buy somebody, you're consciously aware of what you're thinking about. You can make lists of what the considerations are, the pros and cons, and you can articulate what your thought processes are. And afterwards, you can explain to me the basis of your decision, or at least the conscious basis of your decision.

Conscious thought is obviously important, but it has some drawbacks. You can think consciously about only one thing at a time. You can jump around from topic to topic pretty rapidly, but at any given moment, you can think consciously about only one thing. So, imagine that you're driving and you're trying to figure out which turn to take and, while you're trying to figure out where you are and where you're supposed to go, the person is the passenger seat is asking you about what you want for dinner. You simply can't process those 2 streams of information consciously at the same time, in spite of what habitual multi-taskers may tell you. Conscious thought is also rather slow and deliberate. You often can't make instantaneous judgments consciously. So, if you had to rely solely on conscious thought, you wouldn't be able to make moment-to-moment decisions quickly enough to survive.

Fortunately, we also have System 1, the nonconscious system. The nonconscious system can process lots of information simultaneously, and process it all very rapidly. But you're not aware of anything that's going on inside the system until an answer or a reaction pops out. You engage in many behaviors all day long, many of them very complicated behaviors, using the nonconscious system. Just talking is usually totally nonconscious. As you are chatting with someone, your words usually just come rolling out. You aren't choosing your words consciously. Of course, sometimes people do try to manage their speech consciously; when you want to be careful of what you're saying, some conscious thought might be involved. But usually it's not.

Now think of what this says about personality. Many manifestations of your personality—ways in which you tend to feel or behave—are not mediated by conscious thought. You often don't deliberately and consciously decide to act the way you do, to have the reactions that you have, to be the person that you are. It just comes out, with little or no conscious thought or deliberate control on your part. Sometimes you do make deliberate, conscious decisions that reflect aspects of your personality. If you're a highly conscientious person, you might plan things out and purposefully get organized and talk to yourself in ways that keep you on task. Or, if you're facing an ethical dilemma, you might think carefully about your values and make a conscious decision to take one course of action or another. Or if you're a vengeful person, you might lie awake at night consciously plotting how to get back at somebody. So, sometimes, conscious thought can reflect aspects of our personality and create our typical ways of responding.

But much of what determines your personality is entirely nonconscious. It's not the sort of unconscious that Freud was talking about, though. It's not a seething caldron of aggressive and sexual urges that fuels our behavior, although there are certainly motivational inclinations in there. To think about what the nonconscious aspects of personality are, we need to make a distinction between nonconscious processes and nonconscious content.

The processes that occur nonconsciously involve brain mechanisms that process information in ways that you aren't aware of. There's nothing particularly mysterious about this, although it is terribly complicated. Computers can process lots of information all at once to make decisions and run equipment and even drive cars, and they do so presumably without any conscious awareness of what they are doing. They are nonconscious information-processing devices. Your brain isn't exactly like a computer, but it's similar to the extent that it's also an information-processing device. And the analogy helps us to see that mechanisms can process information and make decisions without conscious awareness. So, the fact that you can process information and make decisions nonconsciously isn't too hard to grasp.

The more challenging part is to explain the content of the information that's being processed nonconsciously, because that's what makes people's personalities different. Your brain's nonconscious processes are using somewhat different nonconscious content from the content that my brain uses. So, what's actually in there in your nonconscious? That question is misleading because it implies that the nonconscious is a place in your mind, a dark closet with things in it that you don't know about. In fact, nonconscious processes take place in many different parts of the brain. But the internal content that influences your nonconscious reactions is just stored in memory like other information in your brain.

Let me ask you a question: What color do you associate with the word stop? When the answer popped up in your mind—red—where'd that information come from? And did you have to think consciously about it, or did the answer just come out of nowhere? I suspect that you associated red with stop very quickly without having to think about it consciously. And when you're driving, I suspect that you respond very quickly and automatically, when the light turns red without consciously thinking, "Oh, the light turned red, and red means stop." The association between stop and red is stored in the memory that your conscious mind uses, but your nonconscious processes also have ready access to it.

But that's a very simple association, one that doesn't have much relevance or impact outside of driving, and just about everybody has that same association. But some of our nonconscious associations are idiosyncratic. You and I both automatically associate red with stop, but you may have developed a very different set of automatic associations to certain situations, events, or kinds of people from the associations I have. When you encounter a particular situation or event or kind of person, often some emotion or thought or behavior pops out of your mind just like red popped out when I asked about stop. But that automatic, nonconscious association may be different from the one I would have to the same stimulus. Let me give you one interesting example.

Research has been done on the nonconscious effects of particular stimuli on people who are and are not religious. Presumably, religious people have different associations to certain stimuli and situations from those of nonreligious people. For example, for a Christian, stimuli such as a cross or a lamb or even just the word spirit, have different associations than they do for a non-Christian. Researchers were interested in how far the effects of those associations go. Perhaps just seeing or hearing stimuli with religious associations could start nonconscious processes in religious people yet have no comparable impact on nonreligious people.

Several studies have explored this possibility by exposing religious and nonreligious people to incidental religious stimuli to see how it affects their behavior. A meta-analysis of a number of these studies showed that incidental religious symbols led religious people to behave in a less selfish and more generous way on experimental tasks. But the presence of religious symbols or words had no overall effect on the generosity of nonreligious people. So, just walking through an average day, religious people's behavior may be changed in subtle ways when they experience stimuli with a religious association even if they don't consciously think about it, or even consciously detect it.

I used religious associations as the example here, but all of us carry associations around in our heads that can be triggered nonconsciously and affect our feelings and behavior. And as with religious symbols, we don't have to detect these stimuli consciously. Research shows that stimuli can have these effects on us even if researchers present them subliminally so that research participants don't consciously see them at all. The bottom line is that you and I might respond differently in a particular situation because we have different nonconscious associations to stimuli that are present.

We also might respond differently because we have different motives. As I said, the basic premise of Freud's view of the unconscious was that your behavior is motivated by unconscious urges that you're not aware of, and undesirable, animalistic urges at that. Although he was wrong on the details, modern research shows that people do have motives that they aren't aware of. We call these nonconscious motives implicit to distinguish them from explicit motives that people are aware of and can think about.

The idea that people have motives that they aren't aware of creates a problem for researchers in psychology. As you know, psychologists depend a great deal on questionnaires and interviews to ask people about themselves, and we certainly have well-designed and highly valid self-report measures of people's motives. But by definition, people can report only on their explicit or conscious motives, which leaves us in a bind. How can we find out what people's implicit motives might be—the ones they aren't consciously aware of?

One solution is to use projective tests to get at people's implicit, nonconscious motives. Projective tests provide people with an ambiguous stimulus or unstructured task of some kind, such as an ambiguous picture, or a task that can be accomplished in many different ways. The idea is that people's motives will come out in how they interpret the ambiguous picture or deal with the unstructured task even if they can't identify or verbalize what their motives are. Something inside of the person is leading him or her to respond to the ambiguous, unstructured situation in the way he or she does.

In the case of implicit motives, the most popular measures have been variations of tests modeled on the Thematic Apperception Test—the TAT. The TAT involves a set of drawings of ambiguous situations. For example, one picture shows a woman lying in bed, with a man standing by the bedside shielding his eyes or grasping his forehead—it's not clear. And the respondent is asked to tell a story about the scene. Who are these people? What's going on? What led up to the scene in the picture, and what happened afterwards?

It's fascinating to hear the kinds of stories that people tell. The stories differ a great deal in who respondents think the people in the picture are and what their relationship is. Some think the woman's asleep, some think she's drunk, some think she's dead. Sometimes the man is her husband or lover, sometimes he's a guy who picked her up in a bar last night. Respondents even describe the people's emotions differently. Some think the man is covering his eyes out of guilt; others, that he is rubbing the sleep out of his eyes as he gets up to go to work early.

Of course, you can't tell too much about someone from the story he or she tells about any particular picture. But after coding a person's stories about several of these ambiguous pictures, certain themes often emerge. You can begin to get a sense of how people interpret the world, thereby shining some light on their concerns and motives, even if they can't consciously identify or explain what those motives are. What's interesting is that if you measure a particular motive using this sort of projective technique—let's say you measure the motive to have power and control over other people—and you also administer standard self-report personality scales on which people answer questions about their motives, the scores on the 2 measures often don't correlate very highly. In other words, the nonconscious, implicit motives reflected in the stories people tell on projective tests don't necessarily relate to the explicit motives that they report on questionnaires.

Researchers have spent a lot of time trying to understand why the implicit, projective measures and explicit, self-report measures don't seem to be getting at the same thing. One conclusion might be that one or both of the measures aren't any good, that one or both aren't actually measuring people's motives. But research shows that measures of both implicit motives as measured by the TAT and explicit motives as measured by self-report questionnaires do relate to people's thoughts, behaviors, and emotions. So, measures of both implicit and explicit motives are measuring something that relates meaningfully to people's actual behavior. Both projective tests and self-report questionnaires are valid and predict certain behaviors and reactions.

The best conclusion is that people have 2 sets of motives: one nonconscious implicit set, and one conscious explicit set that may or may not converge, but both sets manifest in people's personalities. Given what we know about nonconscious versus conscious processing—about System 1 and System 2 thinking—it's really not surprising that people can have nonconscious motives that don't necessarily line up with their conscious motives. Sometimes we have automatic, gut-level desires to do something, and sometimes we think carefully about what we should do. And there's no reason that these 2 processes will necessarily lead to the same motivation. In fact, we are sometimes motivated to do something that we consciously tell ourselves we shouldn't be doing, which shows that we can have competing motivational influences.

Another thing we've learned is that implicit, nonconscious motives predict people's long-term outcomes in life better than explicit, conscious motives do, whereas explicit motives predict people's specific choices on particular tasks better than nonconscious motives. For example, scores based on a projective measure of achievement motivation, which is a measure of implicit nonconscious motives, predict long-term success better than a self-report questionnaire does, and a projective measure of power motivation predicts long-term success as a business manager better than a self-report measure of power motivation. My reading of this is that when we're confronted with an explicit decision, something specific that we have to decide right now, we tend to think about it consciously, so our conscious motives figure prominently in our reactions.

But as life unfolds, there are many subtle, seemingly unimportant decisions and choices that we don't think about consciously, and in those unimportant situations, our nonconscious motives are likely to be operating. When we aren't thinking consciously, we go with our gut. So, over the long haul, our nonconscious motives and the decisions we don't think deeply about nudge us along without us even thinking about them.

To conclude, let me mention one other example of how nonconscious processes can influence behavior in ways that make people different from each other: habits.

A habit forms when people are cued to perform a behavior automatically without making a conscious decision to do so. Many of us have the habit of buckling our seatbelt as soon as we get in the car or a habit of following a certain routine as we get ready for work each morning. In each case, a certain contextual cue—getting into the car, or getting out of bed—cues an automatic pattern of behavior. If you have habits for these kinds of things, you don't consciously think to yourself, "Well, I'd better buckle my seat-belt," or sit on the edge of the bed each morning and ponder what to do to get ready for work. You just buckle your seatbelt, or start your day, or whatever without any conscious thought or deliberation. Nonconscious processes are in control. Your day is filled with habitual responses, and they help to make you who you are.

Habits are exceptionally efficient because they allow us to perform certain actions without devoting time or energy to figuring out what to do or how to do it. The downside is that because they're automatic, habits sometimes unfold even though they aren't the best response in a particular situation. So, we sometimes act out of habit even when it is not the optimal thing to do and even when it conflicts with our intentions. I still open the cabinet door under my kitchen sink to throw something in the garbage even though it's been over 10 years since I lived in a house with the garbage can under the sink. Some habits die hard.

Neuroscience research shows that, as habits form and strengthen, control of the behavior shifts from areas of the brain that are associated with conscious thinking and with goal-directed control to brain areas that are involved in perceiving stimuli and initiating actions—the sensorimotor network. That's exactly what we'd expect: Habits take control away from the higher, conscious decision-making levels and give it to brain regions that can perceive and react automatically and nonconsciously.

The fact that much of our personality operates outside of our awareness has a couple of important implications. First, given that nonconscious processes affect our reactions, we can't know for sure why we do certain things. If associations that you don't know you have can be triggered by things that you're not even aware of, you can't be certain why you react as you do. You'll usually be able to give an explanation for your behavior, but all you can report is what you're consciously aware of. You don't know what you don't know.

Second, the fact we aren't privy to nonconscious influences helps to explain why it's often so hard to change our behavior. Let's take a behavior such as procrastination. Many people who procrastinate don't understand why they're always putting things off because they feel like they're motivated to get their work done. They firmly believe that they are motivated to avoid procrastination, and they can't understand why it continues to be a problem. There are many possible explanations, but one is that nonconscious processes are operating that keep them procrastinating. Perhaps they have implicit motives that are being satisfied by putting things off. Who knows? My point is that it's hard to manage your own behavior when you're not aware of all of things that cause it.

Freud would have said that you don't know why you do what you do because the answer is so disturbing that it's locked in your unconscious. But a better answer is that much of your behavior is managed nonconsciously, and you are often not aware, and in fact you can't be aware, of why you do many of the things that you do.

PERSONALITY AND SELF-CONTROL

LECTURE 20

Understanding how people self-regulate is critical to understanding their personalities. Not only do people differ in how well they control their own behavior, but many of the things that make people different from one another involve how they manage their behavior and cope with the challenges they face in life. How good people are at self-regulation is an important determinant of the quality of their lives. High self-control helps people get along better with others and makes them better at avoiding things that will hurt them in the long run. Overall, good self-regulators are happier, healthier, and even live longer than bad self-regulators.

SELF-CONTROL BY INHIBITION VERSUS INITIATION

- At its foundation, self-regulation involves how people manage the process of pursuing their goals. We all have many goals in life. Some are ongoing goals that stretch out over time, such as being financially secure, while other goals are momentary and fleeting, such as getting to a meeting on time.

- At any given moment, many goals can be potentially active. But there are limits on how many goals we can pursue at the same time, and sometimes our goals directly conflict with each other. People who are good at self-regulation manage their behavior in pursuit of their goals better than people who are bad at self-regulation.

- Usually, when we think of people who have poor self-control, we think about people who can't stop themselves from behaving in ways that create problems for themselves or other people—for example, a person who can't resist sweets. These people seem to struggle with the ability to inhibit or resist impulses that are inconsistent with important goals. They're bad at self-control by inhibition; they have trouble inhibiting certain problematic behaviors.

One study found that self-control was the only personality variable among 32 variables studied that significantly predicted grade point average among college students.

- Just as important for self-control as inhibiting yourself from engaging in undesired behaviors is the ability to make yourself take action and initiate desired behaviors. For example, a person who wants to stay fit has to make him- or herself get out the door to work out. This type of self-regulation is called self-control by initiation, and it involves initiating behaviors that move us toward a goal.

- These 2 types of self-regulation tend to go together to some extent. People who are good at initiating behavior also tend to be good at inhibiting behavior, and people who are bad at one also tend to be bad at the other. But self-control by initiation and self-control by inhibition are not as strongly related to each other as you might expect, and different personality variables are associated with each.

- Whether we're talking about initiation or inhibition, people sometimes need to control themselves on an ongoing basis rather than just once. Yet some people are good at initiating or inhibiting just once, but really bad at continuing to initiate or inhibit. To be really good at self-regulation, people not only have to initiate or inhibit a behavior, but they have to be able to keep it up. This requires another set of skills and characteristics called self-control by continuation.

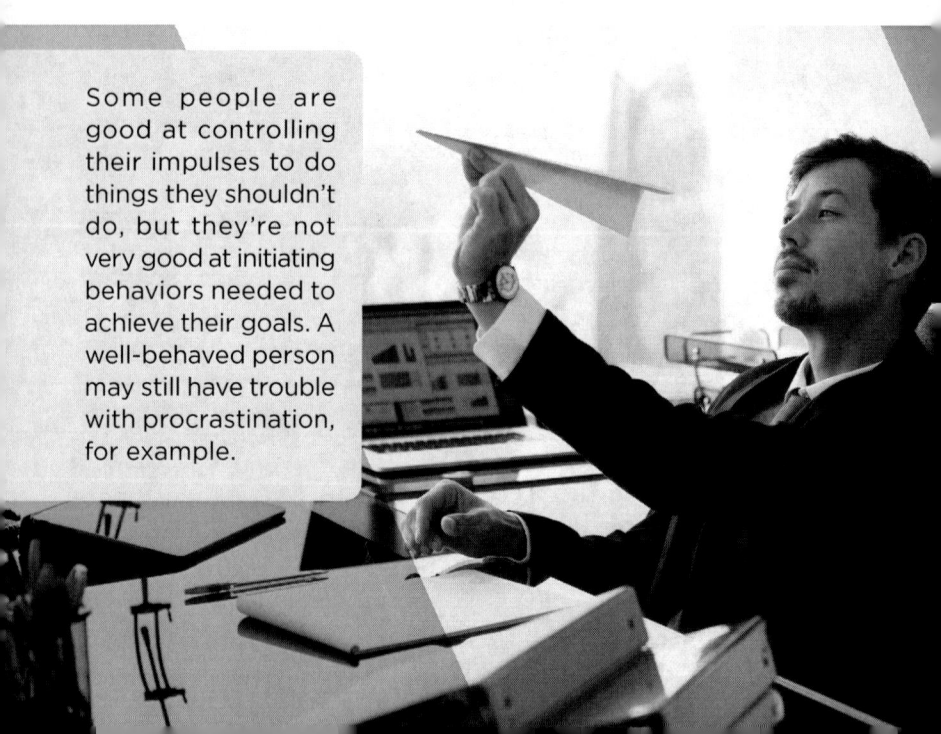

> Some people are good at controlling their impulses to do things they shouldn't do, but they're not very good at initiating behaviors needed to achieve their goals. A well-behaved person may still have trouble with procrastination, for example.

STUDYING SELF-REGULATION

- The scientific study of self-regulation got its start in the late 1960s with research on delay of gratification in children. Delay of gratification refers to the ability to resist the temptation to settle for an immediate reward to get some larger or more important reward sometime in the future. Learning to work toward, and wait for, desired outcomes is essential for achieving most important goals.

- In the early research on delay of gratification, in the so-called marshmallow test—a test of self-control by inhibition—young children were shown a small treat. It wasn't always a marshmallow; it depended on what the child liked. The child was told that the researcher was going to leave the room for a few minutes, and if the child waited and didn't eat the treat until the researcher got back, the child would get 2 of the treats. But at any time while the researcher was gone, the child could ring a little bell that was on the desk and then eat the one treat immediately, in which case he or she wouldn't get any more.

- Dozens of these types of studies have been conducted over the years on children of various ages and using different ways of measuring delay of gratification. These studies have taught us a lot about self-regulation in childhood, but 3 important findings stand out:

    1. Some children were better at self-control than other children were.

    2. Performance on this simple task was correlated with the degree to which children self-regulated in many domains of their lives, meaning that this task measures some basic characteristic or set of characteristics that are related to general self-control.

    3. How well children were able to control themselves when they were young predicted important psychological, educational, and social outcomes both at the time and many years later in adolescence and adulthood.

- If we measure how many seconds a child in elementary school waits before eating the treat, that very simple measure can not only predict reliably how good the child's grades are at the time, but also predict the child's academic performance in high school and how many years of education the child will complete by his or her 20s.

- Furthermore, the better children are able to delay gratification in elementary school, the fewer risky behaviors—such as taking drugs or stealing—they engage in in 9th grade. They also show fewer disruptive behavioral problems, get along better with other people, and are less likely to be overweight.

- Twenty years after doing the marshmallow test, adults who delayed gratification better as children had higher self-esteem, coped better with stress, were less likely to use certain illegal drugs, and had lower rates of obesity.

- People who are generally better at delaying gratification as children fare better in life than those who aren't so good. Clearly, there's some relatively stable personality characteristic related to self-regulation that impacts people's well-being across life.

EXECUTIVE FUNCTIONS

- At the root of all self-control is a set of cognitive skills that are often called executive functions, which include mental abilities that are involved in goal setting, planning, making decisions, monitoring what you do, and managing behaviors that would interfere with your goals. These mental functions are involved any time you try to regulate your own behavior.

- Self-regulation involves separate mental executive functions, including coming up with good goals, coming up with plans for how to achieve those goals, and following through. If people are to be really good at self-regulation, they need to be reasonably good at all of these tasks. If any executive function isn't up to the task, self-regulation will be more difficult and less successful.

- Significantly, these executive functions are highly heritable, so self-regulation has a clear genetic basis. That doesn't mean that people can't get better at these kinds of skills. Research shows that they can. But one reason that some people are better at self-regulation than others from an early age is that they were born that way.

IMPULSIVITY

- Beyond executive functions that are needed for self-regulation, people differ in other ways that are relevant to their ability to control their behavior. A very important trait that predicts self-regulation is impulsivity.

- By the time that children are toddlers, you can see differences in how impulsive they are. Some children run and grab and react without much thought or hesitation, whereas others are more deliberate and controlled. In the same way, some adults are highly impulsive and others are more deliberate, and those who are more impulsive have greater problems with self-regulation.

- When researchers first started studying impulsivity, they regarded it as a single trait. But as it turns out, impulsivity can reflect several different psychological characteristics, each of which is associated with problems in self-regulation for a different reason.

- These characteristics include the tendency to act without thinking or premeditation, an inability to stay focused on what one is doing at the moment, and the tendency to act quickly and with a sense of urgency when something happens—even when a quick reaction isn't necessary.

- Whichever type of impulsivity we're talking about, highly impulsive people tend to have more problems with self-control by inhibition than less impulsive people do.

THE BIG FIVE TRAITS AND SELF-REGULATION

- The big five trait that's most consistently linked to self-regulation is conscientiousness. In fact, research has shown that people higher in conscientiousness are better at self-control by inhibition, self-control by initiation, and self-control by continuation than less conscientious people are.

- Neuroticism is also related to self-control, but the relationship is complex. On one hand, people who are high in neuroticism tend to be inhibited and even overcontrolled at times; they put a lot of effort into self-regulation. But their highly negative emotions can also interfere with self-regulation, and they can struggle with self-control by inhibition when they're upset.

- Agreeableness also relates to self-regulation. Being a highly agreeable person partly involves controlling your negative reactions to other people, such as biting your tongue and letting other people's annoying behavior slide. People who don't self-regulate as well have more trouble controlling these impulses, so they can end up behaving disagreeably when they have problems with other people. Not surprisingly, agreeableness is related most strongly to self-control by inhibition.

- Extraversion also tends to be related to self-regulation, but somewhat more weakly. People higher in extraversion tend to be more outgoing, spontaneous, and uninhibited than people low in extraversion. Those characteristics make extraverts better at self-control by initiation, but those same characteristics can make extraverts a little worse at self-control by inhibition. They sometimes respond impulsively and spontaneously, which means they sometimes don't regulate as well. In the same way, people low in extraversion are better at self-control by inhibition but not as good at self-control by initiation.

- Openness isn't related to self-regulation.

GOALS: PROMOTION- VERSUS PREVENTION-ORIENTED PEOPLE

- Whether people are good or bad at self-regulation, they tend to approach their goals in 2 distinct ways that have implications for how they pursue their goals and how they react when they succeed or fail at what they set out to do.

- Some people are motivated to pursue goals primarily by a desire for positive, pleasant outcomes. These people are promotion-focused; they want to promote positive outcomes. Other people are motivated to pursue their goals primarily by a desire to prevent negative, unpleasant outcomes. These people are prevention-focused because they want to prevent negative things from happening.

- Promotion-oriented people tend to approach their goals with a sense of eagerness because they focus on what they want to get or what they want to have happen. But prevention-oriented people approach goals with caution and vigilance because their goal is mostly to avoid bad things.

- In fact, success and failure mean something different to promotion- and prevention-oriented people. For promotion-oriented people, success is experienced as a gain, as an improvement or reward, so it results in the cheerful kinds of reactions that people have when they get what they want.

- But for prevention-oriented people, success is experienced as the avoidance of a loss. Success means that they didn't fail; they were able to avoid a negative event. So, prevention-oriented people react to success but with relief.

- In the same way, failure means something different to a person who is trying to succeed than it does to a person who's trying not to fail. For promotion-oriented people, failure is a failure to attain some hoped-for goal, so their emotional reaction is disappointment, dejection, or sadness because they didn't get something positive that they were motivated to get. But for prevention-oriented people, failure is having something happen that they didn't want to have happen, so they tend to be anxious and upset by failure.

- Note that the goal itself can be the same. The difference is whether people construe failure as not getting something that they wanted or as getting something that they didn't want. That minor difference has a big effect on how people react to failures to achieve their goals.

- This difference also affects how people look back on their failures. Promotion-oriented people look back and think about what they should have done differently to improve their performance. Prevention-oriented people look back and think about what they shouldn't have done.

A promotion-oriented person wants to be healthy, while a prevention-oriented person wants to avoid getting sick.

- In general, being motivated by the appeal of positive outcomes is better psychologically than trying to be sure that bad things don't happen. People who have mainly a promotion focus tend to be lower in neuroticism than those with a prevention focus. Being promotion-focused is also associated with a lower likelihood of being depressed and with a higher likelihood of being satisfied with one's life.

Suggested Reading

Gottberg, "Promotion or Prevention?"

Jaffe, "Why Wait?"

McMonigal, *The Willpower Instinct.*

Questions to Consider

1. Think of an area of your life in which you are sometimes unable to exercise adequate self-control to make yourself behave in the way that you desire. Is this self-control problem primarily a problem with initiation, inhibition, or continuation—or some combination? Does knowing about the specific source of your self-control problem offer any insights into aspects of your personality that underlie your self-control issue or offer any ideas about how to improve your ability to control this behavior?

2. Are you primarily a promotion-oriented or prevention-oriented person (or an equal mix of both)? What are some examples of how your tendency toward promotion and prevention show up in your behavior?

PERSONALITY AND SELF-CONTROL
LECTURE 20 TRANSCRIPT

One of the biggest psychological differences between human beings and other animals is that we humans are able to exert a certain amount of conscious, deliberate control over our behavior. We're able to contemplate our options and make conscious decisions in ways that other animals can't. And what that means is that we can intentionally decide, at least within limits, how we want to behave. But, as we all know, our efforts to control our behavior often don't work. As hard as we might try, we overeat, we lose our temper, we procrastinate, we can't make ourselves exercise like we should, we give in to all kinds of temptations that we know we ought to resist.

Understanding how people self-regulate is critical to understanding their personalities. Not only do people differ in how well they control their own behavior, but many of the things that make people different from one another involve how they manage their behavior and cope with the challenges they face in life. Importantly, how good people are at self-regulation is also an important determinant of the quality of their lives. For example, self-control promotes achievement and success. As a university professor, it's obvious to me that most students who do poorly in my classes could do the work, but they're having problems with self-regulation. In fact, one study found that self-control was the only personality variable among 32 variables studied that significantly predicted grade point average among college students. And in early adolescence, self-control predicts class grades even better than intelligence does.

High self-control also helps people get along better with others. Self-control can help people refrain from doing things that might hurt their relationships with other people, whether that's blurting out hurtful things or losing one's temper or telling a secret or having an affair. Even in childhood, kids with better self-control are more popular and have higher status among their peers. People who are better at self-regulation are also better at avoiding things that will hurt them in the long run. People who aren't good at controlling how much money they spend end up with financial problems. People who have trouble behaving themselves end up with legal problems. People who don't get things done at work get fired. People who have trouble resisting sexual temptations damage their close relationships. People who have poor self-control tend to eat more and drink more, and they're more likely to take drugs. Of course, most of us have occasional lapses in some of these areas, but overall people who are good at self-regulation are happier and healthier and even live longer than people who are bad self-regulators.

Of all of the aspects of personality that we've discussed in this course, self-regulation ranks near the top in its overall importance in people's lives. Having good self-control doesn't guarantee that a person will be successful, or have good relationships, or be healthy, but the chances of having these things without good self-control are very low.

To understand how personality relates to self-regulation, let's think about what self-regulation actually is. At its foundation, self-regulation involves how people manage the process of pursuing their goals. Self-regulation is all about goal pursuit. We all have many goals in life. Some are ongoing goals that stretch out over time, such as the goal to be financially secure or to get an education or to be healthy. Other goals are momentary and fleeting, such as when we have the goal of finding a parking place or mowing the yard or getting to a meeting on time.

At any given moment, many goals can be potentially active. But there are limits on how many goals we can pursue at the same time—I can't mow the yard and do my taxes at the same time. And sometimes our goals directly conflict with each other. A person on a diet has the goal of losing weight but may also have the goal of enjoying the food at a party. A student might have the goal of studying for tomorrow's test but also want to socialize with friends and get enough sleep. I may have the goal of saving my money but also the goal of buying something I see in the store right now.

We can't do everything, and we can't have everything, so how do we manage our behavior in ways that achieve our goals and maximize our happiness and well-being in the long run? People who are good at self-regulation manage their behavior in pursuit of their goals better than people who are bad at self-regulation. So, the question is this: What aspects of personality help people pursue their goals in a way that maximizes their ability to attain them?

Usually, when we think of people who have poor self-control, we think about people who can't stop themselves from behaving in ways that create problems for themselves or other people: the kid who can't stay in his seat in class, the person who can't resist sweets, or the person who spends too much money. These people seem to struggle with the ability to inhibit or resist impulses that are inconsistent with important goals. They're bad at what we'll call self-control-by-inhibition. They have trouble inhibiting certain problematic behaviors.

Well, that's obviously an important aspect of self-control. But as important as inhibiting yourself from engaging in undesired behaviors is the ability to make yourself take action and initiate desired behaviors. There, the question is: To what extent can a person consciously make him or herself behave in ways that achieve important goals? An employee needs to start the project at work, a student needs to sit down and study, a person who wants to stay fit has to make him- or herself get out the door to work out, and so on. This type of self-regulation is called self-control-by-initiation. It involves initiating behaviors that move us toward a goal.

Of course, these 2 types of self-regulation tend to go together to some extent. People who are good at initiating behavior also tend to be good at inhibiting behavior; and people who are bad at one also tend to be bad at the other. But, self-control-by-initiation and self-control-by-inhibition are not as strongly related to each other as you might expect. So, some people are good at controlling their impulses to do things they shouldn't do, but they're not very good at initiating behaviors needed to achieve their goals. A well-behaved person may still have trouble with procrastination, for example. In the same way, some people have trouble resisting impulses and temptations, but they still initiate behaviors that lead toward certain goals. Even though they struggle with temptations, they can make themselves do what's needed when the time comes. As we'll see in a moment, different personality variables are associated with self-control-by-initiation and self-control-by-inhibition. So you might be good at both, or bad at both, or good at one and bad at the other.

Whether we're talking about initiation or inhibition, people sometimes need to control themselves on an ongoing basis rather than just once. The employee needs to work on the task long enough to make progress, the student has to study long enough, the fitness enthusiast has to work out a sufficiently long time; just running down to the end of the driveway and back isn't going to help. Yet we all know people who are good at initiating or inhibiting just once, but really bad at continuing to initiate or inhibit. To be really good at self-regulation, people not only have to initiate or inhibit a behavior, but they have to be able to keep it up. This requires yet another set of skills and characteristics that we call self-control by continuation. So, self-regulation isn't just a single characteristic. It's a set of characteristics and skills that determine how well people initiate, inhibit, and then continue behaviors that help them achieve their goals.

The scientific study of self-regulation got its start in the late 1960s with research on delay of gratification in children. Delay of gratification refers to the ability to resist the temptation to settle for an immediate reward right now in order to get some larger or more important reward sometime in the future. Learning to work toward, and wait for, desired outcomes is essential for achieving most important goals. Freud talked about this a hundred years ago, saying that children must learn to, and I'm going to quote him here: "...to renounce immediate satisfaction, to postpone the obtaining of pleasure, to put up with a little unpleasure."

In the early research on delay of gratification, which some of you might know as the so-called marshmallow test, young children were shown a small treat. It wasn't always a marshmallow; it depended on what the child liked. It could be little pretzel sticks or a cookie or a few M&Ms or a marshmallow or whatever. The child was told that the researcher was going to leave the room for a few minutes and, if the child waited and didn't eat the treat until the researcher got back, the child would get 2 of the treats. But, at any time while the researcher was gone, the child could ring a little bell that was on the desk and then eat the one treat immediately, in which case he or she wouldn't get any more.

You can see how this experimental set-up could test children's ability to delay gratification. If they could make themselves wait, they'd get 2 treats, or they could have one treat any time they wanted. Just ring the bell. You can think of this as a test of self-control-by-inhibition. How well can the child inhibit the impulse to eat the snack right away? Dozens of these kinds of studies have been conducted over the years on children of various ages, as young as 4 years old, and using different ways of measuring delay of gratification. These studies have taught us a lot about self-regulation in childhood, but for our purposes, 3 important findings stand out.

First, as you can imagine, some kids were better at self-control than other kids were. Some kids gobbled up the snack right away, totally unable to delay gratification even for a few seconds. Others held out for a while, but then ring-a-ding-ding, they gave in and rang the bell and ate the snack. But some kids were able to wait the entire time—to delay gratification—and thereby got 2 treats. Even at age 4, there were clear differences in their ability to self-regulate.

Second, performance on this simple task was correlated with the degree to which children self-regulated in many domains of their lives. For example, how well children did on the marshmallow task was related to how self-controlled their teachers said they were in the classroom and on the playground, and how much self-control they showed at home. That's important because it shows that the marshmallow task measures some basic characteristic or set of characteristics that are related to general self-control.

The third important finding was that how well children were able to control themselves when they were young predicted important psychological, educational, and social outcomes both at the time and many years later in adolescence and adulthood. If we simply measure how many seconds a child in elementary school waits before eating the treat, that very simple measure can not only predict reliably how good the child's grades are at the time, but also predict the child's academic performance in high school, and how many years of education the child will complete by his or her 20s.

Furthermore, the better children are able to delay gratification in elementary school, the fewer risky behaviors they engage in in 9th grade, things like taking drugs, stealing, or doing physically risks things. They also show fewer disruptive behavioral problems, they get along better with other people, and they're less likely to be overweight. And these kinds of effects carry over into adulthood. Twenty years after doing the marshmallow test, adults who delayed gratification better as children had higher self-esteem, coped better with stress, were less likely to use certain illegal drugs, and had lower rates of obesity.

People who are generally better at delaying gratification as children fare better in life than those who aren't so good. Clearly, there's some relatively stable personality characteristic related to self-regulation that impacts people's well-being across life. So, what's going on here? What underlies these kinds of differences?

Well, several things.

At the root of all self-control is a set of cognitive skills that are often called executive functions. That might seem to be a strange term, but if you think of what an executive in a company does, you'll get a general idea of what these mental skills do. The job of an executive is to set goals for the company, to develop plans, to make decisions, to monitor the company's performance, and to keep an eye out for problems that could derail progress toward company goals. In the same way, your brain's executive functions involve mental abilities that are involved in goal-setting, planning, making decisions, monitoring what you do, and managing behaviors that would interfere with your goals. These mental functions are involved any time you try to regulate your own behavior.

Thinking about self-regulation in this way makes it obvious that several distinct skills are involved. It's one thing for an executive at a company to come up with good goals, but it's quite another thing to come up with plans for how to achieve those goals, and then to follow through. And in the same way, self-regulation involves separate mental executive functions. If people are to be really good at self-regulation, they need to be reasonably good at all of these tasks. Self-regulation is only as good as the weakest link in this chain, so if any executive function isn't up to the task, self-regulation will be more difficult and less successful. Significantly, these executive functions are highly heritable, so self-regulation has a clear genetic basis. That doesn't mean that people can't get better at these kinds of skills. Lots of research shows that they can. But one reason that some people are better at self-regulation than others from an early age is that they were born that way.

Beyond executive functions that are needed for self-regulation, people differ in other ways that are relevant to their ability to control their behavior.

A very important trait that predicts self-regulation is impulsivity. By the time that children are toddlers, you can see differences in how impulsive they are. Some kids run and grab and react without much thought or hesitation, whereas others are more deliberate and controlled. In the same way, some adults are highly impulsive and others are more deliberate, and those who are more impulsive have greater problems with self-regulation. When researchers first started studying impulsivity, they regarded it as a single trait. But as it turns out, impulsivity can reflect several different psychological characteristics, each of which is associated with problems in self-regulation for a different reason. The thing you probably think of first when you think of impulsivity is the tendency to act without thinking or premeditation. People who are impulsive in this way just act on their urges without considering the consequences. They don't stop and think.

But some impulsivity reflects an inability to stay focused on what one is doing at the moment. So, I'm working on something important, but then something else pops up: my favorite TV show comes on, or a friend calls asking to go out, or I just get an urge to do something else, and I impulsively drop what I'm doing and run off. Another impulsive characteristic involves the tendency to act quickly, with a sense of urgency, when something happens. Of course, sometimes urgency is fine; when the house is on fire, it's great. But many times, things don't need an immediate reaction. Some people have a tendency to respond quickly, with a sense of urgency, even when they don't need to react quickly, and it might be better to wait a bit. They're thinking about what they're doing, but they're just rushing things a bit.

So, not all impulsive people are alike. In fact, some researchers suggest that we shouldn't use the term, impulsivity, as if it's a single personality characteristic because there are different sorts of impulsive traits. But whichever sort of impulsivity we're talking about, highly impulsive people tend to have more problems with self-control-by-inhibition than less impulsive people do. You probably won't be surprised to know that the big five trait that's most consistently linked to self-regulation is conscientiousness. In fact, it's hard to imagine someone being highly conscientious who isn't reasonably good at making himself or herself do what needs to be done. Lots of research shows a strong link between conscientiousness and people's ability to self-regulate. When researchers have teased apart the individual features of conscientiousness to see which ones relate most strongly to self-regulation, 2 aspects stand out.

One is that conscientious people are more likely to think before taking action. They're more likely to plan ahead, and when immediate action is needed, they're more likely to take a moment to decide the best way to respond, which is obviously an important part of self-regulation. So, people higher in conscientiousness are better at self-control-by-inhibition. The other aspect of conscientiousness that's strongly related to self-regulation is self-discipline: being able to force yourself to act consistently toward your goals. So highly conscientious people are better at avoiding procrastination and at persisting at tasks even if they aren't going well or are unpleasant. They're not only better at inhibition, but they also better at both self-control-by-initiation and self-control-by-continuation than less conscientious people are. To be maximally conscientious you have to do what you should and not do what you shouldn't, and you have to keep doing or not doing it.

Neuroticism is also related to self-control, but the relationship is complex. Researchers were confused initially because some studies showed that people who are high in neuroticism are better at self-regulation, and other studies showed that they were worse. So, which is it? It turns out to be both. On one hand, people who are high in neuroticism tend to be inhibited and even over-controlled at times. Because they're generally more anxious, more self-consciousness, and more concerned about making sure that bad things don't happen, people high in neuroticism may try to do everything just right and to rein in any impulses that would lead them to do things that they shouldn't. So, they put a lot of effort into self-regulation.

But, paradoxically, their highly negative emotions can also interfere with self-regulation. All of us have trouble managing ourselves when we're upset, but because people high in neuroticism experience more negative emotions, their ability to regulate is often derailed by their emotional reactions. When they're anxious or angry or distraught or jealous or upset in some other way, their strong emotions can make it harder for them to control themselves. So people high in neuroticism can struggle with self-control-by-inhibition when they're upset. Not only that, but there's evidence that people higher in neuroticism experience unfulfilled desires more strongly than less neurotic people do. Think about what it feels like not to have something that you want. What most people experience as just a normal desire can feel like an uncomfortable urge, almost like the urge of an addiction, to people who are high in neuroticism. So, when they have the urge to eat something they shouldn't or to buy something that they want or to smoke a cigarette or have a drink, the unfulfilled temptation is so emotionally unpleasant that highly neurotic people are more likely to give in.

So, conscientiousness and neuroticism both relate strongly to self-control. What about the rest of the big five?

Well, agreeableness also relates to self-regulation. If you think about it, being a highly agreeable person partly involves controlling your negative reactions to other people. Highly agreeable people are sometimes agreeable because they're able to restrain some of their negative impulses, to bite their tongues, and choose their battles, and let other people's annoying behavior slide. People who don't self-regulate as well have more trouble controlling these impulses, so they can end up behaving disagreeably when they have problems with other people. Not surprisingly, agreeableness is related most strongly to self-control-by-inhibition.

Extraversion also tends to be related to self-regulation, but somewhat more weakly. As we saw previously, people higher in extraversion tend to be more outgoing, spontaneous, and uninhibited than people low in extraversion. Those characteristics make extraverts better at self-control-by-initiation—they're somewhat better at initiating actions—but those same characteristics can make extraverts a little worse at self-control-by-inhibition. They sometimes respond impulsively and spontaneously, which means they sometimes don't regulate as well. In the same way, people low in extraversion—introverts, if you will—are better at self-control-by-inhibition but not as good at self-control-by-initiation. So, it's a bit of a wash, and the overall relationship between extraversion and self-regulation is weak.

And, in case you're wondering, openness isn't related to self-regulation at all.

Whether people are good or bad at self-regulation, they tend to approach their goals in 2 distinct ways that have implications for how they pursue their goals and how they react when they succeed or fail at what they set out to do. Some people are motivated to pursue goals primarily by a desire for positive, pleasant outcomes. They're motivated to behave in ways that make things better than they are now. We call these people promotion-focused. They want to promote positive outcomes. Other people, though, are motivated to pursue their goals primarily by a desire to prevent negative, unpleasant outcomes. They're motivated to behave in ways that make sure that things don't get any worse than they are now. These people are called prevention-focused because they want to prevent negative things from happening. So, for example, a promotion-oriented student is motivated mostly to get good grades, whereas a prevention-oriented student is motivated mostly to avoid getting bad grades. A promotion-oriented spouse wants to make his or her marriage better; a prevention-oriented spouse is more focused on being sure that it doesn't deteriorate. A promotion-oriented person wants to be healthy; a prevention-oriented person wants to avoid getting sick. Get the idea?

Promotion-oriented people tend to approach their goals with a sense of eagerness because they focus on what they want to get or what they want to have happen. But prevention-oriented people approach goals with caution and vigilance because their goal is mostly to avoid bad things. In fact, success and failure mean something different to promotion- and prevention-oriented people. For promotion-oriented people, success is experienced as a gain, as an improvement or reward, so it results in the cheerful sorts of reactions that people have when they get what they want. But for prevention-oriented people, success is experienced not so much as a gain but rather as the avoidance of a loss. Success means that they didn't fail; they were able to avoid a negative event. So, prevention-oriented people react to success not so much with happiness but with relief. Sure, it's nice that I did well, but mostly I'm relieved that I didn't do poorly.

In the same way, failure means something different to a person who is trying to succeed than it does to a person who's trying not to fail. For a promotion-oriented person, failure is a failure to attain some hoped-for goal. I didn't get something positive that I wanted: success. So, their emotional reaction is disappointment or dejection or sadness because they didn't get something positive that they were motivated to get. But for a prevention-oriented person, failure is having something happen that they didn't want to have happen. I got something that I didn't want: failure. So prevention-oriented people tend to be anxious and upset by failure. Note that the goal itself can be the same. The difference is whether people construe failure as not getting something that they wanted, or as getting something that they didn't want. That minor difference has a big effect on how people react to failures to achieve their goals.

This difference also affects how people look back on their failures. Promotion-oriented people look back and think about what they should have done differently to improve their performance. Prevention-oriented people look back and think about what they shouldn't have done. In general, being motivated by the appeal of positive outcomes is better, psychologically speaking, than trying to be sure that bad things don't happen. People who have mainly a promotion focus tend to be lower in neuroticism than those with a prevention focus, and being promotion-focused is also associated with a lower likelihood of being depressed and with a higher likelihood of being satisfied with one's life.

To recap, the ability to manage our behavior is an important determinant of how well we achieve our goals, both big goals like finishing school and saving for retirement, and little goals like getting the laundry done and paying our bills on time. And as we've seen, self-regulation has many implications for our psychological well-being and satisfaction with life.

That being said, people can sometimes self-regulate too much. People can be too controlled for their own good, which involves at minimum, a lack of spontaneity, or worse, a high level of compulsivity. Trying to exercise deliberate control over everything you do is not healthy. There are times in which people ought not to exercise self-control, and the trick is knowing when self-control will be beneficial and when it will be detrimental to one's well-being. So, on top of everything else, people need to regulate how much they engage in self-regulation.

WHEN PERSONALITIES BECOME TOXIC

LECTURE 21

This course has focused primarily on normal variations in personality. But certain patterns of thought, emotion, and behavior are associated with a high degree of psychological distress, create ongoing problems in people's lives, and make it very difficult for people to function across the important domains of life. These particularly problematic and dysfunctional characteristics are called personality disorders. This lecture will cover 4 of the 10 recognized personality disorders: antisocial, borderline, histrionic, and narcissistic.

PERSONALITY DISORDERS

- A personality disorder is a rigid and inflexible pattern of behavior that a person displays across a wide variety of situations and that leads to ongoing problems and distress in key areas of the person's life, particularly work and social relationships.

    - The person displays a particular pattern of behavior much of the time, even when it's not appropriate for the current situation. In most cases, the behavior could be quite normal under certain circumstances, but the problem is that the pattern of behavior occurs across many situations and over long periods of time, showing that it's a stable personality characteristic.

    - To qualify as a personality disorder, the pattern of behavior has to be self-defeating. It has to interfere with aspects of the person's life and consistently create problems. Personality disorders typically compromise the person's well-being, and they usually make other people unhappy as well.

    - Personality disorders tend to get worse when people are under stress.

- The manual that mental health professionals use to describe and diagnose psychological problems is called the Diagnostic and Statistical Manual of Mental Disorders (DSM). The most recent edition of the DSM recognizes 10 personality disorders, but there are other problems that some researchers classify as personality disorders that don't appear in the official diagnostic manual.

- Personality disorders are often classified into 3 broad clusters that involve dramatic, emotional, and erratic behaviors; behaviors that reflect excessive anxiety; and eccentric behaviors and distorted thinking.

- This lecture will consider the dramatic, emotional, and erratic cluster, which includes 4 disorders: the antisocial, borderline, histrionic, and narcissistic personality disorders. These disorders are grouped together because they all involve problems with emotion regulation and impulse control that have negative effects on other people and on people's social relationships.

Estimates are that, in any given year, around 10% of adults would qualify for a diagnosis of at least one of the 10 personality disorders. And many more people would show the general disordered pattern of behavior, but it wouldn't create enough of a problem for their lives for it to meet the diagnostic criteria.

ANTISOCIAL PERSONALITY DISORDER

◆ Antisocial personality disorder refers to what used to be called psychopathic or sociopathic personalities. At the broadest level, people with antisocial personality disorder regularly disregard and violate the well-being and rights of other people. This disorder is characterized by unemotional callousness and impulsive antisocial motives:

1. People with antisocial personality disorder are rather cold-hearted people; they simply don't care about other people's well-being. They show very little empathy for other people, and they rarely feel guilty when they hurt somebody. They often don't consider the impact of their behavior on other people, and they really don't care if they happen to do things that hurt or disadvantage someone else.

2. When they get the urge to do something that's mean, illegal, or aggressive, they impulsively do it, without much regard for rules, norms, or laws. So, they lie, steal, and cheat more than most people do.

◆ In their dealings with other people, people with antisocial personality disorder tend to be pretty irresponsible and undependable. They're the kind of people who don't follow through on what they say they're going to do, and they certainly don't apologize if their irresponsibility screws you over. They're usually a bit indifferent and detached emotionally, with an edge of intolerance and impatience with other people.

◆ People who act this way usually feel okay about their behavior. In fact, they usually see themselves as free and autonomous people who are not foolish enough to go along with a bunch of silly rules and laws when they don't want to, and they think that the rest of us are dupes for following the rules.

◆ People with antisocial personality disorder consistently score very low in agreeableness; they're cold, unfriendly, and unkind people. They're also very low in conscientiousness; they aren't responsible, dependable, or organized.

- They're also very low in neuroticism. That normally is a good thing, but a certain amount of negative emotion helps keep our behavior in line. People who are very low in neuroticism don't worry much about things, and not feeling much anxiety, guilt, fear, or remorse allows antisocial people not to feel bad about the things they do.

- Finally, they score very low on the trait of honesty-humility. People who are low on this trait are very selfish. In fact, some of the items on the scale that measures honesty-humility look like indicators of psychopathy or antisocial personality.

- Fortunately, people with full-blown antisocial personality disorder are relatively rare. The best estimate is that only about 1 out of 100 people would meet the diagnostic criteria for antisocial personality disorder. Of course, many other people show subclinical signs of being antisocial. Whether they meet formal diagnostic criteria or not, you want to avoid people with antisocial personalities.

Perhaps not surprisingly, a higher percentage of people with antisocial personality disorder are men than women.

BORDERLINE PERSONALITY DISORDER

- Borderline personality disorder is so called because in the 1930s when it was first recognized, some psychiatrists thought that it fell in between being a neurotic disorder (which involves high anxiety and negative emotions) and a psychotic disorder (which involves loss of touch with reality). However, that's not true, so many experts are trying to get it renamed.

- A better term that more accurately describes the borderline personality disorder might be "emotion dysregulation disorder" or "unstable personality disorder" because its central feature involves strong emotions and rapid mood swings in which the person loses control. So, at one moment, the person is interacting easily and happily, and then a moment later, they've lost it in a fit of extreme anger or panic or despair.

- The things that trigger these strong emotional outbursts tend to involve perceiving that other people are being dismissive or rejecting. People with borderline personality disorder are exceptionally sensitive to signs of criticism, disrespect, and rejection. And when they perceive that others are criticizing, disrespecting, or rejecting them, they overreact, lash out at other people, and sometimes behave in vengeful ways to get back at the person. Then, when they calm down, they act more or less as if nothing happened—until the next incident.

- Their reactions are rather paradoxical, though. People with borderline personality disorder very much want other people to like and accept them, but their reactions to signs that they are being negatively evaluated or rejected leads to extreme overreactions that cause other people to avoid or reject them. They want people to accept them, but they continually drive people away.

- The behavior itself is not all that unusual. Many of us lose it every now and then over something that really doesn't matter very much. But it's not our typical way of responding to disagreement or conflict. Only about 1.6% of the population is emotionally unstable enough to meet the diagnostic criteria for borderline personality disorder.

- People with borderline personality disorder often idealize potential friends or lovers at first. They insist on spending a lot of time together and share very intimate information about themselves. But then, they can switch quickly to devaluing the other person when they perceive that the other person doesn't care enough about them or doesn't give enough to the relationship or is not there enough for them.

- For those around them—their partners, children, coworkers, friends (if they have any)—people with borderline personality disorder are pretty maddening. You never quite know which person is going to show up on any particular day: the nice one who seems reasonably normal and accommodating or the vicious one who is out of control.

- And even when the person is acting perfectly fine for a while, other people walk on eggshells worrying about when something will trigger the borderline person's next outburst.

HISTRIONIC PERSONALITY DISORDER

- The central feature of the histrionic personality disorder is chronic and excessive attention-seeking behavior. Wherever they are, whatever they're doing, histrionic people want to be the center of attention, so they monopolize the spotlight in most situations. Of course, most people like attention from time to time, but if you are never happy unless you are the focal point of every social interaction, then you have histrionic tendencies.

- Histrionic people have a very dramatic and lively conversational style. They act like everything they say is very important, and they tell their stories with a great deal of flair, emotion, and exaggeration.

- People with histrionic personality disorder also seek attention by being flirtatious and sexually provocative.

- Sometimes, new acquaintances find histrionic people's enthusiasm, energy, and openness charming, but these characteristics wear thin after a while when histrionic people continually monopolize social interactions. In a conversation, people with histrionic personality disorder tend to ignore what other people say and continually bring the focus back to them.

> The entertainment industry has more than its share of histrionic people.

- And when they aren't at the center of the action, histrionic people may do something dramatic or outlandish to create a scene and get the attention back. After the first few minutes, they're not very enjoyable to interact with, so others often try to avoid dealing with histrionic people.

- Histrionic people don't seem to realize any of this. They generally think of themselves as sociable, charming, and entertaining. And they tend to think that they're well liked and that their relationships with other people are closer and more intimate than they really are.

- The histrionic personality disorder can be really annoying and socially disruptive, and it often interferes with the quality of people's lives, but it doesn't have the strong negative effects on other people that the antisocial and borderline disorders do.

- So, the 2% of the population with histrionic personality disorder usually gets along okay in life, particularly if they are in professions in which their vivaciousness, flamboyance, and exhibitionism don't seem too out of place.

NARCISSISTIC PERSONALITY DISORDER

- The central feature of the narcissistic personality disorder is an excessive sense of superiority and self-importance. Narcissists overestimate their positive characteristics and see themselves as special—and not just in a particular domain. They think that they are special as people.

- Even worse, people who think that they are better than everybody else also think that they are entitled to be treated special. In particular domains, that might be true. If you're the best athlete on the team, maybe you deserve some extra respect and playing time. But if you think you are special as a person, then you walk through life expecting people to treat you special all of the time. And that kind of entitlement often disadvantages other people.

- In fact, people who show signs of narcissistic personality disorder tend to disregard other people's views and rights. And narcissists tend not to feel bad about this inequity because they tend to be low in empathy. They don't care that their self-centeredness and sense of entitlement hurt other people.

- When you first meet narcissists, they often make a very good first impression. They're often charming and confident, and they usually have good social skills. But it doesn't take people too long to realize that narcissists are full of themselves, have a sense of entitlement, and treat others as just an audience for their own self-aggrandizing show.

- By and large, narcissists come across as calm and confident people. In fact, they are so confident that they often seem indifferent to whether other people like them or not. They're often very nonchalant, even when things aren't going well.

- But now and then, when the façade crumbles and they feel that they're under attack, they sometimes exhibit what's known as narcissistic rage: They lose it and overreact, and they might even seek revenge on people who put them down.

- In the mind of narcissists, other people should consistently approve of, adore, and agree with them. Much of the time, narcissists can dismiss any negative reactions they get by simply concluding that other people are stupid or envious or just losers whose opinions don't count anyway.

- But now and then, those defenses break down, and the narcissist becomes enraged by the unfairness of other people's indifference, disrespect, or criticism. We all get angry when we don't think we get what we deserve, but narcissists get angry when they don't get the adoration, respect, and deference that they think someone as special as they are should get.

Parenting and Narcissism

A study conducted in 2015 showed that narcissistic people tend to have parents who overvalued them—who thought they were unusually special—which implies that children seem to acquire narcissism, at least in part, by internalizing their parents' inflated views of them.

The study also showed that parental warmth, not parental overvaluation, seemed to lead to greater self-esteem in the child, supporting the idea that narcissism is different than just having high self-esteem.

- A little more than 2% of the population meets the criteria for a diagnosis of narcissistic personality disorder, but many other people who wouldn't meet the official criteria are still quite narcissistic.

Suggested Reading

Meyer-Lindenberg, "The Roots of Problem Personalities."

Stout, *The Sociopath Next Door*.

Questions to Consider

1. Many people occasionally act in ways that resemble someone with an antisocial, borderline, histrionic, or narcissistic personality disorder, yet we would not conclude that they actually have one of these disorders. Why not?

2. Think of someone you know personally who shows signs of an antisocial, borderline, histrionic, or narcissistic personality disorder. (This person might not qualify for a clinical diagnosis but shows the primary symptoms to some extent.) In what ways does this person's behavior resemble one of these disorders? Are there ways in which his or her behavior does not resemble the disorder? Does considering the possibility that this person has a disorder change how you think about him or her?

WHEN PERSONALITIES BECOME TOXIC
LECTURE 21 TRANSCRIPT

Throughout this course, we have focused primarily on normal variations in personality. Although being high on a particular characteristic might be a bit better or a bit worse for a person overall than being low on that characteristic, such variations are generally not terribly problematic. Of course, all of us have aspects of our personalities that can cause problems for us and that we wish we didn't have, but most of us nonetheless get by and function okay even with all of our quirks. But, some people's personalities create real problems for them. Certain patterns of thought, emotion, and behavior are associated with a high degree of psychological distress, create ongoing problems in people's lives, and make it very difficult for people to function across the important domains of life. We call these particularly problematic and dysfunctional characteristics personality disorders.

I want to distinguish the kinds of personality problems that I'm going to discuss in this lecture from the problems of people who are mentally disturbed in the sense of hearing voices or having hallucinations. Those sorts of problems, such as schizophrenia, aren't really problems with personality in the way we are talking about it. What I'm going to talk about are people who are in touch with reality as most of us know it, but who have problems functioning because of aspects of their personality. Of course, there isn't a clear line that separates normal, flawed personalities that we all have from personalities that are truly disordered and maladaptive in the ways I'm going to discuss. As we have seen, personality characteristics are on a continuum than runs from low to high levels of a trait, and there's no point where we can draw a line and say that you're fine if you're on this side of the line, but you have a disorder if you're on the other side.

Even so, psychiatrists, practicing psychologists, and social workers need to make that determination, and they have formal diagnostic criteria that they use to decide whether someone needs treatment.

We'll use their diagnostic system to talk about personality disorders, but we're going to discuss the problems in looser and more general terms. Many people show signs of having these problems even though they wouldn't technically qualify for a diagnosis of having a personality disorder. So, for our purposes, it's better to think of these disorders as maladaptive patterns of personality rather than as clinical diagnoses.

So, what is a personality disorder, and what makes a personality disorder different from the garden variety of personality problems that we all have?

A personality disorder is a rigid and inflexible pattern of behavior that a person displays across a wide variety of situations, and that leads to ongoing problems and distress in key areas of the person's life, particularly work and social relationships. Let me explain what I mean.

First, when I say that a personality disorder involves a rigid and inflexible pattern of behavior, I mean that the person displays a particular pattern of behavior much of the time even when it's not appropriate for the current situation. In most cases, it's not that the behavior itself is abnormal. In fact, that particular behavior could be quite normal under certain circumstances. The problem is that the person acts that way most of the time. The pattern of behavior occurs across many, maybe most situations, even when it's inappropriate. And it occurs over long periods of time, showing that it's a stable personality characteristic.

Let's take the behavior of being distrustful and suspicious about another person's motives. Sometimes, there are good reasons to be suspicious; there are situations in which being distrustful is entirely appropriate. All of us have been suspicious and maybe even a bit paranoid at times. It's entirely normal. But suspicion becomes a personality disorder when a person is chronically and unreasonably suspicious even when there's no reason to be. That's what I mean by a rigid and inflexible pattern of behavior. It's as if the person is stuck in a personality rut that he or she can't get out of, at least not for very long.

Second, to qualify as a personality disorder, the pattern of behavior has to be self-defeating. It has to interfere with aspects of the person's life and consistently create problems of one kind or another. Personality disorders typically compromise the person's well-being, and they usually make other people unhappy as well. So, to use the same example of distrust, although occasional suspicion is often beneficial, being consistently distrustful of other people makes the paranoid person unhappy, upsets other people who feel falsely accused, and interferes with the quality of their relationships. The person seems to have a disorder rather than normal suspicion.

And, third, personality disorders tend to get worse when people are under stress. So, although these disorders are a problem much of the time, stress increases and amplifies the dysfunctional pattern. In the case of paranoid personality disorder, for example, stress makes paranoid people even more distrustful and suspicious.

The manual that mental health professionals use to describe and diagnose psychological problems is called the Diagnostic and Statistical Manual of Mental Disorders. You'll hear people call it the DSM. The most recent edition of the DSM recognizes 10 personality disorders, but there are other problems that some researchers classify as personality disorders that don't appear in the official diagnostic manual.

As we talk about these disorders, I suspect that you will be able to think of people you know, or that you knew in the past, who fit many of these profiles. Estimates are that, in any given year, around 10% adults would qualify for a diagnosis of at least one of these 10 personality disorders. And many more people would show the general disordered pattern of behavior, but it wouldn't create enough of a problem for their lives for it to meet the diagnostic criteria. So, I hope that learning about these disorders will give you some insight into the personalities of some of the difficult and troubled people you deal with in life.

Let me say one other thing before I talk about these disorders. When we cover these problems in my classes, some of my students invariably start to worry that they show signs of one or more disorders. It's like the first-year students in medical school who think they have symptoms of many of the diseases they learn about in class. You may indeed show signs of some of these disorders, but if you do, keep something in mind. Almost everybody behaves in these ways from time to time. Under the right circumstances, most of them are perfectly normal behaviors. It's only if a person shows them continuously, across many or most situations, and in situations where they are inappropriate, that would we consider them a personality disorder. Remember that it's usually not the behavior that's the problem but the fact that the person is behaving that way when it's not appropriate.

Personality disorders are often classified into 3 broad clusters that involve dramatic, emotional, and erratic behaviors, behaviors that reflect excessive anxiety, and eccentric behaviors and distorted thinking. In this lecture, we'll consider the dramatic, emotional, and erratic cluster, which includes 4 disorders: the antisocial, borderline, histrionic, and narcissistic personality disorders. These disorders are grouped together because they all involve problems with emotion regulation and impulse control that have negative effects on other people and on people's social relationships. We'll start with the antisocial personality disorder.

I'm sure that you've heard the terms, psychopath and sociopath. And I suspect that when you hear these words, you think of a crazed, axe-wielding maniac, probably chopping down a door to attack a bunch of teenagers in some bad horror movie. Well, that's not really what a psychopath or a sociopath actually is, and because those labels have connotations of axe-murderers, we now use the term antisocial personality disorder to refer to what used to be called psychopathic or sociopathic personalities. At the broadest level, people with antisocial personality disorder regularly disregard and violate the well-being and rights of other people. This disorder is characterized by 2 main things.

The first is unemotional callousness. People with anti-social personality disorder are rather cold-hearted people, not so much in the sense that they get pleasure from hurting other people—although that can happen—but rather because they simply don't care about other people's well-being. They show very little empathy for other people, and they rarely feel guilty when they hurt somebody. They often don't consider the impact of their behavior on other people, and they really don't care if they happen to do things that hurt or disadvantage someone else. And if that's not bad enough, their disregard for other people is accompanied by impulsive anti-social motives. What I mean is that when they get the urge to do something that's mean or illegal or aggressive, they impulsively do it without much regard for rules or norms or laws. So, they lie and steal and cheat more than most people do, and as I said, they don't really care about how it affects other people.

So, in their dealings with other people, people with anti-social personality disorder tend to be pretty irresponsible and undependable. They're the kind of people who don't follow through on what they say they're going to do, and they certainly don't apologize if their irresponsibility screws you over. They're usually a bit indifferent and detached emotionally, with an edge of intolerance and impatience with other people. Now, you might wonder how people who act this way can face themselves, but they usually feel okay about it. In fact, they usually see themselves as free and autonomous people who are not foolish enough to go along with a bunch of silly rules and laws when they don't want to, and they think the rest of us are dupes for following the rules and behaving ourselves.

One way to think about a person with anti-social personality disorder is in terms of the major personality traits that we've discussed previously. They have a particular configuration of traits that makes them pretty unpleasant. First, they consistently score very low in agreeableness—they're cold, unfriendly, and unkind people. They're also very low in conscientiousness; they aren't responsible, dependable, or organized. They're also very low in neuroticism. Now that normally sounds like a good thing—nobody wants to be neurotic, right? But a certain amount of negative emotion helps keep our behavior in line. People who are very low in neuroticism don't worry much about things, and not feeling much anxiety, guilt, fear, or remorse allows anti-social people not to feel bad about the things they do. And finally, they score very low on the trait of honesty-humility that we talked about previously. I mentioned that people who are low on this trait are very selfish. In fact, some of the items on the scale that measures honesty-humility look like indicators of psychopathy or anti-social personality. So, when we put this configuration of traits together, we have highly disagreeable and selfish people, who are not conscientious or worried about things, and who don't experience guilt. That's not a great combination.

Fortunately, people with full-blown anti-social personality disorder are relatively rare. The best estimate is that only about 1 out of 100 people would meet the diagnostic criteria for anti-social personality disorder. Perhaps not surprisingly, a higher percentage of those people are men than women. Of course, many other people show subclinical signs of being anti-social. Whether they meet formal diagnostic criteria or not, you really want to avoid people with anti-social personalities.

The borderline personality disorder is just about as problematic. The label borderline is a bit strange, and people sometimes wonder exactly what this disorder is on the border of. The answer is that it's not on the border of anything. It's called borderline personality disorder because back in the 1930s when it was first recognized, some psychiatrists thought that it fell in-between being a neurotic disorder, which involves high anxiety and negative emotions, and a psychotic disorder, which involves loss of touch with reality. In fact, that's not true, so many experts are trying to get it renamed.

A better term that more accurately describes the borderline personality disorder might be something like emotion dysregulation disorder or maybe unstable personality disorder because its central feature involves strong emotions and rapid mood swings in which the person loses control. So, at one moment, the person is interacting easily and happily, and then a moment later, they've lost it in a fit of extreme anger or panic or despair.

The things that trigger these strong emotional outbursts tend to involve perceiving that other people are being dismissive or rejecting. People with borderline personality disorder are exceptionally sensitive to signs of criticism and disrespect and rejection. And when they perceive that others are criticizing or disrespecting or rejecting them, they overreact, lash out at other people, and sometimes behave in vengeful ways to get back at the person. Then, when they calm down, they act more-or-less as if nothing happened until the next incident. Their reactions are rather paradoxical, though. People with borderline personality disorder very much want other people to like and accept them, but their reactions to signs that they are being negatively evaluated or rejected leads to extreme overreactions that cause other people to avoid or reject them. They want people to accept them, but they continually drive people away.

Let me stress again that the behavior itself is not all that unusual. Many of us lose it every now and then over something that really doesn't matter very much. But we don't do it several times a week; it's not our typical way of responding to disagreement or conflict. Only about 1.6% of the population is emotionally unstable enough to meet the diagnostic criteria for borderline personality disorder.

Being in a relationship with someone with borderline personality disorder is quite a roller coaster ride. People with borderline personality disorder often idealize potential friends or lovers at first. They insist on spending a lot of time together and share very intimate information about themselves. But then, they can switch quickly from idealizing the other person to devaluing him or her when they perceive that the other person doesn't care enough about them or doesn't give enough to the relationship or is not there enough for them. You can see the rejection and abandonment theme emerging.

For those around them, their partners, children, coworkers, friends—if they have any—people with borderline personality disorder are pretty maddening. You never quite know which person is going to show up on any particular day; the nice one who seems reasonably normal and accommodating, or the vicious one who is out of control. And even when the person is acting perfectly fine for a while, other people walk on eggshells worrying about when something will trigger the borderline person's next outburst.

The central feature of the histrionic personality disorder is chronic and excessive attention-seeking. Wherever they are, whatever they're doing, the histrionic person wants to be the center of attention, so they monopolize the spotlight in most situations. Of course, most people like attention from time to time, but if you are never happy unless you are the focal point of every social interaction, then you have histrionic tendencies. Histrionic people have a very dramatic and lively conversational style. They act like everything they say is very important, and they tell their stories with a great deal of flair, and emotion, and exaggeration. Everything is a big deal.

People with histrionic personality disorder also seek attention by being flirtatious and sexually provocative. That's one surefire way to get attention. Histrionic women in particular tend to, shall we say, underdress. There are places in which wearing revealing clothing might be perfectly acceptable, maybe even normative. But dressing that way to go to a funeral or the grocery store or your child's school picnic in order to be the center of attention might indicate a rigid pattern of attention-seeking behavior that characterizes a personality disorder.

Sometimes, new acquaintances find histrionic people's enthusiasm, energy, and openness charming, but these characteristics wear thin after a while when histrionic people continually monopolize social interactions. In a conversation, people with histrionic personality disorder tend to ignore what other people say and continually bring the focus back to them. And, when they aren't at the center of the action, histrionic people may do something dramatic or outlandish to create a scene and get the attention back. After the first few minutes, they're not very enjoyable to interact with, so others often try to avoid dealing with histrionic people.

Histrionic people don't seem to realize any of this. They generally think of themselves as sociable and charming and entertaining. They think they're the life of the party. And they tend to think that they're well-liked and that their relationships with other people are closer and more intimate than they really are. The histrionic personality disorder can be really annoying and socially disruptive, and it often interferes with the quality of people's lives, but it doesn't have the strong negative effects on other people that the antisocial and borderline disorders do.

So, the 2% of the population with histrionic personality disorder usually gets along okay in life, particularly if they are in professions in which their vivaciousness, flamboyance, and exhibitionism don't seem too out of place. The entertainment industry has more than its share of histrionic people, and you can probably imagine who some of them are.

The fourth disorder in the dramatic, emotional, and erratic cluster is the narcissistic personality disorder, which is pretty much what it sounds like. The central feature is an excessive sense of superiority and self-importance. Narcissists overestimate their positive characteristics and see themselves as special, and not just in a particular domain. They think that they are special as people. In fact, on measures of narcissism that are based on self-evaluation, they endorse statements such as "I think I am a special person" and "I am an extraordinary person," and "I always know what I am doing."

That sort of self-superiority and arrogance is annoying, but the worst thing is that people who think that they are better than everybody else also think that they are entitled to be treated special. Now, in particular domains, that might be true. If you're the best person at work, maybe you deserve a better office, and if you're the best athlete on the team, maybe you deserve some extra respect and playing time. But if you think you are special as a person, then you walk through life expecting people to treat you special all of the time. And that kind of entitlement often disadvantages other people. In fact, people who show signs of narcissistic personality disorder tend to disregard other people's views and rights. If I'm so great and special, I can do what

I want, and I don't need to be concerned about the rights of lesser people. And narcissists tend not to feel badly about this inequity because they tend to be low in empathy. They don't care that their self-centeredness and sense of entitlement hurt other people.

When you first meet narcissists, they often make a very good first impression. They're often charming and confident, and they usually have good social skills. One study asked research participants to rate the personalities of people who had scored high or low in narcissism after meeting them for the first time. The participants rated the people who had scored high in narcissism as more agreeable, conscientious, open, competent, entertaining, and well-adjusted than the people who had scored low in narcissism. Narcissists made a very good first impression. But as the participants interacted with the narcissists for a longer time and got to know them better, those rosy evaluations disappeared, and they rated the narcissists far less positively. It doesn't take people too long to realize that narcissists are full of themselves, have a sense of entitlement, and treat others as just an audience for their own self-aggrandizing show.

But, here's perhaps the most unsettling finding: The narcissists whom the participants rated most positively at first ended up being the ones who managed to exploit other people most successfully in the long run! I know what a cliché it is to say that you can't judge a book by its cover, but in the case of narcissism, it's certainly the case. Narcissists who make the best first impressions are the most dangerous.

By and large, narcissists come across as calm and confident people. In fact, they are so confident that they often seem indifferent to whether other people like them or not. They're often very nonchalant even when things aren't going well. But now and then, when the façade crumbles and they feel that they're under attack, they sometimes exhibit what's known as narcissistic rage. They lose it and overreact, and they might even seek revenge on people who put them down.

In the mind of a narcissist, other people should consistently approve of, adore, and agree with them. After all, if I'm genuinely a special and superior person, then other people should recognize my specialness and defer to my superior intelligence and judgment. Much of the time, a narcissist can dismiss any negative reactions they get by simply concluding that other people are stupid or poorly-informed or envious or just losers whose opinions don't count anyway. But now and then, those defenses break down, and the narcissist becomes enraged by the unfairness of other people's indifference or disrespect or criticism. We all get angry when we don't think we get what we deserve, and narcissists get angry when they don't get the adoration, respect, and deference that they think someone as special as they are ought to get.

Historically, there have been 2 competing views of the effects of parenting on the development of narcissism. One view is that having parents who are not sufficiently loving and warm creates narcissists, because children who have cold, uncaring parents try to compensate for feeling unloved by telling themselves how great they are. So, from this perspective, narcissism is a defense against feelings of insecurity and being unloved. The other view says, no, narcissism arises when parents evaluate their child too positively. Parents who think that they have an exceptionally special child convey that viewpoint to the child, who believes it and becomes narcissistic.

This has been a hard question to resolve because it requires following a large number of parents and children over time to see what kind of parenting is associated with narcissism: parents who lack warmth or parents who overvalue their child. A study just like that was published in 2015 that clearly showed that narcissistic people tend to have parents who over-valued them, who thought they were unusually special. So, children seem to acquire narcissism, at least in part, by internalizing their parents' inflated views of them. I want to stress that I'm not talking about parents loving their kids; that's great. You can't give your child too much love. I'm talking about parents who believe that their child is a rare and special individual, and who convey that judgment to the kid.

Interestingly, the same study that showed that parental over-evaluation predicted narcissism also found that parental warmth, and not parental over-evaluation, seemed to lead to greater self-esteem in the child. This finding supports the idea that narcissism is quite different than just having high self-esteem. True, narcissists score exceptionally high on measures of self-esteem, but there are plenty of people with high self-esteem who don't show any signs of narcissism. Just over 2% of the population meets the criteria for a diagnosis of narcissistic personality disorder, but again, lots of other people who wouldn't meet the official criteria are still quite narcissistic.

So, we've covered 4 of the 10 recognized personality disorders: anti-social, borderline, histrionic, and narcissistic. Some researchers have suggested that in some ways, these 4 disorders are more of a problem for other people than they are for the person him or herself, but I'm not sure that I agree. Certainly, people with all of these disorders often impose on, take advantage of, and hurt other people.

But all of these disorders are associated with patterns of behavior that undermine the quality of people's lives. People with anti-social personalities often end up with legal problems for aggression, stealing, or not paying their bills. Their irresponsibility creates problems at work, and their cold-heartedness creates relationship problems. All 4 kinds of people create problems in their interpersonal lives and struggle to have close, warm, supportive relationships with others. So, they often don't have the same level of social support that other people have. Yes, all of them affect other people negatively, but each of these disorders also has implications for the people themselves.

AVOIDANCE, PARANOIA, AND OTHER DISORDERS

LECTURE 22

In this lecture, you will learn first about a cluster of 3 personality disorders identified by the Diagnostic and Statistical Manual of Mental Disorder that involve excessive anxiety—the avoidant, dependent, and obsessive-compulsive disorders—and then about a cluster of 3 others that involve eccentric behaviors and distorted or unusual thinking—the paranoid, schizoid, and schizotypal disorders.

AVOIDANT PERSONALITY DISORDER

- Everybody experiences social anxiety from time to time when they become concerned with how they are being perceived and evaluated by other people. But some people are so consistently worried about what other people think of them that their anxiety interferes with their lives on an ongoing basis.

- A person with avoidant personality disorder is chronically preoccupied with being criticized, disapproved of, or rejected across a wide range of social situations. As a result, people with avoidant personality disorder are not only exceptionally anxious, but they also avoid a wide variety of situations in which they have to interact with other people.

- Avoidant people sometimes have satisfying relationships with family members or a close friend, but only if they are certain of being liked and accepted. And even in their closest relationships, they tend to be inhibited because they're afraid of doing something that will lead to disapproval.

- Underlying their extreme anxiety, inhibition, and avoidance are deep feelings of inadequacy. People with avoidant personality disorder see themselves as inept, unappealing, and inferior to other people, so very low self-esteem is a central component.

- People with avoidant personality disorder have somewhat unhappy and unsatisfying lives. They can certainly entertain themselves with their personal interests and activities and can form connections with friends or family members, but their basic needs for acceptance and belonging are not being met, and they go through life feeling alienated.

DEPENDENT PERSONALITY DISORDER

- People differ in how much they need other people's help or support, but when an otherwise normal person has a very needy relationship with just about everybody and can't seem to function on a daily basis without help from other people, the person might qualify for a diagnosis of dependent personality disorder.

- People who qualify for a diagnosis of dependent personality disorder need—or think they need—constant help from other people to function in most major areas of their life. They even have trouble making everyday decisions, such as what to eat for lunch, without advice and reassurance from other people.

- This lack of confidence in their own judgment and ability also leads them to have trouble starting projects or doing things on their own; they're too afraid that they won't know what to do or that they will do it wrong.

- People with dependent personality disorder firmly believe that they are incapable of functioning independently, but they can actually do okay when they know that someone else is supervising and watching over them. So, it's mostly a matter of exceptionally low self-confidence or self-efficacy rather than being truly incompetent.

- People with dependent personality disorder go to great lengths to get nurturance and support from other people. They usually behave in ways that will lead others to help them. For example, they might offer to help other people in unusual or excessive ways. Their goal is to get the other person to reciprocate by being available for them.

- And they have trouble disagreeing with and standing up to other people because they're afraid of losing the person's approval or support. So, they're very nice, helpful, compliant people, but it's motivated by a need to keep other people in their corner.

Teenagers who have dependent personality disorder may display the rather unusual pattern of wanting their parents to decide what clothes they should wear, what they should do in their free time, and who to hang out with.

- People with dependent personality disorder often feel uncomfortable or helpless when they're alone because they're afraid of not being able to handle whatever situations might come up—not being able to take care of themselves. So, they often structure their lives around having other people around for support. And when someone they depend on is not available, they urgently look for somebody else.

- One downside of relying so much on other people—in addition to becoming clingy and annoying—is that highly dependent people often don't learn what they need to know to manage their lives on their own. So, dependency begets more dependency.

OBSESSIVE-COMPULSIVE PERSONALITY DISORDER

- There are 2 psychological problems that have the term "obsessive-compulsive" in their name: obsessive-compulsive personality disorder, which is addressed in this lecture, and obsessive-compulsive disorder (OCD), which is characterized by the presence of true obsessions and/or compulsions.

- Obsessions are recurring and persistent thoughts that are intrusive and unwanted. Compulsions are repetitive behaviors, or sometimes repetitive mental actions, that a person feels that he or she has to perform. Obsessions and compulsions are not tied to normal activities, and they usually create a great deal of stress for the person. But the person with OCD is helpless to stop their unusual, repetitive thoughts or behaviors.

- Obsessive-compulsive *personality* disorder is an obsessive preoccupation with order, perfection, and self-control. In many ways, it's like being exceptionally high in conscientiousness, all the time—even when it doesn't matter and even when one's attention to detail is dysfunctional.

- People who qualify for a diagnosis of obsessive-compulsive personality disorder are preoccupied with organizing the details of their life. And they become quite uncomfortable when things are not organized and orderly.

- Many people have to-do lists and planners to help keep track of important tasks, but people with obsessive-compulsive personality disorder organize their lives in ways that don't matter much. They worry about trivial details and plans. And sometimes, the process of planning and organizing becomes as important as the activities that they're trying to plan and organize.

- Obsessive-compulsive personality disorder is also associated with perfectionism. Doing things well is important, but compulsive perfectionism differs from functional perfectionism in 2 ways: Compulsive perfectionists worry about getting things perfect in areas in which perfection isn't needed, and compulsive perfectionism can interfere with getting many things done because the person won't finish a task until it's absolutely perfect.

- Obsessive-compulsive traits in moderation may be very adaptive, particularly in situations that reward high performance. So, people with this disorder often do a great job on things. But when people overdo it and try to be organized, conscientious, and perfect with everything they do, even when it doesn't matter and even when it interferes with their life, these characteristics can become maladaptive.

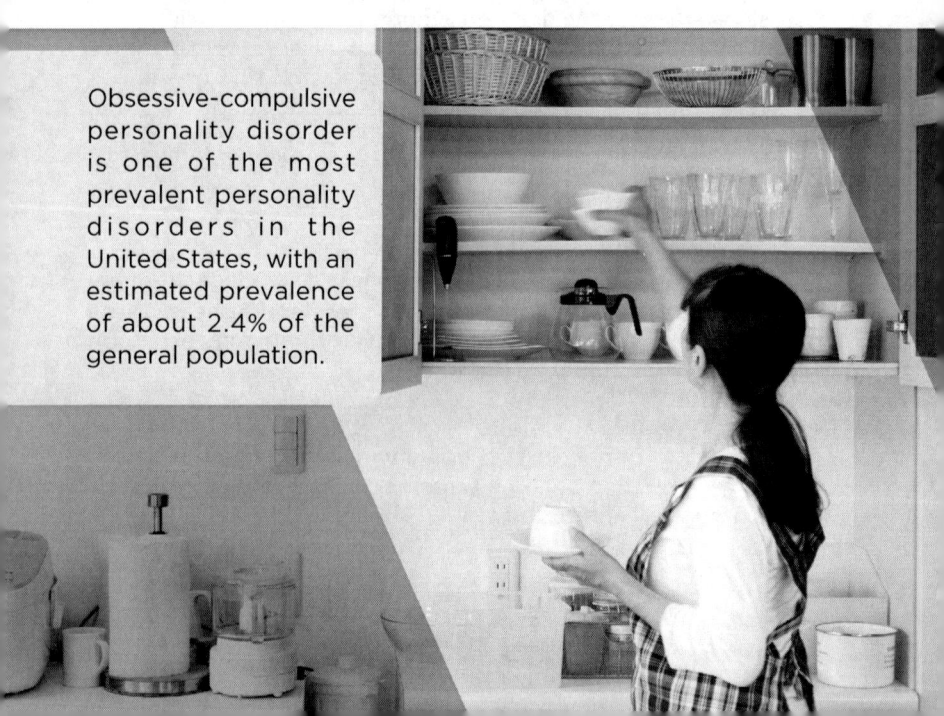

Obsessive-compulsive personality disorder is one of the most prevalent personality disorders in the United States, with an estimated prevalence of about 2.4% of the general population.

PARANOID PERSONALITY DISORDER

- The paranoid personality disorder involves a pervasive distrust of other people. Sometimes being distrustful and suspicious is entirely appropriate, but if you find reasons to distrust many, if not most, of the people that you deal with in life, then the rigidity of your response suggests a personality disorder.

- Paranoid personality disorder manifests in a number of ways. Most importantly, people with paranoid disorder suspect, without sufficient evidence, that people are deceiving, taking advantage of, or harming them—or at least that people might be planning to hurt them. They're preoccupied with doubts about the trustworthiness or loyalty of other people, including their family, friends, and romantic partners.

- In addition, people with paranoid personality disorder have a bias to perceive others' actions as harmful or threatening. They tend to interpret other people's innocuous behaviors or remarks as being insulting or threatening in some way. They often read malevolent intentions into other people's actions.

- Not surprisingly, people with paranoid personality disorder tend to be very private people. They're reluctant to share personal information or confide in other people because they're afraid that the information might somehow be used against them. They also tend to hold grudges against people they think have done something bad to them, and they're less forgiving when someone has hurt them in some way.

- To get a diagnosis of paranoid personality disorder, the person can't show any evidence of schizophrenia or other disorders with psychotic features. Essentially, that means that they can't have lost touch with reality.

SCHIZOID PERSONALITY DISORDER

- People with schizoid personality disorder seem to have little need for other people. They don't care much about social connections, so they're rather detached from normal social relationships.

- Despite its name, schizoid personality disorder doesn't actually resemble schizophrenia very much. Schizophrenia is one of the most serious psychological problems that involves profound disturbances in thought and emotion and that typically includes psychotic symptoms, such as hearing voices, experiencing hallucinations, or having delusional thoughts.

- Instead, schizoid personality disorder is a pervasive pattern of detachment from social relationships. A schizoid person doesn't appear to desire or enjoy close relationships with other people—not even family members.

- People generally enjoy interacting with other people and regard their social relationships as important. Even people who are very introverted are motivated to interact and have close relationships, just not as much as extraverts do.

- But people with schizoid personality disorder seem to lack this basic human motive. They simply don't care about having relationships with other people. They don't even seem to care whether people like them, and they seem rather indifferent to both compliments and criticisms.

- So, not surprisingly, they almost always choose do to things by themselves and live pretty solitary lives. They usually don't have any close friends or confidants, except maybe relatives. And they seem to have little, if any, interest in sexual relationships.

- This pattern of social disconnection and isolation is usually accompanied by flat emotions. They don't take much pleasure in any activities, but they aren't upset by very much either. It's as if they're detached emotionally from their own lives. So, they usually display a bland exterior and come across as aloof and maybe self-absorbed.

> Estimates are that 3% to 5% of adults in the United States would qualify for a diagnosis of schizoid personality disorder.

- Interactions with schizoid people are usually pretty awkward. You not only get the clear sense that they don't care about interacting with you, but their lack of ordinary emotional reactions is unsettling. They don't reciprocate other people's gestures or facial expressions; they don't necessarily wave back when you wave or smile when you smile. More generally, they don't respond appropriately to social cues, so they seem socially inept, awkward, and self-absorbed.

- These social skill problems can create difficulties for their work life, given that most people have to work with other people. But people with schizoid personality disorder may do just fine if they can work under conditions of social isolation.

- You might know some people who could be classified as a secret schizoid, but you wouldn't realize it. Secret schizoids lack the motivation to interact and form close relationships and have flat internal emotional lives. But secret schizoids have learned how to play the part of a normal person, so they may appear to be socially engaged and seem to be interested and involved in interacting, but they still lack any interest in closeness and remain emotionally detached.

SCHIZOTYPAL PERSONALITY DISORDER

- Unlike people who are schizophrenic, people with schizotypal personality disorder don't have hallucinations or delusions, but they do have unusual thoughts and ideas. For example, their interpretations of events are often quite odd. They may explain things that happen or other people's behavior in ways that don't make much sense to anybody else.

- Schizotypal people also tend to have odd magical and superstitious beliefs that most people don't have—usually not things that are downright crazy, but things that are questionable and that most people don't believe.

- Their speech can be idiosyncratic. It's sometimes difficult to follow exactly what they're talking about because they use loose and vague language and digress a lot.

- They also tend to have odd mannerisms and expressions; they might never look at other people when they talk, or they might not nod as you're talking to them. They might bluntly end a conversation by just walking away.

- And they tend to dress in unusual ways. They wear clothes that don't match or don't fit, and it's not because they are making a fashion statement or that they identify with some group that dresses that way. They're not trying to be different—they just are.

- There's not really anything wrong with any of this, and it doesn't hurt anybody—it's just an odd package of eccentricities. The worst thing is that other people think that they're odd and often avoid them.

Why Do Personality Disorders Develop?

As usual, personality disorders develop as a result of a combination of genetic and environmental factors.

Personality disorders appear to be more heritable than most normal personality characteristics. About 50% to 80% of the variability that we see in these disorders seems to be genetic.

Although each of these disorders involves a set of several specific characteristics, it's not likely that the whole syndrome is inherited as a package. Instead, research suggests that the various components of personality disorders are inherited separately.

There are strong genetic predispositions to develop these kinds of problems, but it probably also takes some unusual kinds of environmental influences—probably in the form of parental neglect or abuse or situations in which maladaptive behaviors are rewarded—for a full-blown disorder to appear.

- Not surprisingly, people with schizotypal personality disorder have problems in social interactions and relationships. They usually aren't able to manage interactions in a skilled manner, and they are often stiff or socially inappropriate. They realize that they are different and don't quite fit in, and they're anxious in social situations, particularly those that involve unfamiliar people. They interact when they have to, but they often prefer to keep to themselves when possible.

Suggested Reading

Budd, *I'm OK, You're Not OK*.

Dobbert, *Understanding Personality Disorders*.

Questions to Consider

1. Imagine that you have a family member who is exceptionally well organized. He keeps his house and office neat and clean, with everything in its place and his drawers and closets organized. This person's life is also orderly; he keeps a to-do list and plans his days in advance. He also tries to do most things as well as possible, even everyday tasks, such as mowing his yard. At a family gathering, you hear another family member tease this person about being OCD. Does this person actually show signs of obsessive-compulsive disorder? Why or why not?

2. Some personality disorders are problematic mostly because they disadvantage, annoy, or harm other people, and other personality disorders are problematic mostly because they undermine the quality of the person's own life. Which of the 10 disorders primarily create problems for others? Which ones primarily create problems for the sufferer? Which do both?

AVOIDANCE, PARANOIA, AND OTHER DISORDERS
LECTURE 22 TRANSCRIPT

We previously looked at 4 personality disorders that involve patterns of overly emotional, dramatic, and erratic behaviors: the anti-social, borderline, histrionic, and narcissistic disorders. In this lecture, we'll talk first about a cluster of 3 disorders that involve excessive anxiety, and then a cluster of 3 others that involve eccentric behaviors and distorted thinking.

I'll start with 3 personality disorders that each involve a high level of anxiety: the avoidant, dependent, and obsessive-compulsive disorders. Now, there's absolutely nothing wrong with being anxious or afraid. In fact, anxiety is our friend in that it warns us about possible dangers, and motivates us to take actions that help to keep us safe. But anxiety becomes a problem when it's so persistent that it interferes with a person's life on a regular basis. That's when it becomes a personality disorder.

When we talked about social anxiety earlier, I noted that everybody experiences social anxiety from time to time when they become concerned with how they are being perceived and evaluated by other people. So, many of us feel nervous when giving a talk in front of a group, or being interviewed for a job, or being at a social gathering where we don't know anybody. People differ in how often they feel socially anxious, but social anxiety is perfectly normal. But some people are so consistently worried about what other people think of them that their anxiety interferes with their lives on an ongoing basis. Now, oddly, the Diagnostic and Statistical Manual for Mental Disorders has 2 diagnoses that involve a high level of social anxiety—social anxiety disorder and avoidant personality disorder. But in the DSM, social anxiety disorder is classified as an anxiety disorder, and avoidant personality disorder is classified as a personality disorder. So, given that this lecture is about personality disorders, we're going to look at avoidant personality disorder here.

A person with avoidant personality disorder is chronically preoccupied with being criticized, disapproved of, or rejected across a wide range of social situations. As a result, people with avoidant personality disorder are not only exceptionally anxious, but they also avoid a wide variety of situations in which they have to interact with other people. So for example, they have a great deal of difficulty working in jobs that involve social interaction, and they have trouble meeting people, making friends, and finding romantic partners because they're so afraid of dealing with other people.

Avoidant people sometimes have satisfying relationships with family members or a close friend but only if they are certain of being liked and accepted. And even in their closest relationships, they tend to be inhibited because they're afraid of doing something that will lead to disapproval. Underlying their extreme anxiety, inhibition, and avoidance are deep feelings of inadequacy. People with avoidant personality disorder see themselves as inept and unappealing and inferior to other people. So, very low self-esteem is a central component of this.

This is obviously not a good way to live, and people with avoidant personality disorder have somewhat unhappy and unsatisfying lives. They can certainly entertain themselves with their personal interests and activities and, as I said, they can form connections with friends or family members. But their basic needs for acceptance and belonging are not being met, and they go through life feeling alienated, watching from the sidelines as other people have social lives and friends and romantic partners, but usually being too afraid to jump into the game.

Somewhere along the way, many of us have had a friend or a family member who depended on us too much. They were anxious and really clingy, and they may have driven us a bit crazy by getting in touch too often and asking us to help them with all sorts of things that normal people should be able to handle on their own. Of course, people differ in how much they need other people's help or support, and that's fine. But when an otherwise normal person has this kind of very needy relationship with just about everybody and can't seem to function on a daily basis without help from other people, the person might qualify for a diagnosis of dependent personality disorder.

But where do we draw the line between the normal, and even healthy, ways in which we depend on other people, and the excessive dependency of a person with dependent personality disorder? People who qualify for a diagnosis of dependent personality disorder need, or think they need, constant help from other people to function in most major areas of their life. They even have trouble making everyday decisions, such as deciding which shirt to wear or what to eat for lunch, without advice and reassurance from other people. This lack of confidence in their own judgment and ability also leads them to have trouble starting projects or doing things on their own; they're too afraid that they won't know what to do or that they will do it wrong. For example, teenagers who have dependent personality disorder may want their parents to decide what clothes they should wear, what they should do in their free time, and who to hang out with. That's obviously a rather unusual pattern for teenagers. Highly dependent adults usually depend on a spouse or maybe a parent to help them make these sorts of everyday decisions.

People with dependent personality disorder firmly believe that they are incapable of functioning independently, but they can actually do okay when they know that someone else is supervising and watching over them. So, it's mostly a matter of exceptionally low self-confidence or self-efficacy rather than being truly incompetent. In addition to being too reliant on other people for help and advice, people with dependent personality disorder go to great lengths to get nurturance and support from other people. So they usually behave in ways that will lead others to help them.

So, for example, they might offer to help other people in unusual or excessive ways. They sometimes do favors for other people that are inappropriate. Yes, it was nice they did that, but it was sort of weird. Their goal is to get the other person to reciprocate by being available for them. And they have trouble disagreeing with and standing up to other people because they're afraid of losing the person's approval or support. So, they're very nice, helpful, compliant people, but it's motivated by a need to keep other people in their corner.

There's an emotional component to dependency as well: People with dependent personality disorder often feel uncomfortable or helpless when they're alone because they're afraid of not being able to handle whatever situations might come up, not being able to take care of themselves. So, they often structure their lives around having other people around for support. And when someone they depend on is not available, they urgently look for somebody else. One downside of relying so much on other people, in addition to becoming clingy and annoying, is that highly dependent people often don't learn what they need to know to manage their lives on their own. So dependency begets more dependency.

In some ways, dependent personality disorder may look a little bit like borderline personality disorder in that both disorders involve a fear of being rejected or abandoned. The difference is that people with borderline personality disorder react to the possibility of abandonment with feelings of rage and start making demands, whereas people with dependent personality disorder react by becoming anxious and even more dependent and urgently seeking someone to provide care and support. Dependent personality disorder also looks a little like avoidant personality disorder because people with avoidant personality disorder can become very attached to and dependent on those few individuals with whom they have social connections, and both dependent personality and avoidant personality are characterized by feelings of inadequacy, excessive sensitivity to criticism, and a need for reassurance. But for people with dependent personality disorder, the primary concern is about being taken care of, whereas for avoidant personality disorder, the focus in on avoiding negative evaluation and rejection.

The third disorder in the anxious cluster, obsessive-compulsive personality disorder, is going to take a bit of explanation because there are 2 psychological problems that have the term obsessive-compulsive in their name. There's obsessive-compulsive personality disorder—which is what we're going to talk about here—and there's obsessive-compulsive disorder which is something else entirely. Now that's pretty confusing.

The condition that we aren't going to talk about is obsessive-compulsive disorder—OCD—which is characterized by the presence of true obsessions and/or compulsions. Obsessions are recurring and persistent thoughts that are intrusive and unwanted; the person can't stop thinking certain things. So, obsessions would be things like thinking all the time about germs or getting sick, or obsessing about sex continually to the point where it interferes with normal life, or always thinking about hurting other people. Compulsions are repetitive behaviors, or sometimes repetitive mental actions, that a person feels that he or she has to perform, like obsessively washing your hands dozens of times a day, or having to read the numbers on people's license plates out loud as you drive down the road, or not being able to stop hoarding things.

Obsessions and compulsions are not tied to normal activities, and they usually create a great deal of stress for the person. But the person with OCD is helpless to stop their unusual, repetitive thoughts or behaviors. That's OCD—obsessive compulsive disorder—but that's not exactly a problem with the person's personality. It's not just some extreme pattern of otherwise ordinary behavior. Rather, the thoughts and behaviors that characterize people with OCD typically deal with unusual obsessions and compulsions that don't have much to do with reality. So, we'll set OCD aside.

What we're going to talk about is obsessive-compulsive personality disorder, which is an obsessive preoccupation with order, perfection, and self-control. In many ways, it's like being exceptionally high in conscientiousness all the time, even when it doesn't matter, and even when one's attention to detail is dysfunctional. Obsessive-compulsive personality disorder is like conscientiousness gone wild. People who qualify for a diagnosis of obsessive-compulsive personality disorder are preoccupied with organizing the details of their life. So, they're big fans of lists, schedules, plans, and rules, having everything in its place, doing everything just right. And they become quite uncomfortable when things are not organized and orderly.

Of course, many of us have to-do lists and planners to help us keep track of important tasks, but people with obsessive-compulsive personality disorder organize their lives in ways that don't matter all that much. They worry about trivial details and plans. And sometimes, the process of planning and organizing becomes as important as the activities that they're trying to plan and organize. Obsessive-compulsive personality disorder is also associated with perfectionism. Doing things well is important, but compulsive perfectionism differs from functional perfectionism in 2 ways.

First, compulsive perfectionists worry about getting things perfect in areas in which perfection isn't needed. So, they might have perfectly organized closets or a perfectly manicured lawn or a perfectly planned vacation. Any one of these might be okay, but if you can't help yourself from trying to make everything perfect, you might qualify for a diagnosis of obsessive-compulsive personality disorder. Second, compulsive perfectionism can interfere with getting many things done, because the person won't finish a task until it's absolutely perfect. For example, a person might rewrite and rewrite a report at work to make it perfect without really improving it that much—and, thus, waste time that could be devoted to other projects. So, the person misses deadlines, which creates added distress for someone who is focused on order and planning.

Because of their concern with doing things well, professional people with obsessive-compulsive personality disorder are often so devoted to their work that they don't engage in leisure activities or have much of a social life. They can always do more at work, and they can always do it better. People with obsessive-compulsive personality disorder are often workaholics. And when they do try to relax, these individuals often approach their hobbies and recreational activities as tasks to be mastered. So they plan and organize and schedule and control what should often be spontaneous, enjoyable activities.

Obsessive-compulsive personality disorder is one of the most prevalent personality disorders in the United States, with an estimated prevalence of about 2.4% of the general population.

Now, obsessive-compulsive personality disorder is obviously a double-edged sword. Obsessive-compulsive traits in moderation may be very adaptive, particularly in situations that reward high performance. So, people with this disorder often do a great job on things. But when people overdo it and try to be organized, conscientious, and perfect with everything they do, even when it doesn't matter and even when it interferes with their life, these characteristics can become maladaptive.

The third and final cluster of personality disorders identified by the DSM involves eccentric behaviors and distorted or unusual thinking. In my view, these disorders don't really hang together all that well. They're just 3 more ways in which unusual or extreme patterns of inflexible behavior can create problems for people.

The paranoid personality disorder is pretty clear-cut. As its name indicates, it involves a pervasive distrust of other people. As I mentioned earlier, sometimes being distrustful and suspicious is entirely appropriate, but if you find reasons to distrust many, if not most of the people that you deal with in life—and you're not in the Mafia—then the rigidity of your response suggests a personality disorder.

Paranoid personality disorder manifests in a number of ways. Most importantly, people with paranoid disorder suspect, without sufficient evidence, that people are deceiving or taking advantage of or harming them, or at least that people might be planning to hurt them. So, they're preoccupied with doubts about the trustworthiness or loyalty of other people, including their family, friends, and romantic partners.

In addition, people with paranoid personality disorder have a bias to perceive others' actions as harmful or threatening. For example, they tend to interpret other people's innocuous behaviors or remarks as being insulting or threatening in some way. They often read malevolent intentions into other people's actions. Not surprisingly, people with paranoid personality disorder tend to be very private people. They're reluctant to share personal information or confide in other people because they're afraid that the information might somehow be used against them. They also tend to hold grudges against people they think have done something bad to them, and they're less forgiving when someone has hurt them in some way.

To get a diagnosis of paranoid personality disorder, the person can't show any evidence of schizophrenia or other disorders with psychotic features. Essentially, that means they can't have lost touch with reality. In the case of paranoid schizophrenia, people often have hallucinations in which they hear or see the people who are supposedly out to get them, or their beliefs about the plots against them are clearly not credible. It's not really likely that a foreign government is spying on them. Paranoid schizophrenics can't distinguish what's real from what's going on entirely in their minds. In contrast, people with paranoid personality disorder don't have hallucinations or delusions, and at least on the surface, any particular suspicion they have is not necessarily unreasonable. But once one sees the whole pattern, it's obvious that the person is globally suspicious and distrusting.

Some of the personality disorders we've discussed involve an excessive concern with one's social relationships. So for example, borderline personality disorder reflects extreme reactions to rejection, histrionic personality disorder involves an intense desire for social attention, avoidant personality disorder reflects excessive fear of social interactions, and dependent personality disorder involves excessive dependency on other people. Schizoid personality disorder, the second of our final cluster of disorders, is quite the opposite. People with schizoid personality disorder seem to have little need for other people. They don't care much about social connections, so they're rather detached from normal social relationships.

Schizoid is another one of those unfortunate terms. The word, schizoid, literally means resembling schizophrenia, but schizoid personality disorder doesn't actually resemble schizophrenia very much. Schizophrenia is one of the most serious psychological problems that involves profound disturbances in thought and emotion and that typically includes psychotic symptoms such as hearing voices, experiencing hallucinations, or having delusional thoughts. That's not at all what we're talking about here.

Instead, schizoid personality disorder is a pervasive pattern of detachment from social relationships. A schizoid person doesn't appear to desire or enjoy close relationships with other people, not even family members. People generally enjoy interacting with other people and regard their social relationships as important. Even people who are very introverted are motivated to interact and have close relationships, just not as much as extraverts do. But people with schizoid personality disorder seem to lack this basic human motive. They simply don't care about having relationships with other people. They don't even seem to care whether people like them, and they seem rather indifferent to both compliments and criticisms.

So, not surprisingly, they almost always choose do to things by themselves and live pretty solitary lives. They usually don't have any close friends or confidants, except maybe relatives, such as parents or brothers or sisters. And they seem to have little, if any interest in sexual relationships. If you can think of somebody who is a classic loner and who seems to be okay without close relationships, they might have schizoid personality disorder. This pattern of social disconnection and isolation is usually accompanied by flat emotions. They don't take much pleasure in any activities, but they aren't upset by very much either. It's as if they're detached emotionally from their own lives. So, they usually display a bland exterior and come across as aloof and maybe self-absorbed.

Interactions with schizoid people are usually pretty awkward. You not only get the clear sense that they don't care about interacting with you, but their lack of ordinary emotional reactions is unsettling. They don't reciprocate other people's gestures or facial expressions; they don't necessarily wave back when you wave or smile when you smile. More generally, they don't respond appropriately to social cues, so that they seem socially inept, awkward, and self-absorbed. These social skill problems can create difficulties for their work life, given that most of us have to work with other people. But people with schizoid personality disorder may do just fine if they can work under conditions of social isolation.

Estimates are that 3 to 5% of adults in the United States would qualify for a diagnosis of schizoid personality disorder. If you can't think of anybody who fits that description, it might be because they're not the people that you're likely to run into. They're not out and about. You might, however, know some people who could be classified as a secret schizoid, but you wouldn't realize it. A secret schizoid lacks the motivation to interact and form close relationships, and has a flat internal emotional life, as I just described. But a secret schizoid has learned how to play the part of a normal person. So, they may appear to be socially engaged and seem to be interested and involved in interacting, but they still lack any interest in closeness and remain emotionally detached.

You've probably done this yourself. Think of situations in which you had to interact with other people, but you didn't want to. Maybe you didn't like them, or maybe you were preoccupied by other things and didn't have the energy to deal with people. You were totally unmotivated to be there, and you had no interest in interacting and no emotional connection to the people. But you plastered a fake smile on your face and went in and played the role of someone who cared. That's how the secret schizoid gets by in life all the time.

Many personality disorders aren't immediately obvious to other people. Yes, you may see that a person is being egotistical or socially anxious or intense or detached or a bit of a show-off. But in any given situation, you might not get the impression that the person has a problem. It's only if you interact with such people enough to know that they are almost always that way—that they have only one way of approaching things—that you realize that something is off. Well, in the case of our final disorder, the schizotypal personality disorder, it's pretty obvious from the start that this person is, if not psychologically disturbed, at least different because they're unusual in how they behave, what they think, and often just in how they look. They don't hurt anybody, they're just highly eccentric people.

First, people with schizotypal personality disorder have unusual thoughts and ideas. Unlike people who are schizophrenic, they don't have hallucinations or delusions, but they do have unusual ideas. For example, their interpretations of events are often quite odd. They may explain things that happen or other people's behavior in ways that don't make much sense to anybody else. I knew a guy in high school who, in retrospect, was certainly schizotypal. One day he and I and some other students were wondering why another friend of ours hadn't come to school that day. And the schizotypal guy said, "Maybe he went to Europe." Uh, well...did he say anything about going to Europe? No, in fact, he's probably never been out of the state. But this guy felt fairly sure that maybe he went to Europe. It was just odd.

Schizotypal people also tend to have odd magical and superstitious beliefs that most people don't have; usually not things that are downright crazy, but things that are questionable and that most people don't believe. Their speech can be idiosyncratic. It's sometimes hard to follow exactly what they're talking about because they use loose and vague language and digress a lot. They also tend to have odd mannerisms and expressions; they might never look at other people when they talk, or they might not nod as you're talking to them. They might bluntly end a conversation by just walking away. And they tend to dress in unusual ways. They wear clothes that don't match or don't fit, and it's not to make some sort of fashion statement or because they identify with some group that dresses that way. They're not trying to be different, they just are.

There's not really anything wrong with any of this, and it doesn't hurt anybody, it's just an odd package of eccentricities. The worst thing is that other people think they're odd and often avoid them. If you think of the people that you have known who everybody thought were truly and inexplicably weird, they might have been schizotypal. And, again I'm not talking just about people who were different from you. These people are different from everybody.

Not surprisingly, people with schizotypal personality disorder have problems in social interactions and relationships. They usually aren't able to manage interactions in a skilled manner, and they are often stiff or socially inappropriate. They realize that they are different and don't quite fit in, and they're anxious in social situations, particularly those that involve unfamiliar people. They interact when they have to, but they often prefer to keep to themselves when possible.

In these last 2 lectures, we've covered the 10 official personality disorders. There are obviously other ways in which people's styles of reacting are inflexible or inappropriate or maladaptive, but these are the ones that psychiatrists and practicing psychologists have mostly agreed on.

Well, why do personality disorders develop? As usual, it's a combination of genetic and environmental factors, but a couple of important findings stick out. Personality disorders appear to be more heritable than most normal personality characteristics. When we discussed genetics previously, we saw that most personality variables have heritability coefficients in the 0.3 to 0.6 range. But these 10 disorders have heritabilities in the 0.5 to 0.8 range. That is, 50 to 80% of the variability that we see in these disorders seems to be genetic.

Although each of these disorders involves a set of several specific characteristics, it's not likely that the whole syndrome is inherited as a package. In other words, you probably don't inherit paranoid personality disorder or borderline personality disorder as a unit. Instead, research suggests that the various components of personality disorders are inherited separately. For example, the tendency for emotional dysregulation is inherited separately from the tendency to be impulsive versus inhibited, which is separate from the tendency to be antisocial, which is different from compulsivity, which is separate from low empathy, and so on. Only when a person inherits a certain set of individual tendencies does the pattern for a particular personality disorder appear.

So, there are strong genetic predispositions to develop these sorts of problems, but it probably also takes some unusual sorts of environmental influences, probably in the form of parental neglect or abuse, or situations in which maladaptive behaviors are rewarded, for a full-blown disorder to appear. The ways in which genes and environment interact to create personality disorders have become a very hot topic of research.

THE ENIGMA OF BEING YOURSELF

LECTURE 23

Ever since Aristotle first wrote about authenticity more than 2000 years ago, a variety of philosophers, psychologists, sociologists, and self-help authors have promoted the idea that people should be authentic—they should always behave in ways that reflect their inner beliefs, values, motives, and dispositions. But this lecture considers the possibility that authenticity has some serious problems as a psychological construct: that it's either not what we usually assume it is or that it's not as important as people typically think it is.

AUTHENTIC INCONSISTENCY

- Most people think that being authentic means that a person behaves the same way all of the time. But we shouldn't expect any normal person to show absolute consistency in his or her behavior. Healthy, well-adjusted people are flexible in how they respond. Of course, we see consistencies in how people behave across different situations, but behavioral flexibility is necessary for people to handle the challenges of life effectively.

- If authenticity is going to be a useful construct, it can't require absolute consistency. It has to allow people a good deal of flexibility and latitude—both because people's personalities are multifaceted and contain incompatible characteristics and because well-adjusted people tailor their actions to particular situations.

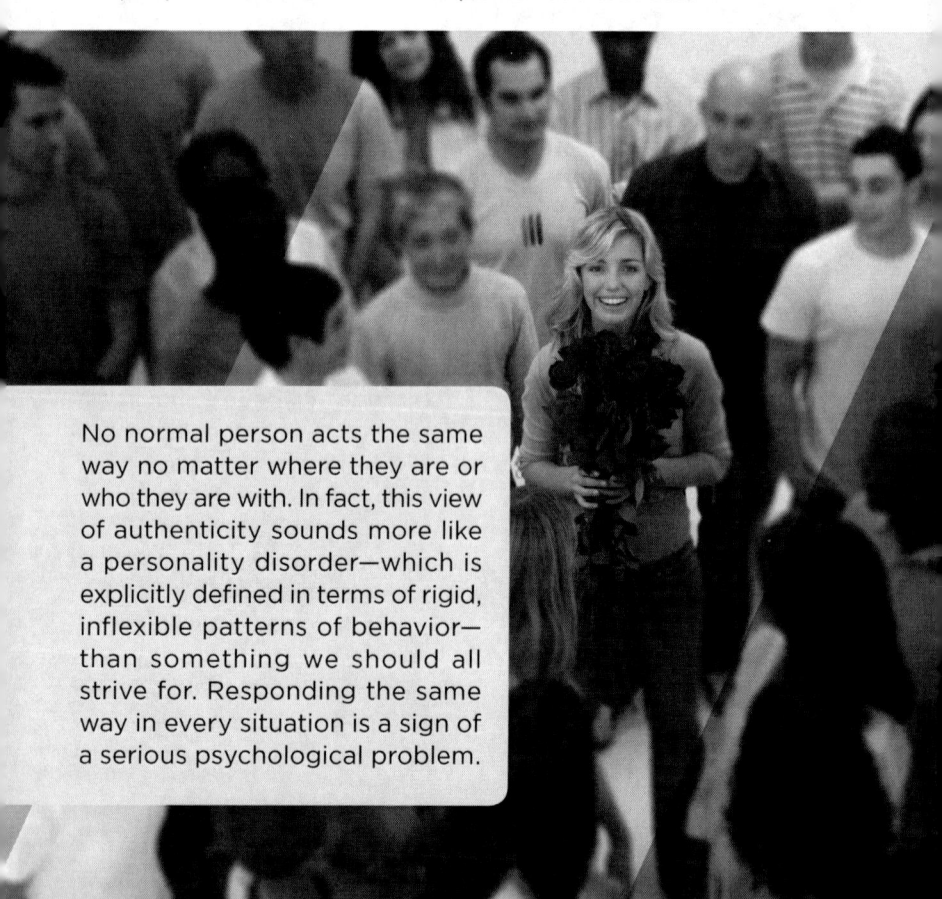

> No normal person acts the same way no matter where they are or who they are with. In fact, this view of authenticity sounds more like a personality disorder—which is explicitly defined in terms of rigid, inflexible patterns of behavior—than something we should all strive for. Responding the same way in every situation is a sign of a serious psychological problem.

- To complicate matters, inconsistency is itself a personality characteristic. People differ in how much their behavior varies across situations. Some people are affected more by situational influences than other people are, so their behavior is less consistent and more variable. Does that mean that they are less authentic than people whose behavior varies less across situations?

- It might seem so, but viewed another way, they may be perfectly authentic because the degree to which people's behavior is affected by situational pressures is itself a personality variable. For people whose personality traits cause them to be strongly affected by the situation they're in, being less consistent is actually more authentic. People can be authentically inconsistent.

SELF-MONITORING

- The personality characteristic that is most closely associated with changing one's behavior to meet situational demands is self-monitoring. People who are high in this characteristic monitor the degree to which they fit whatever situation they are in and behave in ways that are appropriate given the nature of the situation and the characteristics of the people with whom they're interacting.

- In contrast, people who are low in self-monitoring are less influenced by the immediate situation, so their behavior is somewhat more consistent across situations.

- Because they're trying to behave appropriately, people who are high in self-monitoring show greater behavioral variability across situations than people who are low in self-monitoring do. But that doesn't mean that they are less authentic than low self-monitors. In fact, for high self-monitors, a certain degree of inconsistency may be more authentic than consistency is.

- There's a tendency to regard people who mold their behavior to fit the situation that they're in as insecure, duplicitous, or too concerned about social approval. But we all do it, and we absolutely have to in order to manage life effectively.

- On top of that, people can act differently in different situations and still behave in ways that are congruent with their beliefs, values, motives, and dispositions at all times. And for people who are high in self-monitoring, greater variability is even more authentic because that's the way they really are.

UNDERSTANDING OURSELVES

- To strive to be authentic, people have to be able to tell when they are and are not behaving congruently with what they are "really" like. To do that, they have to know about all aspects of their personality, including full details about what motivates their behavior, what they believe, what they value, and all of their psychological characteristics. Without completely understanding themselves and all of the things that influence their behavior, people can't judge whether or not they're being authentic in any particular situation.

- Most of us assume that we have some kind of special insight into what we're like. But our views of ourselves are much less accurate than most people think. Of course, there are some things about yourself that you understand perfectly well, and some aspects of your self-image are right on target. But volumes of research show that people's self-views are not very accurate overall.

- In many studies, researchers have asked people to rate their own personality characteristics and then compared people's self-ratings both with objective measures of their behavior and personality and with ratings of people who know them very well—people who would presumably have deep insight into what the participants were like. People do have some insight into their personalities, so they weren't completely clueless about what they were like, but they weren't entirely accurate either.

- We'd all like to think that we know ourselves reasonably well and that we understand why we do what we do. And sometimes, that's the case. But at other times, it's simply not possible, and we can't tell when we know the truth about ourselves and when we don't.

- Just about everybody sees themselves too positively. We all overestimate our positive qualities and underestimate our negative qualities, and we're biased to attribute our actions to positive, desirable motives rather than negative, undesirable ones. These self-serving biases in our views of ourselves make it virtually impossible to really know who we are. And if that's the case, how do we know when we're being authentic?

INTERNAL COHERENCE

- Most of us fall into the trap of thinking of ourselves as a coherent, unified, integrated person. In other words, we have the sense that we are a single psychologically integrated system and not just some hodgepodge of disconnected values, motives, beliefs, and traits.

- We sense that all of the diverse pieces of our personality are tightly interconnected—that our beliefs are tied to our motives, that our traits are connected to our emotions, that our values and motives are linked, and so on. So, it seems as if our total personality should all work together in some integrated and harmonious way, like the parts of a well-designed machine.

- You also probably have the sense that there's some central mechanism inside you that oversees and controls all of this stuff, some central control unit that integrates and manages all of the different parts of your psychological machinery. You feel like there's somebody in charge of this whole mess, something that oversees all of the parts of your personality and keeps them running smoothly.

- But neither of these perceptions is true. The various parts of your personality are not entirely coherent, integrated, and unified, and there's no one in control of all of it. There isn't any central regulatory mechanism that coordinates all of the different parts of your personality and reactions.

- You have a center of consciousness that you think of as "you" that seems to think your thoughts, feel your emotions, and control your behaviors. But that psychological process that some people think of as their "self" doesn't have much insight into or control over most of what is happening in your brain. Most of what you feel and do operates outside of your conscious self.

- Furthermore, although many of the processes that control your behavior are connected to each other, many of them aren't. Different reactions are mediated by different parts of the brain, which may not be in communication with each other and aren't controlled by a single integrating mechanism.

- And with no central mechanism that coordinates, integrates, and maintains consistency among all of the parts, there's no reason to expect people to be consistent. There's nothing in there that tries to reconcile conflicts between different competing elements of your personality.

Psychologist Robert Kurzban has compared the human mind to a smartphone with lots of different apps. Each little computer program that makes up a phone app contributes a separate, specialized function to the phone. And although these apps use the same operating system and sometimes rely on each other—your maps and weather app might both rely on your GPS location—there's nothing in the phone that forces any coherence among them.

Kurzban says that the human mind works much in the same way: You have many different circuits that do different things, but they can operate somewhat independently. And like a smartphone, there's no central mechanism that forces consistency among the various programs.

- Different parts of your personality can operate somewhat independently while each is doing its job. And you can have a very functional system that processes information and responds without the oversight of a single controller that's trying to maintain consistency among all of the parts.

- So, the notion of authenticity has problems because there's no reason to expect the human mind to display the sort of consistency or internal coherence that the concept of authenticity implies.

AUTHENTICITY AND PERSONALITY

- Maybe we've been thinking about the topic completely wrong in the sense that our notion of authenticity isn't compatible with the way that personality actually works. Perhaps, contrary to how it seems, people are actually *always* authentic. In other words, maybe it makes no sense to think that people could ever behave incongruently with aspects of their personality, motives, values, and beliefs.

- Almost all human behavior is goal-directed—that is, most of your behavior is intended to achieve some goal or fulfill some motive. Sometimes the goal is conscious, and often the goal is not conscious. But it doesn't make much sense to say that you did something for no reason—that your behavior wasn't motivated. You may not know why you did what you did, but there was some reason, motive, or goal.

- Sometimes the goals that are active and operational for us at a given moment are compatible with each other. But sometimes we have goals that are incompatible. One goal is leading us toward one action, and the other goal is leading us toward a different action—maybe even one that's incompatible with the first one.

- But they're both genuine goals, and whichever one you choose, you're acting consistently with one genuine goal and inconsistently with the other genuine goal.

> Most of us think that a person should be honest, and we probably see ourselves as basically honest people, with occasional lapses. When we lie, we're simply pursuing a different goal than to be honest—maybe to get out of trouble or to not hurt somebody's feelings. But the lie is in the service of a genuine goal that we have, so it's as authentic as telling the truth.

- So, when we do things that we don't want to do—or think we shouldn't do—those behaviors are not inauthentic. They're simply motivated by goals that are incompatible with other goals or with our vision of the person we want to be or think we should be.

- People can't help but to behave congruently with their inner beliefs, motives, values, and dispositions. So, all behavior, even if it's inconsistent or duplicitous, would seem to be authentic.

Why You Are Who You Are

THE VALUE OF AUTHENTICITY

- Why do we place such a value on authenticity and urge people to live congruently with their true selves? To make the right choices in life, it helps to know who you are and what you're like as best you can so that you'll increase the chances that you'll make decisions that are congruent with your psychological characteristics.

- Even though some of your characteristics are incompatible with each other and even though you'll never know for certain what you're like or why you do what you do, understanding yourself as well as you can certainly pays off in terms of making good choices in life. It's not a matter of being authentic, but rather a matter of living in a way that best fits your psychological inclinations and thus maximizes your well-being.

- So-called feelings of inauthenticity are often a sign that you don't understand something about yourself. Feelings of inauthenticity aren't telling you that you behaved incongruently with how you really are; instead, those feelings are telling you that you don't know why you did whatever you did.

- If you understood yourself better, you'd realize that your actions were not really incongruent. Your behavior may have been inconsistent with conscious values that you hold, or incongruent with what you were intentionally trying to do, or contrary to the kind of person you want to be, but something inside you led you to do what you did.

> The pressures that we feel to be authentic are functional. They let us know that we don't understand ourselves well enough to know why we did some seemingly incongruent thing. And they caution us when we do things that might lead other people to view us as fake or dishonest.

- Another reason that people take authenticity seriously and have viewed it as a virtue since ancient times is that we are under social pressure to be authentic. Having high-quality social interactions and relationships with other people requires that we understand them reasonably well. We want to know what other people are like, what motivates them, what they believe, and whether they can be trusted. Misperceiving what other people are like almost always leads to problems.

- To know other people well—to know what they're really like—we have to assume that what they say and do is congruent with their actual beliefs, motives, values, and personality. We have to assume that they are conveying accurate and honest impressions of themselves. If they don't—if they appear to be someone they're not—then we'll be at a disadvantage in our interactions and relationships with them.

Suggested Reading

Ibarra, "The Authenticity Paradox."

Mayer, "Know Thyself."

Questions to Consider

1. Do you agree with the proposition that people always behave congruently with some aspect of their traits, beliefs, motives, and values and, thus, people are never truly inauthentic (even when they're being dishonest or trying to appear to be someone they're not)? Why or why not?

2. What situations make you feel inauthentic, like you're not being yourself? Analyze the source of these feelings based on the material covered in this lecture.

THE ENIGMA OF BEING YOURSELF
LECTURE 23 TRANSCRIPT

Should you try to always be yourself—to be authentic—and if so, why? Can you actually tell when you're not being yourself? And what are we really talking about when we say that people should be themselves? Who else's self could they possibly be? Ever since Aristotle first wrote about authenticity more than 2000 years ago, a variety of philosophers, psychologists, sociologists, and self-help authors have promoted the idea that people should strive to always be themselves. In a word, people should be authentic; they should always behave in ways that reflect their inner beliefs, values, motives, and dispositions.

Within psychology, this idea was popularized in the 1950s and 60s by humanistic psychologists like Carl Rogers and Abraham Maslow, who viewed authenticity as a central component of psychological well-being and a necessary ingredient for self-actualization. And, if we took a poll, I suspect we'd find that most people think that it's important to be authentic, to be yourself, to be real.

But in this lecture, I want you to consider the possibility that authenticity has some serious problems as a psychological construct. That it's either not what we usually assume it is, or that it's not as important as people typically think. Let me start off by posing 4 broad questions about authenticity that raise some intriguing issues.

First, if you look at yourself honestly, I think you'll see that your personality includes a fair amount of inconsistency and even contradictory and incompatible features. Are you an agreeable, even-tempered person? Whatever you say—yes I am, or no I'm not—I bet that you act the opposite way a good deal too. Even the most even-keeled people lose it now and then, and most mean, disagreeable people are sometimes perfectly nice.

Are you a truthful person or a liar? Again, I bet that you say many truthful things as well as some things that aren't true.

So, are you agreeable or disagreeable; are you truthful or a liar? Which one is the real you? Incompatible and contradictory traits exist side-by-side in all of us. And if everybody has all sorts of inconsistent and incompatible characteristics, how do you decide which ones are really you and when you're being authentic? Are you authentically agreeable or disagreeable? Are you authentically an honest person or a liar? Who's the real you?

Let's take that a step further: To know whether you are being authentic, you need to know what you're really like. We all think we have a pretty good idea of what we're like and why we do what we do, but do we? And, if we don't know, then how can we really tell whether or not we're being authentic? Remember from our discussion on nonconscious processes that we aren't aware of many of the factors that influence our behavior. If you aren't aware, and can't be aware, of what's causing you to act the way you do, how can you ever know for certain if a particular reaction is authentic or not? Even if some reaction seems foreign to who you think you are and what you think you're like, maybe it was caused by an aspect of yourself that operates nonconsciously. It really was you, but you didn't know it.

Question 3: Is it good to be authentic? Is it good to always behave in ways that are congruent with how we really are, whatever that might be? Is it good advice to tell someone to be yourself? And if so, why? What's wrong with not being yourself? Here I suspect that you might be starting to think "Now wait a minute. Of course, people should be themselves. We don't want lots of fake, inauthentic people walking around."

But look at it this way: Every one of us has some very good, socially desirable characteristics, and each of us has some not-so-good, or even very bad characteristics. Should we always be authentic with respect to our undesirable traits as well? Should we authentically be ourselves when being ourselves means that we act in undesirable ways that may even hurt other people? If the answer to that question is no—that people shouldn't act congruently with their bad values, motives, beliefs, and personality dispositions—then we need to think about whether being authentic is actually a good thing.

And to top off this baffling set of questions, let me ask one more: Do people ever really behave inauthentically? Is it actually possible to be inauthentic?

Think of it this way: What behavior have you ever engaged in that didn't reflect some genuine value, motive, belief, or disposition that you had? Even when you lie, isn't that really you? Weren't you being authentically dishonest? Even if you are forced to do something against your will, with the proverbial gun to your head, isn't your behavior still an authentic reflection of your values, beliefs, motives, or dispositions? What have you ever done that didn't reflect some authentic part of who you are?

Let me warn you that I'm not going to resolve all of these issues by the end of the lecture. But, fortunately, some of these questions are based on common misconceptions about personality and how it works. And once we clear up those misunderstandings, many of these questions will disappear, although they will be replaced by more questions and a view of how personality works that you may find unsettling. To begin to address these quandaries, we have to dispense with the idea that being authentic means that a person behaves the same way all of the time. Most people think of authenticity that way.

In fact, a student of mine did some research that looked at people's beliefs about what it means to be authentic. She gave a national sample of adults different definitions of authenticity and asked how much they agreed with each one. Let me read you the definition that was selected by the highest percentage of her respondents. The most popular description of authenticity said this:

> Being authentic means being yourself in all situations, regardless of what is going on or who else is there. People who are authentic act basically the same way no matter where they are or who they are with because their actions are an expression of who they truly are. Furthermore, the image of themselves that they present to others is the same all of the time. Authentic people express the same personality characteristics and core values in every situation, regardless of who they are with or what situation they are in.

You know enough about personality by now to realize that we shouldn't expect any normal person to show that kind of absolute consistency in his or her behavior. Healthy, well-adjusted people are flexible in how they respond. Sure, we see consistencies in how people behave across different situations, but behavioral flexibility is necessary for people to handle the challenges of life effectively. No normal person acts "the same way no matter where they are or who they are with." In fact, this definition of authenticity that most people endorse sounds more like a personality disorder than something we should all strive for. As we saw previously, personality disorders are explicitly defined in terms of rigid, inflexible patterns of behavior. Responding the same way in every situation is a sign of a serious psychological problem.

So, if authenticity is going to be a useful construct at all, it can't require absolute consistency. It has to allow people a good deal of flexibility and latitude both because people's personalities are multifaceted and contain incompatible characteristics, and because well-adjusted people tailor their actions to particular situations.

To complicate matters, inconsistency is itself a personality characteristic. People differ in how much their behavior varies across situations. We talked previously about the fact that some people are affected more by situational influences than other people are, so their behavior is less consistent and more variable. Does that mean that they are less authentic than people whose behavior varies less across situations?

It might seem so, but viewed another way, they may be perfectly authentic because the degree to which people's behavior is affected by situational pressures is itself a personality variable. For people whose personality traits cause them to be strongly affected by the situation they're in, being less consistent is actually more authentic. People can be authentically inconsistent. The personality characteristic that is most closely associated with changing one's behavior to meet situational demands is called self-monitoring. People who are high in self-monitoring monitor the degree to which they fit whatever situation they are in and behave in ways that are appropriate given the nature of the situation and the characteristics of the people with whom they're interacting.

In contrast, people low in self-monitoring are less influenced by the immediate situation, so their behavior is somewhat more consistent across situations. Because they're trying to behave appropriately, people who are high in self-monitoring show greater behavioral variability across situations than people low in self-monitoring do. But that doesn't mean that they are less authentic than low self-monitors. In fact, for high self-monitors, a certain degree of inconsistency may be more authentic than consistency is.

There's a tendency to regard people who mold their behavior to fit the situation that they're in as insecure or duplicitous or too concerned about social approval. But we all do it, and we absolutely have to in order to manage life effectively. On top of that, people can act differently in different situations and yet still behave in ways that are congruent with their beliefs, values, motives, and dispositions at all times. And as I noted, for people who are high in self-monitoring, greater variability is even more authentic because that's the way they really are. So, as we move forward in this lecture, I urge you to abandon the idea that being authentic means that a person should always act the same way.

As I said, to strive to be authentic, people have to be able to tell when they are and when they're not behaving congruently with what they are really like. To do that, they have to know about all aspects of their personality, including full details about what motivates their behavior, what they believe, what they value, and all of their psychological characteristics. Without completely understanding themselves and all of the things that influence their behavior, people can't judge whether or not they're being authentic in any particular situation. Most of us assume that we have some kind of special insight into what we're like. But our views of ourselves are far less accurate than most people think. Sure, there are some things about yourself that you understand perfectly well, and some aspects of your self-image are right on target.

But, volumes of research show that people's self-views are not very accurate overall. In many studies, researchers have asked people to rate their own personality characteristics and then compared people's self-ratings both with objective measures of their behavior and personality and with ratings of people who know them very well, people who would presumably have deep insight into what the participants were like. Of course, people do have some insight into their personalities, so they weren't completely clueless about what they were like. But they weren't entirely accurate either.

You can certainly see this when you look at other people. You probably know people who see themselves in a certain way or think that their behavior is motivated by certain things when everybody else can see that those beliefs are not accurate. We just have a harder time seeing those discrepancies in ourselves.

I personally find all of this rather unsettling. We'd all like to think that we know ourselves reasonably well and that we understand why we do what we do. And sometimes, that's the case. But, at other times, it's simply not possible, and we can't tell when we know the truth about ourselves and when we don't. In addition to the fact that it's impossible to know everything about ourselves and that so much of our personality operates nonconsciously, just about everybody sees themselves too positively. We all overestimate our positive qualities and underestimate our negative qualities, and we're biased to attribute our actions to positive, desirable motives rather than negative, undesirable ones. These self-serving biases in our views of ourselves make it virtually impossible to really know who we are. And if that's the case, how do we know when we're being authentic?

Let me mention one other issue that enters into people's beliefs about authenticity. Most of us fall into the trap of thinking of ourselves as a coherent, unified, integrated person. That is, we have the sense that we are a single, psychologically integrated system and not just some big hodgepodge of disconnected values, motives, beliefs, and traits. We sense that all of the diverse pieces of our personality are tightly interconnected, that our beliefs are tied to our motives, that our traits are connected to our emotions, that our values and motives are linked, and so on. So, it seems like our total personality should all work together in some integrated and harmonious way, something like the parts of a well-designed machine. Not only that, but you also probably have the sense that there's some central mechanism inside you that oversees and controls all of this stuff, some central control unit that integrates and manages all of the different parts of your psychological machinery. You feel like there's somebody, or something, in charge of this whole mess, something that oversees all of the parts of your personality and keeps them running smoothly.

But, neither of these perceptions is true. The various parts of your personality are not entirely coherent and integrated and unified, and there's no one in control of all of it. There isn't any central regulatory mechanism that coordinates all of the different parts of your personality and reactions. Yes, you have a center of consciousness that you think of as you that seems to think your thoughts, and feel your emotions, and control your behaviors. But that psychological process that some people think of as their self doesn't have much insight into or control over most of what is happening in your brain. Most of what you feel and do operates outside of your conscious self.

Furthermore, although many of the processes that control your behavior are connected to each other, many of them aren't. Different reactions are mediated by different parts of the brain, which may not be in communication with each other, and aren't controlled by a single, integrating mechanism. And, with no central mechanism that coordinates, integrates, and maintains consistency among all of the parts, there's no reason whatsoever to expect people to be consistent. There's nothing in there that tries to reconcile conflicts between different competing elements of your personality.

Psychologist Robert Kurzban has compared the human mind to a smartphone: to a cell phone with lots of different apps. Each little computer program that makes up a phone app contributes a separate, specialized function to the phone; there's one for news, one for maps, another for weather, one for alarms, one for email, one to surf the web, and so on. Yet, although these apps use the same operating system and sometimes rely on each other—your maps and weather app might both rely on your GPS location—there's nothing in the phone that forces any coherence among them. In fact, if you have

3 weather apps, they might give you slightly different temperatures or forecasts. And if you have different news apps, they might put entirely different spins on the news. Each app does its own thing without much concern for what other apps are doing. Kurzban says that the human mind works much in the same way. You have many, many different circuits that do different things, but they can operate somewhat independently. And like a smartphone, there's no central mechanism that forces consistency among the various programs.

We don't want to take the phone app metaphor too far, but it makes the point that different parts of your personality can operate somewhat independently while each doing its job. And it shows that you can have a very functional system that processes information and responds without the oversight of a single controller that's trying to maintain consistency among all the parts. So, the notion of authenticity has problems because there's no reason to expect the human mind to display the sort of consistency or internal coherence that the concept of authenticity implies.

As I've struggled with these issues surrounding authenticity, it's occurred to me that maybe we've been thinking about the topic completely wrong in the sense that our notion of authenticity isn't compatible with the way that personality actually works. I can't present any concrete data to support this, but I've started to think that, contrary to how it seems, people are actually always authentic. Or to say it differently, maybe it makes no sense to think that people could ever behave incongruently with aspects of their personality, motives, values, and beliefs.

Look at it this way: Almost all human behavior is goal-directed. That is, most of your behavior is intended to achieve some goal or fulfill some motive. Sometimes the goal is conscious—you know what you're trying to achieve by doing something—and often the goal is not conscious—you do things for reasons that you're not consciously aware of. But it doesn't make much sense to say that you did something for no reason whatsoever—that your behavior wasn't motivated. You may not know why you did what you did, but there was some reason, some motive, some goal.

Sometimes the goals that are active and operational for us at a given moment are compatible with each other. Maybe I'm motivated to be healthy, and I'm motivated to lose weight, so I eat a salad for dinner. But sometimes we have goals that are incompatible. One goal is leading us toward one action, and the other goal is leading us toward a different action, maybe even one that's incompatible with the first one. Maybe I have the goal to be healthy, but I'm also motivated to enjoy a delicious fatty and sugar-filled meal. But they're both genuine goals, and whichever one I choose, I'm acting consistently with one genuine goal and inconsistently with the other genuine goal. Different apps on the cell phone of my mind are open, but only one can control my behavior at a time.

So, when we do things that we don't want to do, or think we shouldn't do, those behaviors are not inauthentic. They're simply motivated by goals that are incompatible with other goals or with our vision of the person we want or think we ought to be. For example, most of us think that a person should be honest, and we probably see ourselves as basically honest people, with occasional lapses. When we lie, we're simply pursuing a different goal than to be honest, maybe to get out of trouble or to not hurt somebody's feelings. But the lie is in the service of a genuine goal that we have, so it's as authentic as telling the truth. I can't prove that all intentional behavior is authentic, but as a psychologist, I can't see any other way to think about it. People can't help but to behave congruently with their inner beliefs, motives, values, and dispositions. So all behavior, even if it's inconsistent or even duplicitous, would seem to be authentic.

Let me summarize a few major points before I move on. First, a certain degree of inconsistency is perfectly normal, as well as adaptive and functional. We're complex, multi-faceted individuals whose personalities contain features that are inconsistent and even incompatible. That's just the way we are. And there's no central psychological mechanism that coordinates or maintains consistency among the parts. In fact, in many cases, the various parts of our personalities operate pretty independently and can push our behavior in contradictory directions. And, finally, in my view, it doesn't make much psychological sense to think that people can ever do things that are incongruent with how they really are. If I'm right, then every action is authentic in the sense of being congruent with genuine aspects of who we are, and it's impossible to ever be inauthentic.

But if the human mind is designed in a way that leads to inconsistent behavior, and there's no mechanism that maintains consistency or congruence, and we can't ever judge whether we are behaving authentically, then why do people sometimes feel inauthentic? And why do we place such a value on authenticity and urge people to live congruently with their true selves? Let me give you 2 reasons.

The first is that, in order to make the right choices in life, it helps to know who you are and what you're like as best you can so that you'll increase the chances that you'll make decisions that are congruent with your psychological characteristics. Even though some of your characteristics are incompatible with each other and even though you'll never know for certain what you're like or why you do what you do, understanding yourself as well as you can certainly pays off in terms of making good choices in life. It's not a matter of being authentic but rather a matter of living in a way that best fits your psychological inclinations and thus maximizes your well-being.

So-called feelings of inauthenticity are often a sign that you don't understand something about yourself. It's like a warning that says: You don't know yourself well enough to understand why you did what you did. Feelings of inauthenticity aren't telling you that you behaved incongruently with how you really are. Instead, those feelings are telling you that you don't know why you did whatever you did. If you understood yourself better, you'd realize that your actions were not really incongruent. Your behavior may have been inconsistent with conscious values that you hold, or incongruent with what you were intentionally trying to do, or contrary to the kind of person you want to be, but something inside you led you to do what you did.

You know, when people do something bad or behave in a way that goes against their conscious values, they sometimes say something like, "Oh, that wasn't really me." Yes, it was! And if you understood all of your beliefs, values, motives, and dispositions fully, you'd be able to see how it was congruent with genuine aspects of yourself. It might have been incompatible with some of your characteristics as well, but it wasn't actually inauthentic.

The second reason that people take authenticity seriously and have viewed it as a virtue since ancient times is that we are under social pressure to be authentic. Having high-quality social interactions and relationships with other people requires that we understand them reasonably well. We want to know what other people are like, what motivates them, what they believe, whether they can be trusted, what their game is. Misperceiving what other people are like almost always leads to problems.

To know other people well, to know what they're really like, we have to assume that what they say and do is congruent with their actual beliefs, motives, values, and personality. We have to assume that they are conveying accurate and honest impressions of themselves. If they don't—if they appear to be someone they're not—then we'll be at a disadvantage in our interactions and relationships with them.

So, we're all under social pressure to be reasonably upfront about who we are and what we're like. People who are viewed as fake, who appear to be trying to lead others to form impressions of them that are not true, are mistrusted, disliked, and avoided. So, when we feel inauthentic, it's often an indication that we need to be careful about how we are being viewed by others—that we might be appearing fake to other people. Of course, we're all fake from time to time, saying things that we know we don't believe and doing things that are inconsistent with our values and motives. But again, this isn't a question of authenticity; we are authentically being fake. But the feelings that we interpret as inauthenticity help to warn us about how we're coming across and caution us to tread carefully.

The bottom line is that the pressures that we feel to be authentic are functional. They let us know that we don't understand ourselves well enough to know why we did some seemingly incongruent thing. And they caution us when we do things that might lead other people to view us as fake or dishonest. So the psychological processes that underlie the feelings that we interpret as authenticity and inauthenticity are a useful part of our personalities. But not for the reasons that most people assume.

THE WELL-ADJUSTED PERSONALITY

LECTURE 24

This lecture will examine the relationship between personality and what most psychologists consider healthy psychological adjustment. It's best not to think of psychological adjustment itself as a trait; instead, it's more useful to view the degree to which people are well adjusted or poorly adjusted as dependent on particular patterns or configurations of traits. Adjustment also shouldn't be thought of as something that's a permanent and unchanging part of a person's personality; our level of psychological adjustment can vary a great deal across time as situations change and as we change.

5 CRITERIA OF PSYCHOLOGICAL ADJUSTMENT

- There's no definitive list of characteristics that define an adjusted, well-functioning person, but most psychologists would agree that 5 key ingredients are necessary:

  1. a lack of genuine psychopathology or mental illness
  2. the ability to get along with other people and maintain some supportive close relationships
  3. the ability to pursue and achieve one's goals
  4. the ability to cope with problems that arise in life
  5. a sense of subjective well-being.

- A person who meets all 5 of these criteria is functioning reasonably well. If any one of them is missing over a period of time, however, the person is probably struggling psychologically.

- The first criterion—lack of psychopathology or mental illness—seems obvious. A person who currently has some serious psychological problem is clearly not functioning well at the moment. In addition to personality disorders, other serious problems, such as schizophrenia, bipolar disorder, PTSD, and depression, can compromise an individual's well-being.

- The second characteristic that signals good psychological adjustment is an ability to get along with other people and have some close, supportive, high-quality relationships. People who can't get along with others, whose social interactions are full of conflict and negative emotions, and who can't maintain stable and supportive relationships with friends, romantic partners, family members, and people at work are not dealing effectively with a central feature of human life.

- Healthy, well-adjusted people generally get along with other people, have mostly positive interactions, and have at least a few strong and supportive relationships that help promote their well-being.

- Being higher in agreeableness and lower in neuroticism is associated with having higher-quality relationships of all kinds.

> Nobody glides through life without psychological difficulties of one kind or another.

Being low in agreeableness and high in neuroticism is associated with more conflict, negative social interactions, and unhappy relationships. These traits also predict the stability of friendships and romantic relationships. People lower in agreeableness and higher in neuroticism have more trouble maintaining their relationships over time.

- People's beliefs about other people—for example, their general tendency to trust others—and the value they place on relationships also influence how they approach their interactions and relationships with other people.

- In addition, characteristics that are associated with socioemotional intelligence predict the quality and length of people's relationships. Socioemotional intelligence involves skills that are needed to interact effectively with other people, such as the ability to read and understand other people, to empathize with others' problems and feelings, and to carry on meaningful conversations, as well as the willingness to compromise. So, people who are more empathic, more socially skilled, and less self-centered tend to have better relationships.

- Self-regulation is also important for relationships. People who are better at controlling their reactions to other people get along better with others.

- Third, well-adjusted people are able to pursue and achieve the goals they set for themselves. The point is not that everybody should necessarily try to achieve great things or always strive to be the best. Those goals are okay for some people, but for other people, they aren't congruent with what's most important to them. Rather, from the standpoint of psychological adjustment, the important thing is that people should be reasonably effective at pursuing whatever goals they do have.

- Two characteristics are essential for achieving one's goals, almost without regard to what they are: conscientiousness and the ability to self-regulate. In addition, it helps if people have an internal locus of control. People with an internal locus of control believe that their outcomes are due to their own efforts rather than external, outside influences, so they're more likely to take action and to stick with tasks that become challenging.

- It also helps to have high self-efficacy—to believe that you're able to accomplish what you want to accomplish. Not having confidence that one can achieve a particular goal undermines motivation, keeps people from getting started, and leads them to give up quickly when problems arise. Being too confident can also create problems, but in general, people with higher self-efficacy, either in general or on a particular task, are more likely to accomplish the goals they set for themselves.

- The fourth requirement for psychological adjustment is to be able to cope with the problems that inevitably arise in life. Being well adjusted means being able to cope with life events emotionally and to take appropriate actions to solve problems that arise when possible.

- The word "resilient" is often used to describe people who handle their problems well and who bounce back quickly after major problems and traumatic events. Like adjustment, resilience isn't actually a personality characteristic as much as it's a description of how people respond when they confront problems and stressful events.

None of us handles every problem with equanimity and grace, but people who regularly have trouble coping emotionally with their problems or have trouble doing what's needed to deal with them effectively struggle in life.

- To respond in a resilient fashion, it helps a great deal to be relatively low in neuroticism. People lower in neuroticism still get frustrated, upset, and stressed out when things fall apart, but their reactions are weaker and don't last as long as those of people who are higher in neuroticism. They're also less likely to ruminate about their problems when there's nothing that can be done at the moment, and they tend to worry less about things that might or might not ever happen in the future.

- In addition to low neuroticism, optimism predicts how well people cope with stressful events. It helps to get through tough times if you're optimistic that things will eventually get better.

- Certain styles of coping also promote well-being. Research has identified many ways that people try to deal with problems and stressful situations. And personality predicts the strategies that people tend to use.

- For example, both extraversion and conscientiousness predict a greater use of problem solving and cognitive restructuring (that is, reframing problems in a more positive way), whereas neuroticism is associated with lower use of these strategies. Neuroticism predicts strategies that tend to be less effective, such as wishful thinking and withdrawal, although it also predicts seeking support from other people.

- Some coping strategies are more effective and more adaptive than others, but evidence also shows that people who are flexible in the coping strategies that they use cope better overall.

- Different types of problems and stressors call for different strategies. Even strategies that have gotten a bad reputation for being maladaptive and ineffective—such as distracting yourself, avoiding the problem, and denying that the problem even exists—may sometimes be appropriate and effective. We don't know much about the particular characteristics that help people cope flexibly, but researchers are studying them.

- The final thing that people need for adjustment is high subjective well-being—the general sense that life is going reasonably well. You might think that if the other 4 criteria are fulfilled, people will naturally feel good about their lives and about themselves, but that's not necessarily the case.

> A meta-analysis of more than 100 studies showed that flexibility was related to psychological adjustment, well-being, and mental health.

- The world is full of people who are free of psychopathology, have good relationships with other people, are effective at achieving goals, and deal effectively with problems but still are not satisfied and happy. This signals that something is amiss that is undermining the person's well-being, despite the fact that things seem to be going reasonably well.

- What undermines a sense of well-being is that people are talking to themselves in their own minds in particular, dysfunctional ways. They're adding a layer of thinking and evaluation on top of their lives that's mostly unnecessary and making things harder on themselves than they need to be. Many of the sources of poor adjustment are self-inflicted as people who should be reasonably satisfied think themselves into unnecessary unhappiness.

WELL-ADJUSTED PERSONALITY TYPES

- In the broadest sense, who are the most well-adjusted people, and what are they like? To answer this question, researchers have used methods that statistically compare people across a large number of personality characteristics simultaneously. These studies repeatedly reveal 3 qualitatively different types of people, and these 3 basic types of people differ mostly in terms of their psychological adjustment.

- First, all of the studies identified a personality type that is reasonably well adjusted. The researchers called these people the resilient type. The data show that resilient people are low in neuroticism and higher than average in conscientiousness, extraversion, agreeableness, and openness. They also tend to have higher self-esteem and to score low in shyness. Overall, this resilient group had a personality profile showing that they were secure, conscientious, adaptable, and flexible people who had good relationships with others. These characteristics map pretty well onto the features of adjustment mentioned previously in this lecture.

- The other 2 personality types involved people who are less well adjusted than the resilient group, but they are less well adjusted in different ways. One group—called the overcontrolled personality type—is characterized by high neuroticism. Overcontrolled people not only experience a good deal of negative emotion, but they tend to be inhibited and shy. They also score lower in extraversion, and they're less sociable. They have fewer relationships, and the relationships they do have tend to be less close and less secure. They seem to show an insecure attachment style and have lower self-esteem.

- The third personality type is the undercontrolled personality. Undercontrolled people also score higher than average in neuroticism, although not as high as the overcontrolled type, but their primary characteristic is low conscientiousness. Undercontrolled people are impulsive, undependable, and prone to engaging in risky behavior. They also tend to be low in agreeableness, sometimes to the point of behaving in mean and antisocial ways.

◆ None of the studies directly measured self-regulation, but one gets the sense that undercontrolled people have problems doing what they're supposed to do and behaving themselves. The studies showed that people who fit the undercontrolled personality profile have fewer close relationships, their relationships are less close and more difficult, and their relationships tend not to last as long. They also tend to be less popular among their peers.

◆ Addressing psychological adjustment by classifying everybody into one of 3 personality types is an oversimplification that misses nuances and differences among people within each of these types. But it does reveal a few things about personality and adjustment:

1. In general, there is only one basic way to be well adjusted but 2 basic ways in which to be poorly adjusted. Fundamentally, the difference between being well adjusted and poorly adjusted lies in how high people are in neuroticism and how well they get along with other people.

2. The specific characteristics that create the resilient, overcontrolled, and undercontrolled personality types are correlated in nonrandom ways that produce these patterns. In other words, the various characteristics that create each of these 3 types of people tend to go together. People who have one of the characteristics in a profile also tend to have the others.

3. As we deal with problems in ourselves and in other people, it may be helpful to think about the degree to which those problems reflect the overcontrolled profile versus the undercontrolled profile. Looking beneath the behavioral and emotional manifestations of adjustment problems allows us to think about the psychological characteristics and processes that undermine adjustment and lower well-being in any particular case.

> Extreme childhood trauma can affect well-being, but as long as parents or other adults provide the needed emotional support and rational guidance, a certain amount of stress, struggle, and adversity in childhood actually promotes better long-term adjustment than if the child has no negative experiences.

- Most of the traits that make some people better adjusted than others have a genetic basis. People are genetically predisposed not only to be relatively well adjusted or poorly adjusted, but people who are poorly adjusted are genetically predisposed to be prone to either the overcontrolled or undercontrolled pattern. Genes account for no more than about half of the variability in these traits, so environment and experience also play a role.

- Adjustment and resilience generally develop naturally during childhood and adolescence as long as things don't happen that interfere and mess up their development.

- Setting genetics aside, the most important thing that contributes to long-term adjustment is effective parenting, and it seems to do so by helping the development of important adaptive systems. Two dimensions of parenting in particular are critical: warmth and support on one hand and reasonable, explicit expectations on the other. This combination has repeatedly been shown to result in positive psychological adjustment.

Suggested Reading

Catalino and Fredrickson, "A Tuesday in the Life of a Flourisher."

Kaufman, "Which Personality Traits Are Most Predictive of Well-Being?"

Weir, "Maximizing Children's Resilience."

Questions to Consider

1. This lecture identified 5 primary determinants of psychological adjustment: a lack of psychopathology or mental illness, the ability to get along with other people and maintain supportive relationships, the ability to pursue and achieve one's goals, the ability to cope with problems in life, and a sense of subjective well-being. In thinking about yourself, which of these 5 is the weakest link? Which one is the greatest impediment to having optimal psychological well-being?

2. No matter how well adjusted you are, when you experience psychological or behavioral problems, do they tend to be of the overcontrolled or undercontrolled variety? Do you see any links between your personality characteristics and whether your struggles primarily reflect an overcontrolled or undercontrolled personality?

THE WELL-ADJUSTED PERSONALITY
LECTURE 24 TRANSCRIPT

When we dig deeply into people's personalities, we find remarkable complexity: a large variety of traits, motivations, emotional tendencies, beliefs, self-evaluations, styles of thinking, self-regulatory processes, and more. Appreciating that complexity gives us greater understanding of the fascinating variations in human behavior. Yet when we step back and look at the totality of people's personalities—how all of these characteristics play out in people's lives—it's clear that some people's personalities work better for them than other people's personalities do. Certain patterns of characteristics are associated with effective behavior and a high level of psychological well-being, and other patterns of characteristics are associated with emotional and behavioral struggles.

I'm not talking here about personality disorders or other psychological problems that qualify people for clinical diagnoses like those we've discussed previously. I'm talking about more common, run-of-the-mill problems that otherwise normal people have. In this final lecture, we're going to draw upon much of what we've learned throughout the course to take a look at the relationship between personality and what most psychologists consider healthy psychological adjustment.

It's best not to think of psychological adjustment itself as a trait, as if it's a single personality characteristic that's associated with how well people function in their lives. Instead, it's more useful to view the degree to which people are well-adjusted or poorly-adjusted as dependent on particular patterns or configurations of traits. Some combinations of traits promote psychological well-being, and other combinations diminish it. To understand adjustment, we have to look for personality patterns that are associated with effective behavior and emotional well-being. We also shouldn't think of adjustment as something that's a permanent and unchanging part of a person's personality. People's level of psychological adjustment can vary a great deal across time, so that at some points in their life, they're managing things just fine. But at other times, they're struggling psychologically. Nobody glides through life without psychological difficulties of one kind or another.

Our level of adjustment can change over time for 2 reasons. The first is that situations change. Our personality might have worked well under one set of circumstances; in fact, we might have even been flourishing. But then, when the circumstances of life changed—we lost our job or had children or moved to a new city or were promoted into a position at work with too much responsibility—those same personality characteristics were not as adaptive as they once were. Or maybe the opposite happened: maybe you struggled psychologically when you were younger, but once you got out on your own, you managed life just fine. Our level of adjustment also changes over time because we change. Sometimes we change in ways that help us function better. We learn new strategies, have new experiences, become more mature, read self-help books, or talk to a counselor.

And, sometimes we change in ways that lead us to function worse than we did before. Maybe something shakes our self-confidence, or we become too depressed to manage life, or we have a traumatic experience that leaves us with post-traumatic stress disorder. So, our psychological adjustment can wax and wane. But even so, at any particular time, some people are more adjusted than other people are, and that's what we want to examine here.

To talk usefully about personality and adjustment, we have to define what it means to be well-adjusted. There's no definitive list of characteristics that define an adjusted, well-functioning person, but let me tell you what I see as 5 key ingredients that I think most psychologists would agree are necessary in order to say a person is well-adjusted. Let me just list them first, and then we'll go through them one-by-one and talk about the personality characteristics that are needed in each case.

I think it's safe to say that the main requirements of being well-adjusted are:

1. A lack of genuine psychopathology or mental illness.

2. The ability to get along with other people and maintain some supportive close relationships.

3. The ability to pursue and achieve one's goals.

4. The ability to cope with problems that arise in life.

5. A sense of subjective well-being.

A person who meets all 5 of these criteria is functioning reasonably well. If any one of them is missing over a period of time, however, the person is probably struggling psychologically. Let's go through these aspects of adjustment one-by-one and think about the characteristics that predispose people to meet or fail to meet each criterion.

The first criterion for being well-adjusted—lack of psychopathology or mental illness—seems obvious. A person who currently has some serious psychological problem is clearly not functioning well at the moment. We've talked about personality disorders, which clearly compromise well-being, and there are other serious problems that are obvious indicators that people are not doing well, such as schizophrenia, bipolar disorder, PTSD, and depression. But these sorts of problems are topics for a course in abnormal or clinical psychology, and they're not fundamentally about personality characteristics, so we won't go into detail about them here.

The second characteristic that signals good psychological adjustment is an ability to get along with other people and having some close, supportive, and high quality relationships. People who can't get along with others, whose social interactions are full of conflict and negative emotions, and who can't maintain stable, supportive relationships with friends, romantic partners, family members, and people at work are not dealing effectively with a central feature of human life. Healthy, well-adjusted people generally get along with other people, they have mostly positive interactions, and they have at least a couple of strong, supportive relationships that help to promote their well-being. The question is: What psychological characteristics do people need in order to have positive relationships with other people?

Most notably, being higher in agreeableness and lower in neuroticism is associated with having higher quality relationships of all kinds. Or to look at it the other way, being low in agreeableness and high in neuroticism is associated with more conflict, negative social interactions, and unhappy relationships. And these traits also predict the stability of friendships and romantic relationships. People lower in agreeableness and higher in neuroticism have more trouble maintaining their relationships over time. People's beliefs about other people, for example, their general tendency to trust others—at least until someone shows they can't be trusted—and the value they place on relationships also influence how they approach their interactions and relationships with other people.

In addition, characteristics that are associated with socio-emotional intelligence predict the quality and length of people's relationships. Socio-emotional intelligence involves skills that are needed to interact effectively with other people, such as the ability to read and understand other people, to empathize with others' problems and feelings, and to carry on meaningful conversations, as well as the willingness to compromise. So, people who are more empathic, more socially skilled, and less self-centered tend to have better relationships.

As we discussed previously, self-regulation is also important for relationships. People who are better at controlling their reactions to other people get along better with others. In brief, there's a relatively small set of traits, beliefs, values, and skills that lead to better relationships with other people and thereby promote well-being.

Third, well-adjusted people are able to pursue and achieve the goals they set for themselves, whatever those goals happen to be. They tend to behave in ways that help them perform up to their level of ability in school, and they tend to do a good job at work. The point is not that everybody should necessarily try to achieve great things or always strive to be the best. Those goals are okay for some people, but for other people, they aren't congruent with what's most important to them. Rather, from the standpoint of psychological adjustment, the important thing is that people should be reasonably effective at pursuing whatever goals they do have.

As we saw when we talked about self-regulation, 2 characteristics are essential for achieving one's goals, almost without regard to what they are. One is conscientiousness. It's pretty difficult to achieve any goal if you're not reasonably conscientious. The other characteristic is the ability to self-regulate. As we discussed earlier, to achieve any goal, people have to make themselves take action, inhibit behaviors that would interfere with achieving the goal, and stay on task until it's accomplished. People who have difficulty with self-control skills involving initiation, inhibition, and continuation often have difficulty achieving their goals.

In addition, it helps if people have an internal locus of control. You may recall that people with an internal locus of control believe that their outcomes are due to their own efforts rather than external, outside influences. So, they're more likely to take action and to stick with tasks that become challenging. It also helps to have high self-efficacy—to believe that you're able to accomplish what you want to accomplish. Not having confidence that one can achieve a particular goal undermines motivation, keeps people from getting started, and leads them to give up quickly when problems arise. Being too confident can also create problems but, in general, people with higher self-efficacy, either in general or on a particular task, are more likely to accomplish the goals they set for themselves.

The fourth requirement for psychological adjustment is to be able to cope with the problems that inevitably arise in life. If your life is anything like mine, rarely a day goes by without some problem or frustration or hassle. It's always something. Fortunately, most of these things are rather minor, but life also has its share of big, serious problems as well. Being well-adjusted means being able to cope with these kinds of events emotionally and to take appropriate actions to solve problems that arise when possible. None of us handles each and every problem with equanimity and grace, but people who regularly have trouble coping emotionally with their problems or have trouble doing what's needed to deal with them effectively struggle in life.

You sometimes hear the word resilient used to describe people who handle their problems well and who bounce back quickly after major problems and traumatic events. Like adjustment, resilience isn't actually a personality characteristic as much as it's a description of how people respond when they confront problems and stressful events. So, what does it take to cope well and to respond in a resilient fashion?

First, it helps a great deal to be relatively low in neuroticism. People lower in neuroticism just tend to take things in stride better. Sure, they get frustrated, upset, and stressed-out when things fall apart, but their reactions are weaker and don't last as long as those of people who are higher in neuroticism. And they're also less likely to ruminate about their problems when there's nothing that can be done at the moment, and they tend to worry less about things that might or might not ever happen in the future. In addition to low neuroticism, optimism predicts how well people cope with stressful events. It helps to get through tough times if you're optimistic that things will eventually get better.

Certain styles of coping also promote well-being. Research has identified many ways that people try to deal with problems and stressful situations. For example, some people try to reframe the situation in a positive way; others take action to try to solve the problem; still others distract themselves so they don't think about it, or they deny that there is a problem, or seek support from other people; and so on. Personality predicts the strategies that people tend to use. For example, both extraversion and conscientiousness predict a greater use of problem-solving and cognitive restructuring—that is, reframing problems in a more positive way—whereas neuroticism is associated with lower use of these strategies. Neuroticism predicts strategies that tend to be less effective, such as wishful thinking and withdrawal, although it also predicts seeking support from other people.

Researchers have generally assumed that some coping strategies are more effective and more adaptive than others, which is certainly true. But evidence also shows that people who are flexible in the coping strategies that they use cope better overall. A meta-analysis of over 100 studies showed that coping flexibility was related to psychological adjustment, well-being, and mental health. Different sorts of problems and stressors call for different strategies. Even strategies that have gotten a bad rap for being maladaptive and ineffective, such as distracting yourself, avoiding the problem, and denying that the problem even exists, may sometimes be appropriate and effective. We don't know much about the particular characteristics that help people to cope flexibly, but researchers are now studying them.

The final thing that people need for adjustment is high subjective well-being—the general sense that life is going reasonably well. You might think that if the other 4 criteria are fulfilled, people will naturally feel good about their lives and about themselves. But that's not necessarily the case. A person can be free of psychopathology, have good relationships with other people, be effective at achieving goals, and deal effectively with problems, yet still not be satisfied and happy. The world is full of such people, and it signals that something is amiss that is undermining the person's well-being, despite the fact that things seem to be going reasonably well.

Sometimes it's tied up in people's expectations about themselves: expectations of how good they should be, or how much they should accomplish, or what their lives should be like. Some people's expectations are so high that they will never feel satisfied with themselves and with their lives, no matter what. In other cases, people have internalized such negative beliefs about themselves that they can't ever feel good about things even when life is going well. People whose parents neglected, rejected, or abused them as children are particularly likely to carry negative self-images through their life.

Still other people struggle to find meaning in life. They can see that their lives are objectively going well, but they lack a sense of purpose or meaning. I could go on, but you get the idea. What all of these things have in common that undermines a sense of well-being is that people are talking to themselves in their own minds in particular, dysfunctional ways. They're adding a layer of thinking and evaluation on top of their lives that's mostly unnecessary and making things harder on themselves that they need to be. Many of the sources of poor adjustment are self-inflicted as people who ought to be reasonably satisfied think themselves into unnecessary unhappiness.

If your life is such that you are free of serious psychological problems; you get along well with other people and have supportive, rewarding relationships; you're reasonably effective at pursuing and accomplishing goals that are important to you; you handle most problems that arise reasonably well; and you're generally happy and satisfied with life, then I'd say that, number 1, you're a very fortunate person, and number 2, you're pretty well-adjusted. But what makes a person that way?

I've mentioned some of the specific personality characteristics that affect well-being, but typically any single trait isn't enough to make someone well-adjusted. It's broader patterns of traits that contribute to adjustment. But which patterns? In the broadest possible sense, who are the most well-adjusted people and what are they like?

To answer this question, researchers have used methods that statistically compare people across a large number of personality characteristics simultaneously. If you and I complete measures of, say, 20 characteristics of various kinds, we can calculate a statistic that indicates how similar you and I are across this set of 20 attributes. How much does my profile of personality characteristics, as a whole, resemble your profile? How much do we tend to score low and high on the same traits? Imagine that we did this not just for you and me but for several hundred people. We could calculate a statistical index of how much each person resembled every other person across this set of 20 characteristics. Looking at each pair of people in a sample of 100 individuals gives us millions of comparisons.

With all of these comparisons in hand, researchers then conduct analyses that cluster people into groups of individuals whose profiles are very similar to each other. If you and I have similar psychological profiles, the analysis would put us in the same group, but if our profiles differ, we'll end up in different groups. Essentially, this process identifies types of people based on their personality profiles. You may remember that I said previously that personality researchers don't talk about types of people very often, because most personality characteristics are not categorical types. Instead, we think of personality in terms of continuous trait dimensions.

But in this case, when we're dealing with many different traits simultaneously, it makes sense to see whether we can identify types of people who share the same patterns of traits. These analyses tell us whether there are clusters or groups of people who resemble each other in their profiles of traits. If there are, then researchers examine how those groups of people, how those different types, differ from one another psychologically.

The interesting thing is that, across several studies, conducted by different researchers on diverse samples of participants of different ages from around the world, the same 3 groups show up again and again. These studies repeatedly reveal 3 qualitatively different types of people. In every study, the researchers also tested models that included fewer and more than 3 types, but the results consistently showed that people fall into 3 large clusters. And for our purposes, the important thing is that those 3 basic types of people differ mostly in terms of their psychological adjustment.

First, all of the studies identified a personality type that is reasonably well-adjusted. The researchers called these people the resilient type. The data show that resilient people are low in neuroticism, which makes sense, but they're also higher than average in conscientiousness, extraversion, agreeableness, and openness. They also tend to have higher self-esteem and to score low in shyness. Overall, this resilient group had a personality profile showing that they were secure, conscientious, adaptable, and flexible people who had good relationships with others. These characteristics map pretty well onto the features of adjustment I just described.

The other 2 personality types involved people who are less well-adjusted than the resilient group, but they are less well-adjusted in different ways. One group, called the over-controlled personality type, is characterized by high neuroticism. Over-controlled people not only experience a good deal of negative emotion, but they tend to be inhibited and shy. They also score lower in extraversion, and they're less sociable. Not surprisingly, then, over-controlled people have fewer relationships, and the relationships they do have tend to be less close and less secure. They seem to show an insecure attachment style, and like insecurely attached people, they have lower self-esteem. The picture one gets of the over-controlled type is of a person who tends to be unhappy and anxious and somewhat lonely, and who is not very sociable or secure with other people.

The third personality type revealed in these studies is the under-controlled personality. Under-controlled people also score higher than average in neuroticism, although not as high as the over-controlled type, but their primary characteristic is low conscientiousness. Under-controlled people are, well, under-controlled. They're impulsive, undependable, and prone to engaging in risky behavior. They also tend to be low in agreeableness, sometimes to the point of behaving in mean and antisocial ways. None of the studies directly measured self-regulation, but one gets the sense that under-controlled people have problems doing what they're supposed to and behaving themselves. The studies showed that people who fit the under-controlled personality profile have fewer close relationships, that their relationships are less close and more difficult, with significantly more conflict, and their relationships tend not to last as long. They also tend to be less popular among their peers.

Obviously, talking about psychological adjustment by classifying everybody into one of 3 personality types is an over-simplification that misses nuances and differences among people within each of these types. But it does reveal a couple of things about personality and adjustment. First, in general, there is only one basic way to be well-adjusted but 2 basic ways in which to be poorly adjusted. Fundamentally, the difference between being well-adjusted and poorly adjusted lies in how high people are in neuroticism and how well they get along with other people.

Second, the specific characteristics that create the resilient, over-controlled, and under-controlled personality types are correlated in nonrandom ways that produce these patterns. In other words, it's not the case that people develop a variety of separate characteristics, some good and some bad, and people who just happen to end up with a greater number of less adaptive characteristics have more adjustment issues. Instead, the various characteristics that create each of these 3 types of people tend to go together. People who have one of the characteristics in a profile also tend to have the others.

Third, as we deal with problems in ourselves and in other people, it may be helpful to think about the degree to which those problems reflect the over-controlled profile versus the under-controlled profile. Looking beneath the behavioral and emotional manifestations of adjustment problems allows us to think about the psychological characteristics and processes that undermine adjustment and lower well-being in any particular case. So, people differ in adjustment in 3 basic ways. But where do these patterns come from? Why are some people better-adjusted than other people are?

You won't be surprised that most of these traits have a genetic basis. We've already talked about the fact that all of the big five personality traits have sizable heritabilities, which is also true of characteristics that underlie self-regulation. So, people are genetically predisposed not only to be relatively well-adjusted or poorly-adjusted, but people who are poorly adjusted are genetically predisposed to be prone to either the over-controlled or under-controlled pattern. But, of course, genes account for no more than about half of the variability in these traits, so environment and experience clearly play a role. I won't rehash what I've already said about environmental and experiential causes of these characteristics, but let me say a couple of things about childhood development.

Early work on adjustment and resilience tended to view people who deal particularly well with life as somehow unusual or special. Researchers had the sense that children who grow up to be well-adjusted adults must have some special genetic predispositions or have had some highly unusual parents or experiences. But as time went on, it became clear that adjustment and resilience generally develop naturally during childhood and adolescence as long as things don't happen that interfere and mess up their development.

Setting genetics aside, the most important thing that contributes to long-term adjustment is effective parenting, and it seems to do so by helping the development of important adaptive systems. Two dimensions of parenting in particular are critical. First, parents who are responsive and nurturing, who are warm, understanding, and empathic both provide support to their children and model positive social behaviors. Children need ongoing love and support to become well-adjusted. At the same time, parents foster adjustment by having age-appropriate expectations for their children. Parents who have a rational approach to parenting in which they discuss their expectations and rules with the child foster a child's ability to understand the reasons for rules and to regulate his or her own behavior.

This combination of warmth and support on one hand and reasonable, explicit expectations on the other has repeatedly been shown to result in positive psychological adjustment. This parenting style doesn't necessarily assure that a child will grow up to be well-adjusted—many other things can intrude—but lack of warmth, support, and appropriate guidance certainly interferes with good adjustment. Parents who are cold, distant, and rejecting lower children's long-term adjustment, as do parents whose expectations are either too lax or too strict.

By the way, although researchers once assumed that adverse, stressful experiences in childhood undermine adjustment and resilience, we now know that the relationship between childhood adversity and adjustment is more complex. Certainly, extreme trauma can affect well-being, but as long as parents or other adults provide the needed emotional support and rational guidance, a certain amount of stress, struggle, and adversity in childhood actually promotes better long-term adjustment than if the child has no negative experiences at all.

At heart, we all want mostly the same sorts of things: to be healthy and happy, to have good relationships, to achieve our goals, and to cope with all the stuff that happens. But because of our genetics and upbringing and experiences, we each develop our own ways of thinking, feeling, and behaving as we deal with the opportunities and challenges of life. I hope that gaining a better understanding of the great diversity in people's traits, motives, emotions, beliefs, values, and other characteristics helps you to make a little more sense out of other people's behavior. I think it can also serve as a reminder that, underneath all of these differences, we're all just trying to get by.

Many of the problems we encounter in life are fundamentally problems with how people think, feel, and behave. I'm hopeful that you can use what you've learned in this course to think about personality—your own personality and the personalities of the people around you—in a more informed and effective way.

BIBLIOGRAPHY

Altemeyer, Robert. *The Authoritarians*. 2006. https://theauthoritarians.org/options-for-getting-the-book/ A free online book on the authoritarian personality by the expert on right-wing authoritarianism.

———. *The Authoritarian Specter*. Cambridge, MA: Harvard University Press, 1996. A summary of research on the authoritarian personality and its impact on society from a leading expert on the topic.

Baker, Catherine. *Behavioral Genetics: An Introduction to How Genes and Environments Interact through Development to Shape Differences in Mood, Personality, and Intelligence*. New York: American Association for the Advancement of Science and the Hastings Center, 2004. https://www.aaas.org/page/behavioral-genetics-publications. An introduction to behavioral genetics for nonscientists, along with a discussion of its ethical and social implications. Free download.

Bargh, John. *Before You Know It: The Unconscious Reasons We Do What We Do*. New York: Simon and Schuster, 2017. An engaging look at unconscious influences on behavior by an influential researcher on this topic.

Bartz, Andrea. "Sense and Sensitivity (A Guide to the Highly Sensitive Person)." *Psychology Today*, July 5, 2011, 72–76. https://www.psychologytoday.com/articles/201107/sense-and-sensitivity. Explains people who are emotionally sensitive.

Baumeister, Roy F., Jennifer D. Campbell, Joachim I. Krueger, and Kathleen D. Vohs. "Does High Self-Esteem Cause Better Performance, Interpersonal Success, Happiness, or Healthier Lifestyles?" *Psychological Science in the Public Interest* 4, no. 1 (2003): 1–44. Reviews research suggesting that high self-esteem does not have most of the positive effects that have been attributed to it.

Bem, Daryl J., and Andrea Allen. "On Predicting Some of the People Some of the Time: The Search for Cross-Situational Consistencies in Behavior." *Psychological Review* 81, no. 6 (1974): 506–520. A classic article on the consistency of personality across situations.

Boyce, Christopher. J., and A. M. Wood. "Personality Prior to Disability Determines Adaptation: Agreeable Individuals Recover Lost Life Satisfaction Faster and More Completely." *Psychological Science* 22, no. 11 (2011): 1397–1402. A study of the relationship between personality and coping with disability.

Briley, Daniel A., and Eliot M. Tucker-Drob. "Genetic and Environmental Continuity in Personality Development: A Meta-Analysis." *Psychological Bulletin* 140, no. 5 (2014): 1303–1331. A meta-analytic review of research on the genetic and environmental determinants of personality across the life span.

Budd, Linda S. *I'm OK, You're Not OK: Experiences of Having a Loved One with a Personality Disorder*. North Charleston, SC: CreateSpace, 2013. A look at the impact that people with personality disorders have on those around them, with insights on how to deal with people who have a personality disorder.

Buss, David M. "Human Nature and Culture: An Evolutionary Psychological Perspective." *Journal of Personality* 69, no. 6 (2001): 955–978. Extends evolutionary analyses of personality to an understanding of human culture.

Cain, Susan. *Quiet: The Power of Introverts in a World That Can't Stop Talking*. New York: Broadway Books, 2013. An examination of the benefits of being introverted.

Carver, Charles S., and Teri L. White. "Behavioral Inhibition, Behavioral Activation, and Affective Responses to Impending Reward and Punishment: The BIS/BAS Scales." *Journal of Personality and Social Psychology* 67, no. 2 (1994): 319–333. An article describing the development of a measure to assess BAS and BIS tendencies.

Catalino, Lahnna I., and Barbara L. Fredrickson. "A Tuesday in the Life of a Flourisher: The Role of Positive Emotional Reactivity in Optimal Mental Health." *Emotion* 11, no. 4 (2011): 938–950. Report of a research study by the leading expert on positive emotions showing how patterns of behavior and personality relate to flourishing.

Cheng, Cecilia, Hi-po B. Lau, and Man-pui, S. Chan. "Coping Flexibility and Psychological Adjustment to Stressful Life Changes: A Meta-Analytic Review." *Psychological Bulletin* 140, no. 6 (2014): 1582–1607. A meta-analysis of all studies from 1978 to 2013 on the relationship between coping flexibility and psychological adjustment.

Clyman, Ronald I., R. S. Roth, Susan H. Sniderman, and J. Charrier. "Does a Belief in a Just World Affect Health Care Providers' Reactions to Perinatal Illness?" *Journal of Medical Education* 55, no. 6 (1980): 538–539. A study of the relationship between the degree to which health-care providers believe in a just world and their assumptions about parents' role in perinatal diseases.

Cohen, Sheldon, Cuneyt M. Alper, William J. Doyle, John J. Treanor, and Ronald B. Turner. "Positive Emotional Style Predicts Resistance to Illness after Experimental Exposure to Rhinovirus or Influenza A Virus."

Psychosomatic Medicine 68, no. 6 (2006): 809–815. Report of study described in lecture 6 in which happier people were less susceptible to the common cold.

Cohen, Taya R., Abigail T. Panter, and Nazli Turan. "Guilt Proneness and Moral Character." *Current Directions in Psychological Science* 21, no 5. (2012): 355–359. A summary of research on the link between the tendency to feel guilty and moral behavior.

Collier, Lorna. "Growth after Trauma: Why Are Some People More Resilient Than Others—And Can It Be Taught?" *Monitor on Psychology*, Nov. 2016. http://www.apa.org/monitor/2016/11/growth-trauma.aspx. Examines instances in which trauma enhances people's well-being.

Dahl, Melissa. "How Much Can You Really Change after You Turn 30?" *New York* (The Science of Us), November 24, 2014. http://nymag.com/scienceofus/2014/11/how-much-can-you-really-change-after-30.html. A look at personality change in adulthood.

Diagnostic and Statistical Manual of Mental Disorders (DSM-5). New York: American Psychiatric Association, 2013. The official diagnostic manual for psychological and psychiatric problems, including personality disorders.

Diener, Ed, and Christie N. Scollon. "The What, Why, When, and How of Teaching the Science of Subjective Well-Being." *Teaching of Psychology* 41, no. 2 (2014): 175–183. A highly accessible overview of basic findings about psychological well-being.

Dobbert, Duane L. *Understanding Personality Disorders: An Introduction*. New York: Rowman and Littlefield, 2010. A layperson's introduction to how to identify and deal with people who have personality disorders.

Donnellan, M. Brent, and Richard W. Robins. "Resilient, Overcontrolled, and Undercontrolled Personality Types: Issues and Controversies." *Social and Personality Psychology Compass* 4, no. 11 (2010): 1070–1083. A look at the 3 fundamental personality types that emerge when people's profiles of traits are examined as a whole.

Fleeson, William. "Towards a Structure- and Process-Integrated View of Personality: Traits as Density Distributions of States." *Journal of Personality and Social Psychology* 80, no. 6 (2001): 1011–1027. Research on the relationship between personality and within-person variability in behavior.

Fleeson, William, and Patrick Gallagher. "The Implications of Big Five Standing for the Distribution of Trait Manifestation in Behavior: Fifteen Experience-Sampling Studies and a Meta-Analysis." *Journal of Personality and Social Psychology* 97, no. 6 (2009): 1097–1114. A set of studies on the relationship between people's personality traits and how they behave in everyday life.

Fraley, R. Chris. *A Brief Overview of Adult Attachment Theory and Research*. https://internal.psychology.illinois.edu/~rcfraley/attachment.htm. An expert on attachment style summarizes the most important findings on attachment in adulthood.

Friedman, L. F. "The Perks of Feeling So-So: Embracing Emotional Ambiguity Does More for You Than Thinking Positively All the Time." *Psychology Today*, Sept.–Oct. 2012, 44. A brief article on the benefits of mixed emotions.

Funder, David. *The Personality Puzzle*. New York: Norton, 2016. A comprehensive and readable textbook that covers the field of personality psychology by a leading researcher in personality science. You can learn more about many of the topics covered in the course from this book.

Furnham, Adrian, and Edward Procter. "Belief in a Just World: Review and Critique of the Individual Difference Literature." *British Journal of Social Psychology* 28, no. 4 (1989): 365–384. A review and critique of research on belief in a just world.

Geary, David C. *Male, Female: The Evolution of Human Sex Differences*. 2nd ed. Washington, DC: American Psychological Association, 2010. Discusses the evolution of sex differences throughout the animal kingdom, with a focus on differences between human men and women.

Gottberg, Kathy. "Promotion or Prevention? What's Your Focus and Why It Matters." *SmartLiving 365*. https://www.smartliving365.com/promotion-prevention-whats-focus-matters/. Explains promotion- versus prevention-focused goals and offers lists to help you determine whether you are a promotion- or prevention-focused person.

Graziano, William G., J. Bruce, Brad E. Sheese, and Renee M. Tobin. "Attraction, Personality, and Prejudice: Liking None of the People Most of the Time." *Journal of Personality and Social Psychology* 93, no. 4 (2007): 565–582. Describes studies on the relationship between personality, prejudice, and prosocial behavior, with a focus on the trait of agreeableness.

Haidt, Jonathan. *The Righteous Mind: Why Good People Are Divided by Politics and Religion*. New York: Pantheon, 2012. A best-selling books that applies Haidt's moral foundations theory to political attitudes and religious beliefs.

Hepler, Justin, and Delores Albarracin. "Attitudes without Objects: Evidence for a Dispositional Attitude, Its Measurement, and Its

Consequences." *Journal of Personality and Social Psychology* 104, no. 6 (2013): 1060–1076. Report of research on the dispositional attitude described in lecture 6.

Hofstede, Geert. "Dimensionalizing Cultures: The Hofstede Model in Context." *Online Readings in Psychology and Culture* 2, no. 1 (2011). https://doi.org/10.9707/2307-0919.1014. An introduction to Hofstede's model of cultural values.

Holmes, Bob. "How Dogs Are Helping Decode the Genetic Roots of Personality." *New Scientist*, March 15, 2017. Why dogs are ideal research subjects for understanding how personality is encoded in genes.

Hoyle, Rick H., ed. *Handbook of Personality and Self-Regulation*. New York: Wiley, 2010. Contains 21 chapters on scholarly research on self-regulation from personality, developmental, and social psychology.

Hoyle, Rick H., and Erin K. Davisson. "Varieties of Self-Control and Their Personality Correlates." In *Handbook of Self-Regulation*, 3rd ed., edited by Kathleen D. Vohs and Roy F. Baumeister, 396–413. New York: Guilford Publications, 2016. A discussion of the distinctions among initiation, inhibition, and continuation as forms of self-control.

Hyde, Janet S. "The Gender Similarities Hypothesis." *American Psychologist* 60, no. 6 (2005): 581–592. A review of research on gender differences showing that men and women tend to be more similar than different.

Ibarra, Herminia. "The Authenticity Paradox." *Harvard Business Review*, January–February 2015. https://hbr.org/2015/01/the-authenticity-paradox. Considers the role of authenticity and inauthenticity in effective leadership.

Jaffe, Eric. "Why Wait? The Science behind Procrastination." *APS Observer*, April 2013. http://www.psychologicalscience.org/observer/why-wait-the-science-behind-procrastination. Summarizes research on why people procrastinate.

Jarrett, Christian. "Different Nationalities Really Have Different Personalities. *BBC Future*, April 13, 2017. http://www.bbc.com/future/story/20170413-different-nationalities-really-have-different-personalities. A summary of research on differences in personality around the world.

John, Oliver, Richard Robins, and Lawrence Pervin, eds. *Handbook of Personality*. 3rd ed. New York: Guilford Publications, 2008. The authoritative reference for researchers and students of personality in which leading authorities review the state of the science.

Johnson, Wendy, Eric Turkheimer, Irving I. Gottesman, and Thomas J. Bouchard Jr. Beyond Heritability: Twin Studies in Behavioral Research. *Current Directions in Psychological Science* 18, no. 4 (2009): 217–220. A brief summary of the value of research on twins in exploring genetic and environmental influences on personality and behavior.

Kashdan, Todd. *Curious? Discover the Missing Ingredient to a Fulfilling Life*. New York: Harper Collins, 2009. An intriguing look at the nature and benefits of curiosity.

Kaufman, Scott B. "Which Personality Traits Are Most Predictive of Well-Being?" *Scientific American,* Jan. 21, 2017. https://blogs.scientificamerican.com/beautiful-minds/which-personality-traits-are-most-predictive-of-well-being/. An expert offers his view on the 11 personality traits that are central to well-being.

Khazan, Olga. "Why Self-Compassion Works Better Than Self-Esteem." *The Atlantic*, May 6, 2016. https://www.theatlantic.com/health/archive/2016/05/why-self-compassion-works-better-than-self-esteem/481473/. An article on the benefits of being self-compassionate.

Lahey, Benjamin B. "Public Health Significance of Neuroticism." *American Psychologist* 64, no. 4 (2009): 241–256. Reviews evidence showing that neuroticism not only undermines psychological well-being but also contributes to a variety of health problems.

Larsen, Randy, and David M. Buss. *Personality Psychology: Domains of Knowledge about Human Nature*. New York: McGraw-Hill, 2015. An excellent overview of personality theory and research.

Layton, Julia. "How Fear Works." *HowStuffWorks.com*, September 2005. http://science.howstuffworks.com/life/inside-the-mind/emotions/fear.htm. A look at the emotion of fear, with special attention to how fears can be classically conditioned.

Leary, Mark R. *The Curse of the Self: Self-Awareness, Egotism, and the Quality of Human Life*. New York: Oxford University Press, 2004. A look at the ways in which our thoughts about ourselves undermine the quality of our lives and create a variety of personal and social problems.

Leary, Mark R., and Rick H. Hoyle, eds. *Handbook of Individual Differences in Social Behavior*. New York: Guilford Press, 2009. A collection of chapters about 37 important personality variables written by experts on each characteristic. Most of the personality characteristics discussed in this course are covered in detail.

Leary, Mark R., Kaitlin T. Raimi, Katrina P. Jongman-Sereno, and Kate J. Diebels. "Distinguishing Intrapsychic from Interpersonal Motives in Psychological Theory and Research." *Perspectives in Psychological*

Science 10, no. 4 (2015): 497–517. An examination of the importance of distinguishing between intrapsychic and interpersonal motives in understanding human behavior.

Leary, Mark R., Kate J. Diebels, Erin K. Davisson, Katrina P. Jongman-Sereno, Jennifer C. Isherwood, Kaitlin T. Raimi, Samantha A. Deffler, and Rick H. Hoyle. "Cognitive and Interpersonal Features of Intellectual Humility." *Personality and Social Psychology Bulletin* 43, no. 6 (2006): 793–813. Describes 4 studies of personality variables that are related to intellectual humility and the ways in which people who are low versus high in intellectual humility differ in how they process information.

Lee, Kibeon, and Michael C. Ashton. *The H Factor of Personality: Why Some People Are Manipulative, Self-Entitled, Materialistic, and Exploitive—And Why It Matters for Everyone.* Waterloo, Ontario: Wilfrid Laurier University Press, 2012. A readable introduction to the trait of honesty-humility, the sixth trait of the HEXACO model discussed in lecture 3.

Lilienfeld, Scott O., James Wood, and Howard N. Garb. "The Scientific Status of Projective Techniques." *Psychological Science in the Public Interest* 1, no. 2 (2000): 27–66. A critique of projective personality tests, such as the Thematic Apperception Test (TAT).

Lilienfeld, Scott O., S. J. Lynn, John Ruscio, and Barry L. Beyerstein. "Myth #27: In Romance, Opposites Attract." *Association for Psychological Science.* http://www.psychologicalscience.org/media/myths/myth_27.cfm. Debunks the myth that opposites attract by explaining why people with opposite personality characteristics seldom get along well.

Lynam, Donald R., Avshalom Caspi, Terrie E. Moffitt, Per-Olaf H. Wikström, Rolf Loeber, and Scott Novak. "The Interaction between Impulsivity and Neighborhood Context on Offending: The Effects of Impulsivity Are Stronger in Poorer Neighborhoods. *Journal of Abnormal Psychology* 109, no. 4. (2000): 563–574. The study discussed in lecture 1 showing that impulsivity was related to juvenile offending only for boys living in poor neighborhoods.

Lyubomirsky, Sonja. *The How of Happiness.* New York: Penguin, 2007. A readable excursion into the nature of happiness by a foremost authority on the topic.

Masten, Ann S. "Ordinary Magic: Resilience Processes in Development." *American Psychologist* 56, no. 3 (2001): 227–238. A summary of research on the processes that promote resilience in children.

Mayer, John. "Know Thyself." *Psychology Today*, April 4, 2014, 64–71. The cocreator of the concept of emotional intelligence discusses the importance of personal intelligence.

McMonigal, Kelly. *The Willpower Instinct: How Self-Control Works, Why It Matters, and What You Can Do to Get More of It.* New York: Penguin, 2012. The science of self-control, drawing on research in psychology, neuroscience, and economics.

Melchers, Martin, Christian Montag, Martin Reuter, Frank Spinath, and Elizabeth Hahn. "How Heritable Is Empathy? Differential Effects of Measurement and Its Subcomponents." *Motivation and Emotion* 40, no. 5 (2016): 720–730. A study showing the differential heritability of cognitive and affective aspects of empathy.

Meyer-Lindenberg, Andreas. "The Roots of Problem Personalities." *Scientific American Mind*, April 2, 2009. http://integral-options.blogspot.com/2009/04/sciam-mind-roots-of-problem.html. Explains the origins of borderline personality disorder.

Mischel, Walter. "Toward an Integrative Science of the Person." *Annual Review of Psychology* 55 (2004): 1–22. A review and resolution of the controversy regarding the consistency of personality by the psychologist who started the debate.

Mischel, Walter, and Yuichi Shoda. "Toward a Unified Theory of Personality: Integrating Dispositions and Processing Dynamics within the Cognitive Affective Processing System." In *Handbook of Personality*, 3rd ed., edited by Oliver P. John, Richard. W. Robins, and Lawrence Pervin, 208–241. New York: Guilford Publications, 2008. An overview of the CAPS (if-then) model of personality.

Moffitt, Terrie E., Avshalom Caspi, Jay Belsky, and P. A. Silva. "Childhood Experience and the Onset of Menarche: A Test of a Sociobiological Model." *Child Development* 63, no. 1 (1992): 47–58. Research on a possible conditional evolutionary adaptation in which girls in high-stress environments reach puberty earlier.

Morell, Virginia. "A Kingdom of Characters." *Psychology Today*, January–February 2014, 70+. A fascinating excursion through the personalities of other species.

Olson, James M., Philip A. Vernon, Julie Aitken Harris, and Kerry L. Jang. "The Heritability of Attitudes: A Study of Twins." *Journal of Personality and Social Psychology* 80, no. 6 (2001): 845–860. A research study demonstrating that attitudes, like personality traits, can have a genetic basis.

Ozer, Daniel, and Veronica Benet-Martinez. "Personality and the Prediction of Consequential Outcomes." *Annual Review of Psychology* 57 (2006): 401–421. An overview of research on the implications of personality for health, relationships, occupational performance, political ideology, crime, spirituality, and other important outcomes.

Parks-Leduc, Laura, Gilad Feldman, and Anat Bardi. "Personality Traits and Personal Values: A Meta-Analysis." *Personality and Social Psychology Review* 19, no. 1 (2015): 3–29. A review of research dealing with the relationships between traits and values.

Pinker, Steven. "My Genome, My Self." *New York Times Sunday Magazine*, January 11, 2009. http://www.nytimes.com/2009/01/11/magazine/11Genome-t.html?mcubz=3. The benefits and downsides of learning about your genetic predispositions.

Plomin, Robert. "Behavioral Genetics." *Serious Science*, January 26, 2017. http://serious-science.org/behavioral-genetics-7975. A pioneer in the study of the genetic bases of personality describes his work and overviews the field.

Prinzie, Peter, Geert J. M. Stams, Maya Dekovic, Albert H. A. Reijntjes, and Jay Belsky. "The Relations between Parents' Big Five Personality Factors and Parenting: A Meta-Analytic Review." *Journal of Personality and Social Psychology* 97, no. 2 (2009): 351–362. A meta-analysis of studies of the relationship between the big five traits and 3 dimensions of parenting: warmth, control, and support.

Reiss, Stephen. "The Multifaceted Nature of Intrinsic Motivation: The Theory of 16 Basic Desires." *Review of General Psychology* 8, no. 3 (2004): 179–193. Introduces a theory of human motivation that proposes 16 basic motives.

Roberts, Brent W., and Daniel Mroczek. "Personality Trait Change in Adulthood." *Current Directions in Psychological Science* 17, no. 1 (2008): 31–35. Summarizes research on how personality changes over the life span.

Saucier, Donald A., and Russell J. Webster. "Social Vigilantism: Measuring Individual Differences in Belief Superiority and Resistance to Persuasion." *Personality and Social Psychology Bulletin* 36, no. 1 (2010): 19–32. The article that introduced the construct of social vigilantism.

Schwartz, Shalom. H. "An Overview of the Schwartz Theory of Basic Values." *Online Readings in Psychology and Culture* 2, no. 1 (2012). https://doi.org/10.9707/2307-0919.1116. An overview of research on the 10 universal values described in lecture 8.

Siever, Larry J. "The Frontiers of Pharmacology: Key Personality Traits Are Linked to the Brain's Neurotransmitters." *Psychology Today*, January 1, 1994. https://www.psychologytoday.com/articles/199401/the-frontiers-pharmacology. A summary of research on the link between neurotransmitters and personality.

Singal, Jesse. "How Well Do You Handle Uncertainty?" *New York* (The Science of Us), December 29, 2015. http://nymag.com/scienceofus/2015/12/this-quiz-shows-how-well-you-handle-uncertainty.html. An article on tolerance for ambiguity, along with a test to assess your own ability to handle uncertainty.

Smits, Jill C. "Goody Two-Shoes." *Psychology Today*, March–April, 2012, 30. A look at moral hypocrisy.

Stout, Martha. *The Sociopath Next Door*. New York: Broadway Books, 2012. An exploration of antisocial personality disorder.

Sullivan, Andrew. "The He Hormone." *New York Times Magazine*, April 2, 2000. http://www.nytimes.com/2000/04/02/magazine/the-he-hormone.html?mcubz=3. The ways in which testosterone relates to behavior and personality.

Svoboda, Elizabeth. "A Field Guide to the Cynic." *Psychology Today*, November 2006. https://www.psychologytoday.com/articles/200611/field-guide-the-cynic. Personality variables that underlie dispositional cynicism.

Tedeschi, James T., Barry R. Schlenker, and Thomas V. Bonoma. "Cognitive Dissonance: Private Ratiocination or Public Spectacle?" *American Psychologist* 26, no. 8 (1971): 685–695. A classic article that reinterpreted cognitive dissonance as an interpersonal rather than an intrapsychic phenomenon.

Triandis, Harry C., and Eunkook M. Suh. "Cultural Influences on Personality." *Annual Review of Psychology* 53 (2002): 133–160. A review of research on the links between culture and personality.

Turkheimer, Eric. "Three Laws of Behavior Genetics and What They Mean." *Current Directions in Psychological Science* 9, no. 5 (2000): 160–164. A brief summary of general findings in behavioral genetics, with a focus on why genes account for more variability in personality than family variables.

Vazire, S., and Erika N. Carlson. "Self-Knowledge of Personality: Do People Know Themselves?" *Social and Personality Psychology Compass* 4, no. 8 (2010): 605–620. Reviews research regarding the accuracy of people's perceptions of their own personality.

Vernon, Philip, Vanessa Villani, Leanne Vickers, and Julie Schermer. "A Behavioral Genetic Investigation of the Dark Triad and the Big Five." *Personality and Individual Differences* 44, no. 2 (2008): 445–452. Report of a study that investigated the degree to which genetic factors underlie narcissism, Machiavellianism, and psychopathy.

Vukasovic, Tena, and Dennis Bratko. "Heritability of Personality: A Meta-Analysis of Behavior Genetic Studies." *Psychological Bulletin* 141, no. 4 (2015): 769–785. A meta-analytic review of 134 studies that tested the genetic bases of personality traits.

Weir, K. "Maximizing Children's Resilience." *Monitor on Psychology*, September 2017, 40–46. A summary of the steps that parents, teachers, grandparents, and others can take to promote a resilient personality in children.

Westerhoff, Nicholas. "The 'Big Five' Personality Traits." *Scientific American*, December 17, 2008. https://www.scientificamerican.com/article/the-big-five/. An extended introduction to the big five traits.

Wilson, Sylia, Catherine B. Stroud, and C. Emily Durbin. "Interpersonal Dysfunction in Personality Disorders: A Meta-Analytic Review." *Psychological Bulletin* 143, no. 7 (2017): 677–734. A meta-analysis of studies on the relationship between personality disorders and particular interpersonal problems.

Wilson, Timothy. *Strangers to Ourselves: Discovering the Adaptive Unconscious*. Cambridge, MA: Harvard University Press, 2002. Examines why people often do not know themselves very well and what they can do to increase self-knowledge.

Winter, David G. "Things I've Learned about Personality from Studying Political Leaders at a Distance." *Journal of Personality* 73, no. 3 (2005): 557–584. The importance of motives and personality traits in political leaders, including U.S. presidents.

Wrightsman, Larry S. *Assumptions about Human Nature*. Newbury Park, CA: Sage, 1992. A summary of 3 decades of research on beliefs about human nature from the leading expert on the topic.

Zuckerman, Miron, Kathleen C. Gerbasi, R. I. Kravitz, and Ladd Wheeler. "The Belief in a Just World and Reactions to Innocent Victims. *JSAS Catalog of Selected Documents in Psychology* 5 (1975): 326. Brief description of an experimental study of victim derogation.

IMAGE CREDITS

3	©KatarzynaBialasiewicz/iStock/Thinkstock.
7	©Chad Baker/Ryan McVay/ Photodisc/Thinkstock.
8	©ShutKatya/iStock/Thinkstock.
9	©Ajr_images/iStock/Thinkstock.
10	©Monkeybusinessimages/iStock/Thinkstock.
12	©Sandorgora/iStock/Thinkstock.
26	©Ridofranz/iStock/Thinkstock.
29	©Rawpixel/iStock/Thinkstock.
31	©Saiko3p/iStock/Thinkstock.
33	©Monkey Business Images Ltd/Thinkstock.
35	©Photodisc/Thinkstock.
49	©SanneBerg/iStock/Thinkstock.
51	©G-stockstudio/iStock/Thinkstock.
53	©Highwaystarz-Photography/iStock/Thinkstock.
54	©Eraxion/iStock/Thinkstock.
56	©Moodboard/Thinkstock.
58	©Thomas Northcut/DigitalVision/Thinkstock.
72	©Dolgachov/iStock/Thinkstock.
74	©Jasam_io/iStock/Thinkstock.
76	©Urestock/Purestock/Thinkstock.
77	©Zanskar/iStock/Thinkstock.
77	©Nerthuz/iStock/Thinkstock.
77	©Ismagilov/iStock/Thinkstock.
77	©Tero Vesalainen/iStock/Thinkstock.
79	©Gpointstudio/iStock/Thinkstock.
81	©A.collectionRF/Model released/Thinkstock.
95	©Zinkevych/iStock/Thinkstock.
97	©Demaerre/iStock/Thinkstock.
99	©LightFieldStudios/iStock/Thinkstock.
100	©McIninch/iStock/Thinkstock.
101	©Liderina/iStock/Thinkstock.
102	©P_ponomareva/iStock/Thinkstock.
117	©Eskaylim/iStock/Thinkstock.
119	©Ralf Nau/DigitalVision/Thinkstock.
121	©Mike Watson/moodboard/Thinkstock.
122	©ThinkstockDMEPhotography/iStock/Thinkstock.
124	©Photos.com/Thinkstock.
126	©RoterPanther/iStock/Thinkstock.
141	©G-stockstudio/iStock/Thinkstock.

143	©Wavebreakmedia Ltd/Thinkstock.
144	©Top Photo Corporation/Thinkstock.
144	©Pixelheadphoto/iStock/Thinkstock.
145	©HASLOO/iStock/Thinkstock.
146	©LuminaStock/iStock/Thinkstock.
148	©Fizkes/iStock/Thinkstock.
150	©Monkey Business Images Ltd/Thinkstock.
164	©amanaimagesRF/amana images/Thinkstock.
165	©Wavebreakmedia Ltd/Thinkstock.
166	©Diego_cervo/iStock/Thinkstock.
168	©Paul/F1online/Thinkstock.
168	©Filipefrazao/iStock/Thinkstock.
169	©Thomas Northcut/Photodisc/Thinkstock.
170	©Fizkes/iStock/Thinkstock.
172	©Kieferpix/iStock/Thinkstock.
186	©Panic_attack/iStock/Thinkstock.
188	©Vadimguzhva/iStock/Thinkstock.
190	©LggyLee/iStock/Thinkstock.
193	©Petrenkod/iStock/Thinkstock.
195	©Max-kegfire/iStock/Thinkstock.
209	©Milkos/iStock/Thinkstock.
210	©David De Lossy/Photodisc/Thinkstock.
210	©dragana991/iStock/Thinkstock.
211	©Deeepblue/iStock/Thinkstock.
212	©UberImages/iStock/Thinkstock.
214	©Kazoka30/iStock/Thinkstock.
215	©LSOphoto/iStock/Thinkstock.
215	©AntonioGuillem/iStock/Thinkstock.
217	©Creatas Images/Thinkstock.
219	©Diego_cervo/iStock/Thinkstock.
233	©G-stockstudio/iStock/Thinkstock.
234	©Pixland/Pixland/Thinkstock.
236	©Jupiterimages/ PHOTOS.com>>/Thinkstock.
239	©Ljupco/iStock/Thinkstock.
241	©Ajr_images/iStock/Thinkstock.
242	©Cathy Yeulet/Hemera/Thinkstock.
256	©Feedough/iStock/Thinkstock.
258	©Max-kegfire/iStock/Thinkstock.
260	©MariaDubova/iStock/Thinkstock.
262	©Fizkes/iStock/Thinkstock.
263	©Wavebreakmedia Ltd/Thinkstock.
263	©Mangpor 2004/Thinkstock.
264	©Ridofranz/iStock/Thinkstock.
265	©Moodboard/Thinkstock.

NOTES

NOTES

NOTES

NOTES

WHY YOU ARE WHO YOU ARE

Investigations into Human Personality

Mark Leary, Ph.D.

THE GREAT COURSES®

PUBLISHED BY:
THE GREAT COURSES
Corporate Headquarters
4840 Westfields Boulevard, Suite 500
Chantilly, Virginia 20151-2299
Phone: 1-800-832-2412
Fax: 703-378-3819
www.thegreatcourses.com

Copyright © The Teaching Company, 2018

Printed in the United States of America
This book is in copyright. All rights reserved.
Without limiting the rights under copyright reserved above,
no part of this publication may be reproduced, stored in
or introduced into a retrieval system, or transmitted,
in any form, or by any means
(electronic, mechanical, photocopying, recording, or otherwise),
without the prior written permission of
The Teaching Company.